George Basil Dixwell

Premises of free trade examined

Also reviews of Bastiat's

George Basil Dixwell

Premises of free trade examined
Also reviews of Bastiat's

ISBN/EAN: 9783337284152

Printed in Europe, USA, Canada, Australia, Japan

Cover: Foto ©Suzi / pixelio.de

More available books at **www.hansebooks.com**

PREMISES OF FREE TRADE EXAMINED;

ALSO REVIEWS

OF

BASTIAT'S "SOPHISMS OF PROTECTION,"

OF

PROFESSOR SUMNER'S ARGUMENT AGAINST "PROTECTIVE TAXES,"

OF

PROFESSOR PERRY'S "FARMERS AND THE TARIFF,"

OF

PROFESSOR SUMNER'S SPEECH BEFORE THE TARIFF COMMISSION,

AND OF

"PROGRESS AND POVERTY."

BY

GEORGE BASIL DIXWELL.

———•———

CAMBRIDGE:

JOHN WILSON AND SON.

University Press.

1883.

THE PREMISES OF FREE TRADE EXAMINED.

As the text-books from which political economy is taught in most of our colleges are generally by English authors, or by Americans who have adopted the English views, it is not surprising that we should meet with a great many highly educated men who believe the trans-Atlantic ideas to be invulnerable. They have been taught that economical phenomena are too complex to be investigated by the *a posteriori* method, and that nothing can be relied on but reasoning from assumptions; and they have accepted with delight certain most attractive argumentations, in which the wasteful futility of protection appears to be demonstrated, just as the mathematician demonstrates that the three angles of a triangle are in all cases equal to two right angles. But deductive reasoning has its own liability to error. Very eminent authors may change the *subject* or change the *premises* or reason from an apparent *axiom*, which upon careful examination is found little better than a blunder, or an identical proposition. The writer believes that all these logical faults are to be found in the supposed demonstrations above alluded to; and he proposes in this paper to point out a few of them, in the hope that some able minds may be led to review their conclusions, and to read or read again, with a candid spirit, what has been urged by Rae, Phillips, Carey, List, Bowen, Seaman, Thompson, Greeley, E. P. Smith, Kelly, Elder, and many others who have written in favor of protection.

Let us first examine Mr. J. R. McCulloch's apparent demonstration that absenteeism is not financially injurious to a country. He argued in this way: —

1st. "We get nothing from abroad except as an equivalent for something else; and the individual who uses only Polish wheat, Saxon cloth, and French silks and wine, gives, by occasioning the exportation of an equal amount of British produce, precisely the same encouragement to industry here as he would give were he to consume nothing not directly produced among us. The Portuguese do not send us a single bottle of port, without our sending to them, or to those to whom they are indebted, its worth in cottons, hardware, or some sort of produce; so that whether we use the wine or its equivalent is, except as a matter of taste, of no importance whatever."

But if it be indifferent whether an Irish landlord residing in Dublin consumes an Irish or a foreign product, it is evidently indifferent whether he consumes the one or the other in Dublin or in Paris. Therefore, absenteeism, as far as its financial effects are considered, is a matter of entire indifference to the Irish people.

If the premises be correct, the conclusion appears to be inevitable; but in this, as in other cases, where the result of reasoning contradicts the almost universal opinion of mankind, it is well to look again very closely at the premises. Let us do this, and, in order not to perplex ourselves by interposing money, let us suppose that the annual produce of the land of Ireland is equivalent to 30,000,000 bushels of wheat, and that the landlord's portion for rent is ten per cent, or 3,000,000 bushels of wheat. If this ten per cent of the rude product of the land be sent off in the form in which it is raised, it is evident that it might as well be burned, as far as the people of Ireland are concerned. The people will have raw products to consume equivalent to 27,000,000 bushels of wheat. This we will call case first.

Now, alter the supposition, and let the 3,000,000 bushels of wheat be exchanged for Irish manufactured products, and these last be exported. Then, clearly, the people of Ireland will have available for consumption one-ninth part more of the products of the land than they had under the first supposition. This is case second.

Now, vary the supposition yet again. Bring home the landlords, and confine them and their dependents to the use of Irish manufactures. The people of Ireland will then have for consumption the same quantity of wheat as in the last case, and *also* the manufactured products which are exported under case second. This we will call case third.

In the first case, the raw produce constituting rent is sent abroad. It might as well have been burned. In the second case, it is given to productive laborers, who give in exchange manufactured products, which are exported. Here the Irish people get 3,000,000 bushels of wheat to consume in addition to what they had under case first. In the third case, the Irish people, altogether, have for consumption the additional 3,000,000 bushels of wheat (the same as in case second), and *also* an equal value of other products, subject only to a deduction of what the landlords and their wives and children actually use themselves; and, if we go through the expenditures of a wealthy family, we shall find this deduction to be very trivial. A very large part of their incomes are exchanged for professional and personal and commercial services. Those who render such services constitute, according to the census of the United States, more than one hundred and thirty distinct classes, and are over one-fourth part of the whole working population.

Mr. McCulloch saw very clearly that the landlords living in Paris would only obtain services and commodities by exchanging for them their rents or other Irish products into which their rents were converted: what he appears to have overlooked is that the landlords, when living in Dublin, would obtain *Irish* commodities and services only in exchange for their rents or other Irish products into which those rents were converted. The producer of Dublin stout will not give a single bottle of it, except in exchange for other commodities, any more than will the Portuguese producer of port. It would appear, then, that the premises of Mr. McCulloch were quite inaccurate, and that the conclusion drawn from them must be abandoned. Mr. J. S. Mill, in his "Logic," in book v. chapter iv., end of paragraph 4, has a similar error. He says it is indifferent whether an Englishman buys British or French silks, because British commodities must be produced and ex-

·ported to pay for the French silks. He forgets that the necessaries, conveniences, &c., of the British weavers are as much British commodities and employ as much industry to produce them as do the commodities which pay for the French silks in the other case. The only difference is, that in one case the British weavers are deprived of their support, and in the other case they are not. Everything else remains the same, except that the consumer may get the French silks a trifle cheaper, — a matter altogether too trivial to be compared with the national loss.

Professor Cairnes, in his book entitled "Some Leading Principles of Political Economy," repeats this mistake, and props it up with the remark that if it be an error, " we seem to have made a mistake in repealing our protective laws ; nor were protectionists, after all, so very wrong in seeking to encourage native industry by compelling expenditure towards domestic productions !" See part ii. chap. i., note at the end.

Mr. Mill makes use of the error to prop up the free-trade doctrine, and Professor Cairnes makes use of the free-trade doctrine to prop up the error.

Let us now examine another specimen of reasoning : the doctrine that a universal glut of all commodities is impossible, — not a permanent glut, but *any* glut. This doctrine makes a business man open his eyes wide with astonishment. They get at it in this way : —

1st. " Human desires are unlimited.

2d. " Commodities are paid for by commodities.

3d. " He who has produced a commodity has therefore the means of purchasing the other commodity he desires. Double the number of products, and everybody would bring a double demand as well as supply. It is a sheer absurdity that all things should fall in value, and that all producers should, in consequence, be insufficiently remunerated."

Thus says Mr. John Stuart Mill ; and Professor J. E. Cairnes, in his work entitled " Some Leading Principles of Political Economy," before alluded to, maintains that with regard to commodities, demand and supply, as general phenomena, as aggregates, cannot be discriminated. He says:

. "An article is produced and is offered in the market: it is now supply; but the possession of the article confers upon the owner a purchasing power, and this power being exercised, the article becomes a source of demand; *nor is there any other source from which demand can spring.* Demand as an aggregate cannot increase without supply, nor supply without demand. This," he says, "is fundamental in the theory of exchange; and all assumptions to the contrary must be regarded as baseless and absurd."

Now, every business man knows that the aggregate demand for commodities is sometimes greater and sometimes less; so much so, that the quantities in stock are sometimes greatly reduced and sometimes greatly increased, — even to the extent that is called a glut. What, then, has perplexed the abstract reasoners? The doctrine of value appears to be the culprit. The value of anything, they say, is what it ˙will exchange for in other things; it is a ratio; and so, of course, it is absurd to say that all values can rise or all fall together. Hence Mr. Mill and Professor Cairnes maintain that the supply of commodities cannot outrun the demand. But it is just here, in applying to commodities the arguments applicable to values, that the reasoning breaks down, and is found to consist in changing the subject. That all values cannot rise or fall together may be perfectly true; but it does not follow that all commodities — the total annual product — may not rise or fall in exchangeable value; because the totality of commodities does not constitute the totality of values. Besides commodities, there are the rights to incomes, and the totality of fixed capital, the possession of which gives incomes. The annual product in the United States being taken at 6,000,000,000, those other values are estimated at 30,-000,000; and, in fixing their minds upon commodities alone, the eminent authors in question overlooked five-sixths of the values which the money power has constantly to measure. Let no one suppose that Messrs. Mill and Cairnes intended to include all these under the term "commodities." They meant to include nothing beyond the annual product, as would be abundantly evident if there were space to copy their arguments *in extenso.* They argued the case as if there existed nothing besides commodities, and as if men had no desires for anything else, — overlooking that most pervasive and persistent instinct of man to increase his income or better his condition, of which Adam Smith remarks, "that it comes with man when he issues from the womb, and continues with him until he enters the grave."

Now, the action of this instinct sometimes causes an increased demand for commodities, and sometimes a great diminution and a glut. When many possessors of property yielding an income arrive at the conclusion that the country has outgrown its fixed capital, — that it needs more houses, farms, mills, forges, &c., — they can descend into the market, sell or pledge a portion of their bonds, shares, or other property, and proceed to the construction of new railroads, houses, cities, mills, forges, &c.; and this movement will involve the fuller employment of the community, a consequent diminution in the stocks of commodities, and an advance in their exchangeable value. It seems to be of the nature of such movements to run to excess, as each onward step causes a larger and larger demand and stimulates more and more to an increased production by making the earlier enterprises profitable; but, finally, just as the most prudent give up looking for a crash, it comes. It suddenly reveals itself to the community that more fixed capital has been formed than can for the time being be profitably used. Then comes a violent reflux of opinion. Men rush into the belief that more has been done in that direction than the country will require for twenty years. Every new enterprise falls into discredit; the population which was engaged in converting floating into fixed capital, — that is, engaged in converting a portion of the annual product into instruments designed to increase the future product, — this portion of the population is dismissed into idleness, and is thereby forced to diminish enormously its demand for commodities; and here we find ourselves face to face with a *glut*. The productive energies, which had adapted themselves to meet the effective demand of a fully employed community, find themselves in excess in presence of the diminished demand of a community only partially employed. There is over-production or under-consumption ; and, as a necessary consequence, the exchangeable value of the whole annual product suffers a great diminution. Those who had been producing upon borrowed capital find themselves unable to meet their obligations ; there are failures, panic, forced liquidations. The possessors of fixed capital next find their incomes diminished. They, for the time being, are no longer able to save ; no longer able even to maintain their previous scale of expenditures. *These* are next diminished, with the effect of throwing more people out of employment, diminishing still farther the aggregate demand for commodities, and consequently their aggregate exchangeable value. Next, or coincidently, all instruments of production decline ; the productive energies adapt themselves after a while to the new conditions ; a new scale of exchangeable values is evolved ; a smaller gross annual product, involving a smaller average annual net individual income, issues, and the community gradually and slowly settles itself upon a lower level, from which in time to take a fresh start. To trace the steps of recovery, and see how a progressive community, after a number of years, works back to its former level and beyond it, might or might not be interesting, but would exceed the limits and go beyond the object of this paper, which in this portion is simply to show, not that gluts do occur, for this everybody knows, but that just reasoning ought to have anticipated them, — ought to have seen that in the present state of our knowledge they are inevitable and likely to be of considerable duration. The panic of 1873 was not entirely over before 1879.

The next specimen of abstract reasoning is the free-trade argument published by Adam Smith in 1775, and repeated in a somewhat modified form by Mr. J. S. Mill three quarters of a century later.

It will shorten the examination if we first establish one or two preliminary points.

Between 1860 and 1865 the Northern States supplied the government with commodities or money, which, directly or indirectly, was converted into commodities of the value of about $4,000,000,000 in currency, or say $3,000,000,000 gold value, in four years. The inducement was government bonds promising a continuous income. Suppose, now, that instead of government bonds issued to carry on a war, there had been offered to the community new industries promising to yield as great an income. It is evident that in the same time $3,000,000,000 would have been forthcoming for the development of those industries, — a sum greater than the whole fixed and floating capital employed in 1860 in the manufacturing and mechanical industries of the United States. The country, then, could have doubled those industries in four years. That the annual product of commodities does not increase with this rapidity is not, then, because of the inability to find capital, but because men do not discover mutual wants so rapidly. Perhaps more than one-third of the annual product falls to the share of those who desire to save rather than increase their annual consumption. They must be tempted to spend by the discovery of new products or new services, or by the gradual growth of a more liberal scale of living. Failing this, a portion of the annual product remains in stock, diminishing profits and holding in check the expansion of the known industries. This it is which limits the field of industry in a community still possessed of a vast amount of undeveloped resources. Industry, then, as a matter of fact, is not held in check by the want of capital, but by the want of a sufficiently profitable field of employment, and by the accumulated stocks of finished products and of materials awaiting conversion. The legitimate loans of banks of issue are made chiefly upon these; and these loans in the United States, we all know, exceed $1,000,000,000.

Mr. Mill recognized that these stocks of goods were unemployed capital; but, in spite of this, he, as well as Adam Smith, argues the free-trade question upon the assumption that, in a normal condition of things, every atom of the actual and potential capital of a country is and must be fully employed upon productive industry, so that anything taken for new industries must be taken or withheld from the old.

We come now to the argument of Adam Smith, contained

in the second chapter of the fourth book of his " Inquiry into the Nature and Causes of the Wealth of Nations." The limits of space forbid the quotation of his whole chapter, which contains a great deal of rhetorical repetition ; but nothing shall be passed over which demands reply.

In his first paragraph he calls protected industries monopolies. This they may have been in his time, when almost every trade and manufacture was a close guild ; but this they are not in our time and country, with 50,000,000 of people free to exercise them. To use the word now is anything but complimentary to the intellect of the listener or reader.

His third paragraph maintains that

" The general industry of the society never can exceed what the capital of the society can employ. As the number of workmen that can be kept in employment by any particular person must bear a certain proportion to his capital, so the number of those that can be continually employed by all the members of a great society must bear a certain proportion to the whole capital of that society, and never can exceed that proportion. No regulation of commerce can increase the quantity of industry in any society beyond what its capital can maintain. It can only divert a part of it into a direction into which it might not otherwise have gone ; and it is by no means certain that this artificial direction is likely to be more advantageous to the society than that into which it would have gone of its own accord."

But the number of workmen that can be kept in employment by any particular person does not bear a certain proportion to his capital. When the market for his products is dull, a large part of his capital is locked up in unsold goods ; he must then lessen his production and dismiss some of his workmen. Quicken the demand for goods, and his ability to employ workmen increases ; and the same is true of society taken together. In a normal condition of things there may be, for instance, a stock of goods equal to two months' consumption of the whole community, — a value in the United States at the present time (1881) considerably exceeding a thousand millions of dollars. And observe that these stocks of commodities are the very things — the food, the raiment, 'the tools, &c. — which are requisite, and in fact used, in carrying out any new undertakings. The proposition, then, that "industry never can *exceed* what the capital of the society *can* support" is totally irrelevant.* One-half of the capital normally unemployed is ample for the inauguration of gigantic enterprises, and these, if within the strength of the community, will not prevent anything being done which would otherwise have been done. On the contrary, the previously existing industries will be stimulated to larger production.

Let us suppose that the United States at the end of 1879 were producing and consuming commodities equal to a value of $6,000,000.000 for the year, and with a surplus stock equal to a value of $1,000,000,000. If at that time they commenced forming new instruments (mills, forges, farms, houses, and railroads) to an annual value of $300,000,000 over and beyond the regular and normal movement, there would be, as we see, $1,000,000,000 of unemployed floating capital out of which to take the funds ; but these funds would go to recompense the producers of the new instruments, and would be by them expended for the most part for commodities, thus relieving the capitalists of a portion of their stocks and placing them in a position to employ more labor for the sake of enlarging their production of commodities. But whatever they thus expended for labor would lead to the production of more than twice the value expended in labor,† and it might well have happened that at the end of 1880 the gap made in the stock of unemployed floating capital was quite repaired, and the country as ready to continue a similar movement in 1881 as it was to commence it a year before. Meanwhile, the extra recompense to labor during the year would have been not less than $600,000.000.

Vary the amounts if you please, but you will find that any

* It never can, for any considerable time, be nearly as great as the capital can support ; for, if it were, there would be no stock of commodities, which would cause such high prices and such high rates of interest as must inevitably moderate the industrial movement.

† The census of 1870 gave, as the total value added to materials by the mechanical and manufacturing industries, $1,744,000,000, of which $776,000,000 went to labor.

new enterprise not out of proportion to the existing surplus stock of commodities will result, 1st, in an enlarged employment of laborers; and, 2d, in the creation of new subsidiary capital, or say rather of new instruments of production, which would not otherwise have come into existence. But a free-trader may say, How do you know that there is any surplus stock of commodities? and we should reply that, in the first place, we know it as a matter of fact, which can be verified, any day you please to take evidence, in State Street or Wall Street or anywhere else. But as our free-trade brethren do not like facts, nor believe in them unless they agree with conclusions deduced from postulates admitted by their own authors, we will try to show that in an industrial community there must be normally a stock of commodities or of unemployed capital.

First, then, take industry A. Those who commenced it did so for the sake of profit. But, so long as they obtained a satisfactory profit, the same motive would lead them to enlarge their production. If one man did not, another would; and so the increase of the industry would go on until it overran the demand. A stock would then accumulate, bringing down profits and locking up a portion of the producer's capital at the same moment. But what is true of industry A is true of B, C, D, &c.; and we thus arrive at the conclusion that each carries along a surplus stock. When this stock is diminished by a novel or increased demand, prices rise, and the industry is stimulated; when the stock is increased, prices fall, and the industry is checked.

No economist, so far as we know, has noticed the vast aggregate amount of these stocks, nor the manner in which they regulate the play of the industrial forces; and yet, without knowing about them, it is impossible to understand what happens upon the commencement of a great war, or of a great industrial movement. When we have ascertained what the ordinary average stock is, — whether equal to two or three or more months' consumption, — it will become possible to form a rational opinion as to how far any industrial movement can be pushed without bringing on a scarcity of floating capital and a stringency in the money market.

But, meanwhile, it is something to have satisfied ourselves that such stocks must and do exist, and that systems framed in ignorance or disregard of them are necessarily erroneous. Such a system is that of Adam Smith in his third paragraph above quoted. He starts with a self-evident axiom that " the general industry of the society never can *exceed* what the capital of the society *can* employ." He then repeats the idea in different words three several times; and then, mistaking apparently this rhetorical artifice for logic, he draws his conclusion that " a regulation of commerce can only divert a portion of the capital of the society into directions into which it might not otherwise have gone." This conclusion will follow from his axiom, whenever an industrial community shall be found in which there exists no unemployed capital, and no funds, which, though originally intended for private expenditure, are capable of being diverted to the support of productive labor the moment a protective law affords a sufficient motive for doing so. Until such a community be found, the conclusion does not follow from the premises. His argument, if it can by any stretch of courtesy be called an argument, does not cohere.

In the next four paragraphs he argues from the supposed interests and motives of men that they would in certain cases act in accordance with the public interest, and he thence concludes that they are "led by an invisible hand to promote an end which was no part of their intention."

This is a stupendous generalization to be jumped at from a few very uncertain coincidences. Had he inquired, after the inductive method laid down by Bacon, as to whether the selfish private acts of men coincided generally with the interests of the society, he would have found that innumerable negative instances forbade any such conclusion.

His next paragraph argues that men can judge what is for their own interest better than any statesman can. This does not seem to be very evident, in light of the fact that over ninety per cent of business men fail ; and, if it were evident, it has been noted already that there is no scientific basis for the assumption that individual private interests generally coincide with those of the public. All that is evident is, that a statesman cannot undertake to attend to the private affairs of each individual, who, therefore, is left to manage for himself, under the restraint of general laws. These, however, forbid him to build unsafe ships or houses, to encroach upon or prevent the laying out of a public way, to set up lotteries or gambling-houses, to tie up property indefinitely, to use other than certain weights and measures, &c., *ad infinitum*. Uninstructed common sense recognizes everywhere that the immediate interest of the individual is, in an immense number of instances, quite opposite to the interest of the community ; and one of the instances is, when the individual buys of the foreigner at the smallest difference of price, while his fellow-citizen, who could make the article, sits idle or becomes a charge upon the society.

In the next two paragraphs Adam Smith argues that

" It is the maxim of every prudent master of a family never to attempt to make at home what it will cost him more to make than to buy," and that " What is prudence in the conduct of every private family can scarce be folly in that of a great kingdom. If a foreign country can supply us with an article cheaper than we can make it ourselves, better buy it of them with some part of the produce of our own industry, employed in a way in which we have some advantage. The general industry of the country, being always in proportion to the capital which employs it, will not thereby be diminished, no more than that of the above-mentioned artificers, but only left to find out the way in which it can be employed to the greatest advantage."

Here are two fallacies of confusion. The first is in comparing a nation which, by his own supposition, is *not* fully occupied, with an individual who, by his own supposition, *is* fully occupied. Let us correct this by supposing the individual to have employment only four days out of six. He will then be a very *imprudent* and thriftless master of a family if he sits idle two days in the week, because somebody else excels him in all save his special trade. He will set himself about something, will gradually acquire skill and become more independent ; and his income all the time will be augmented. The second fallacy is introduced by the use of the word *cost*. We immediately figure to ourselves what the article *would* cost, calculating his labor at what he earns during his four occupied days; but what he makes while he would otherwise be idle costs him nothing; and what a nation makes with labor otherwise idle and with capital which would otherwise be lying unemployed, or which perhaps would never have come into existence, costs the *nation* nothing. By producing the article it would otherwise import, it adds to the national revenue the total gross value of the article produced, or rather the total value of what would have otherwise been exported. The argument that industry will not be diminished because it is always in proportion to capital, would be good if true, but is good for nothing after we have found out that industry is held in check, not by the want of capital, but by the want of a field of employment sufficiently profitable to attract capital.

Adam Smith continues: —

"Though for the want of such (protective) regulations the society should never acquire the proposed manufacture, it would not, on that account, necessarily be the poorer in any period of its duration. In every period of its duration its whole capital and industry might still have been employed, though upon different objects, in the manner that was most advantageous at the time. In every period its revenue might have been the greatest which its capital could afford, and both capital and revenue have been augmented with the greatest possible rapidity."

This would be correct, were the facts as to capital such as he imagined. He knew nothing of the normal existence of unemployed capital; nothing of the rapidity with which new capital can be taken from income; nothing of the impetuosity with which the savers rush upon and occupy every field of employment which promises a profit.

But the world has learned something in a hundred years; and in the light of the newly observed facts, we know that in consequence of such regulations the nation will in every period of its duration enjoy a larger revenue and acquire a larger capital.

We come now to the anti-protectionist argument of Mr. John Stuart Mill. He says: —

"There can be no more industry than is supplied with materials to work up and food to eat. Self-evident as the thing is, it is often forgotten that the people of a country are maintained and have their wants supplied, not by the produce of present labor, but of past. They consume what has been produced, not what is about to be produced. Now, of what has been produced, a part only is allotted to the support of productive labor; and there will not and cannot be more of that labor than the portion so allotted (which is the capital of the country) can feed and provide with the materials of production.

"Yet, in disregard of a fact so evident, it long continued to be believed that laws and government, without creating capital, could create industry."

This is Adam Smith's argument over again, and is, in brief: —

1st. Industry cannot *exceed* what capital *can* maintain.

2d. Industry, therefore, cannot increase until new capital has been created.

3d. Laws and governments cannot create capital.

4th. Therefore laws and governments have no power to increase industry.

But to make the later propositions flow from the first, a vast gap has to be filled up: it requires to be proved that in a normal condition of things there is no unemployed capital, and no funds, which, although intended for unproductive consumption, are capable of being instantly turned to the support of production the moment that a new industry, intrenched by a protective law, presents a profitable field of employment.

This is a question of fact; and the moment we inquire into the facts, we find that the unemployed capital in the United States is vast, probably much exceeding $1,000,000,000; and that the ability to reinforce this out of the funds intended for unproductive consumption within the year is also vast, probably a good deal over $700,000,000. Before these facts the whole argument falls to pieces.

Mr. Mill continues as follows: —

3

"Not by making the people more laborious, or increasing the efficiency of their labor : these are objects to which the government can in some degree contribute. But, when the people already worked as hard and as skilfully as they could be made to do, it was still thought that the government, without providing additional funds, could create additional employment."

These are wonderful words, as showing how far the most conscientious man may be led in misrepresenting his opponent's positions. The protectionist does not maintain that the government can increase the industry of a people who *already* work as hard and as skilfully as they can be made to ; but that of a people who do *not* already work as hard and as skilfully as they can be made to. Indeed, to suppose that they who already did all they could might still be made to do more (whether the government provided additional funds or not), seems to be one of those blunders or bulls which one would hardly expect to find in the deliberate composition of one who has written so admirably upon logic.

Mr. Mill continues : —

"A government would, by prohibitory laws, put a stop to the importation of some commodity ; and when by this it had caused the commodity to be produced at home, it would plume itself upon having enriched the country with a new branch of industry, would parade in statistical tables the amount of produce yielded and labor employed in the production, and take credit for the whole of this, as a gain to the country, obtained through the prohibitory law. Although this sort of political arithmetic has fallen a little into discredit in England, it flourishes still in the nations of continental Europe. Had legislators been aware that industry is limited by capital, they would have seen that, the aggregate capital of the country not having been increased, any portion of it which they by their laws had caused to be embarked in the newly acquired branch of industry must have been withdrawn or withheld from some other, in which it gave, or would have given, employment to probably about the same quantity of labor which it employs in its new occupation."

Here the cat jumps out of the bag, and we see how Mr. Mill made out his proposition, which he called invulnerable. He translates his original proposition that industry cannot *exceed* what capital can maintain, into the words, " industry is limited by capital," which are ambiguous. In one sense they are identical with his original and fundamental proposition ; but his conclusions, as we have seen, cannot be deduced from this. In the other sense they mean that, in point of fact, industry does not increase because there is not any unemployed capital nor any other funds which can be at once turned into capital. His conclusions would logically follow from this proposition ; but this proposition, as we have seen, is not true. But, by converting his first and fundamental proposition into an ambiguous form, he misled himself and his readers, and seemed to prove that, when millions of practical men believed they had been enriched by a protective law, they were only as many millions of idiots for thinking so. In doing this, he committed precisely the error which he denounced in his " Logic," chap. vi. sec. 4, where he says : —

" The commonest and certainly the most dangerous fallacies of this class, are those which do not lie in a single syllogism, but slip in between one syllogism and another in a chain of argument, and are committed by *changing the premises.* A proposition is proved, or an acknowledged truth laid down, in the first part of an argumentation ; and in the second a farther argument is founded, not on the same proposition, but on some other resembling it sufficiently to be mistaken for it. Instances of this fallacy will be found in almost all the argumentative discourses of unprecise thinkers," &c.

But here an instance is found in his own argument : a great logician, when closely examined, is seen committing a capital error in logic, and thereby teaching us how signally unreliable is the purely abstract system of reasoning, and how constantly it requires to be checked and verified by comparison with facts.

The absurdities into which abstract reasoning may run by overlooking important economical facts is curiously shown by another doctrine, enforced at great length by Mr. J. S. Mill. This is the doctrine that a demand for commodities " does not and cannot create any employment, except at the expense of other employment which existed before." This flies in the face of two economical facts. First, that people are constantly striving to save; and, second, that there always, in a normal condition of society, exists a stock of unsold goods or of materials awaiting transformation, — in short, a vast aggregate of unemployed capital. He argues thus: —

"A consumer may expend his income either in buying services or commodities; he may employ part of it in hiring journeymen bricklayers to build a house, or excavators to dig artificial lakes, or laborers to make plantations and lay out pleasure-grounds; or, instead of this, he may expend the same value in buying velvet and lace."

If he does the latter, Mr. Mill concludes that the additional quantity of velvet which his demand causes to be produced could not be produced at all were it not that the bricklayers, &c., being now without work, their demand for necessaries, &c., ceases, and hence the production of those necessaries, &c., ceases; and hence the precise amount of capital necessary for a larger production of velvet is set free. "There was," he says, "capital in existence to do one of two things, — to make the velvet or produce necessaries for the bricklayers, — but not to do both!"

Imagine the case of a young man, who, being imbued with these doctrines, is thrown into practical life in the United States, and obliged to consider business problems into which enters as a factor the probable amount of the capital unemployed at the moment, he being utterly ignorant of the fact that the aggregate is generally very large and sometimes enormous. What grave blunders he would make, and at how fearful an expense would he unlearn what he had been taught at school or college! If we take Mr. Mill's consumer as merely the embodiment of the totality of consumers, we know that in one phase of the revolving phenomena of society he may have been saving until the general glut of commodities has reduced all profits so low that there is no longer a sufficient inducement to save. If, then, he sets his bricklayers at work and buys his velvet, his purchases will relieve the velvet maker of a portion of the stock of goods which held his industry in check, and will enable him to make more velvet;

and the bricklayers, now employed, will purchase a portion of the overstock of necessaries, and enable their producers to augment their production. And this can go on until the production of commodities has become so profitable that it may appear desirable to increase the aggregate of productive instruments; and the employment of men to construct these will cause a further demand for commodities, a further diminution of the unemployed capital, a further rise in profits, concurrent with a greatly increased demand for labor.

But our young man has been taught that an increased supply of commodities is impossible, unless at the same time there is an equal diminution in the demand for services, or for other commodities; that a glut is impossible; that demand cannot in the aggregate increase beyond supply, nor supply beyond demand; that no new industry can be introduced except by diminishing or preventing some other industry; that the demand for labor cannot increase suddenly, but only gradually and slowly, as capital is, little by little, saved out of income. He has been taught these and other errors, which tend to seriously mislead him in practical life, and may ruin him, if he wants that quick perception and almost intuitive interpretation of facts which are needed to place him where he would have been had he never studied these subjects abstractly.

In Professor Cairnes's book, entitled " Some Leading Principles of Political Economy,'' already alluded to, we have an elaborate work, designed evidently to affect public opinion in the United States and on the continent of Europe in favor of free trade. Let us examine its logic. He says, part iii., chapter i., paragraph iii. : —

" Secondly, when it is said that international trade depends on the difference in the comparative, not in the absolute, cost of producing commodities, the costs compared, it must be carefully noted, are the costs in each country of the commodities which are the subjects of exchange, not the different costs of the same commodity in the exchanging countries. Thus, if coal and wine be the subjects of a trade between England and France, the comparative costs on which the trade depends are the comparative costs of coal and wine in France as compared with the comparative costs of the same articles in England. England might be able to raise coal at one-half the amount of labor and abstinence needed in France; but this alone would not render it profitable for France to obtain her coal from England. If her disadvantage in procuring other commodities was as great as in producing coal, she would gain nothing by an exchange of products, and the conditions of a trade between the two countries would not exist. But, supposing she was, in the case of some other commodity, under a less disadvantage than in that of coal, still more, if she had, with regard to that other, — as in wine, — a positive advantage, it would at once become her interest to employ this commodity as a means of obtaining through trade her coal from England, instead of producing coal directly from her own mines."

All that this proves is, that in *some* cases it will be advantageous for France to get its iron from England in exchange for wine. That it will not be so in all cases is easily shown, as follows: Let the utmost requirements of England for wines be £2,000,000 sterling; let the requirements of France for iron be £10,000,000 sterling. She (France) can in this case obtain from England iron somewhat more cheaply, — we say *somewhat*, because the advantages would be divided between the two countries, — but she would have to *go without* four-fifths of the iron she required. Her saving of labor and abstinence upon the iron she did get from England would be a considerable percentage, of the value of, let us say, 100,000 tons of iron; her loss would be the enormously greater value of 400,000 tons of iron.

Professor Cairnes's reasoning, then, leads only to a *particular conclusion*, and can be used only as a particular, not as a universal, premise.

Further on in the same paragraph Professor Cairnes quotes the instance of Barbadoes buying to advantage its food in New York, and paying in tropical products, notwithstanding that it could raise food also more cheaply than New York.

Here is another particular instance from which no general conclusion can be drawn. It may or may not be well for a small island inhabited by a handful of people to purchase their food and clothing and other conveniences, by giving for them sugar and coffee and spices; but scarcely even a lunatic would propose to 100,000,000 of people to do the same thing; because the quantity of sugar and coffee and spices which they could find a market for would not procure them a twentieth part of what they required in other things.

We come now to Professor Cairnes's chapter iv., entitled "Free-Trade and Protection." Unfortunately he based the main portion of his argument upon the statistical deductions of Mr. David A. Wells. The Professor probably did not know how roughly these had been handled in Congress; but, being a prominent economist, he ought, one would think, to have distrusted the accuracy of figures which appeared to prove that the real wages of the people of the United States had declined twenty per cent between the years 1860 and 1868. However, he accepted them in full faith, and based upon them his main argument, which amounts to this:—

So great a deterioration in the condition of the people must have a cause. I look about in every direction, and cannot find anything to attribute it to, except the MORRILL TARIFF. Here we have a sufficient cause. It puts on duties averaging forty-seven per cent.

"Every article, therefore, produced in the United States, which would not have been produced there but for the protective tariff, represents an expenditure of labor and capital greater than would have been necessary to obtain the same article had it been obtained under free trade. In a word, American labor and capital, as a whole, have, effort for effort and outlay for outlay, been producing smaller results since 1861 than formerly; and, this being so, what other explanation do we need of the actual facts which we encounter, — of diminished returns on American industry, of a fall in the real wages of labor?"

Scores of times it has been shown by American writers that, when an industry has been raised up by protective duties, its products have been often cheapened and scarcely ever augmented by the amount of the duties. Scores of times the free-trader has replied, Where, then, was the necessity for the duty? and scores of times they have been told,. The duty was necessary in the first place to establish the industry, and afterwards to prevent it from being maliciously overwhelmed by English goods sold at a loss, which was to be more than made up by the higher prices obtainable when we no longer were able to help ourselves.

It by no means follows, then, that forty-seven per cent was added to the cost of articles caused to be produced by the Morrill Tariff. It is almost certain that with the tariff we have still to offer in foreign markets as great a surplus of the commodities " in raising which we have an advantage " as can be well sold ; that, if we offered a larger quantity, the net returns would be less in the aggregate than they are now ; and, if so, the commodities produced by reason of the tariff are just so much clear gain. The question was, " Are protective laws a burthen to the country imposing them ? " and the Professor surely made a grave slip in undertaking to prove they were, by assuming that they were ! If the statement of Mr. Wells had been a fact, and the average real wages of the inhabitants of the United States had actually been reduced twenty per cent, there are many other conceivable causes besides a tariff. In 1874 to 1879 there was a serious fall in the rate of wages as measured by money, and also probably as measured by commodities ; but there has recently (1881) been an enormous advance. Did the tariff cause both the decline and the advance? We certainly are not called upon to draw any such absurd conclusion. The fall in 1873–74 was sufficiently accounted for by the sudden cessation by the community from the construction of new instruments of production, and the recent advance is sufficiently accounted for by the movement in the opposite direction now going on. When the community is fully employed, the gross annual product is large : there is much to divide, and wages and profits advance together. When a portion of the community is dismissed into idleness, the annual product is diminished : there is less to divide, and wages and profits fall together.

Professor Cairnes feels great anxiety about the Illinois farmer, lest he should not get enough for his corn, and have to pay too much for other things. He and M. Mongredien would like to have us confine ourselves to that in which we have an advantage, and take the other things from England. The farmers could take $1,000,000,000, and the rest of the community converted into farmers could take another $1,000,-000,000; and, twenty-five years hence, when we number 100,000,000 of people, we could take twice as much, or say $4,000,000,000 of other things. What would be the price of the other things under such circumstances, — whether double or treble what it is now, — and what the price of the corn, — whether two-thirds or half of what it is now, — ought not to trouble political economists!

On looking further, I see I am in error, and that Professor Cairnes does not agree with M. Mongredien. He does not expect us all to become farmers; on the contrary, he tells us that —

" (1) As regards the industries of raw produce, protection does not call into existence a single branch of production which would not equally have existed under free trade, — it merely alters the proportions in which such industries are carried on, hindering their natural and healthy development ; (2) in the domain of manufacturing industry it is equally inefficacious as a means of creating variety of pursuits, — for if on the one hand it secures a precarious existence for certain kinds of manufactures, on the other, by artificially enhancing the price of raw material, it discourages other kinds which in its absence would grow and flourish ; while (3) over and above all these injurious effects, it vitiates the industrial atmosphere by engendering lethargy, routine, and a reliance on legislative expedients, to the great discouragement of those qualities on which, above all, successful industry mainly depends, — energy, economy, and enterprise. To conclude, having regard to the geographical position, extent of territory, and extraordinary natural resources of the United States, as well as to the character of its 'people, trained in all the arts of civilization, and distinguished beyond others by their eminent mechanical and business talents, there seems no reason that they should not take a position of commanding influence 'in the world of commerce, — a position to which no other people on earth could aspire. But, to do this, they must eschew the miserable and childish jealousy of foreign competition which is now the animating principle of their commercial policy. If they desire to command a market for their products in all quarters of the world, they must be prepared to admit the products of other countries freely to their markets, and must learn to seek the benefits of international trade, not in the vain ambition of underselling other countries, and so making them pay tribute in gold and silver to the United States, but in that which constitutes its proper end and only rational purpose, — the greater cheapening of commodities and the increased abundance and comfort which result to the whole family of mankind."

But the "world of commerce" in which we are invited to partake is a world in which Great Britain, by immense efforts, — warlike, industrial, diplomatic, social, and literary, — has been able to find markets for only about twelve hundred millions of dollars in value of the products of her mechanical and manufacturing industries; while our own market, which we are invited to share with Great Britain, is now some four or five times as great, and pretty sure to be ten times as great in twenty-five years. The invitation has a humorous aspect, and might be passed over with a good-natured smile, if the matter were not one of such transcendant importance. Any attempt to put his recommendations in practice would place in peril a large proportion of our capital and industry, and also the high rate of real wages which we have thus far been able to sustain. The farmer is not very likely to sanction it. He knows too well what protection he gets from the removal of nearly half the population from the soil; and he knows too well how his farm rises in value when the mill or the forge settles down beside him. No! the men who thoughtlessly favor such movements are professional and literary men and the possessors of incomes. All these are apt to think it would be well if they could get their clothing and other conveniences cheaply from England. They forget that with a diminution of the rate of wages must also come a diminution of fees, salaries, profits, and incomes. When the incomes from mills, forges, railroads, houses, all fell off, they would lament the day that they assisted to inaugurate so perilous, so pernicious, an experiment.

Professor Cairnes tells us that protection does nothing to diversify industries. His reasoning has been found exceedingly liable to error in other instances, and is exceedingly unsubstantial in this. Facts all over the world confute him.

Let us now turn over the leaves of a livelier author, M. Bastiat. He, at all events, entertains us. He gives us a most amusing petition from the manufacturers of gas for the abolition of sunshine. We laugh ; but we remember that no one proposes to employ labor to produce an inferior substitute for what can be had for nothing. Nor does anybody propose to raise pineapples under glass as a substitute for the tropical product. The climate is too much against us, except indeed when the article to be produced is of sufficient importance to make it worth our while to set civilization against sunshine, as was done in the case of sugar from the beet, and done with complete success.

Another point which Bastiat urges with great wit and vivacity is that our object in building railroads and steamships and telegraphs is to facilitate intercourse, — to remove impediments to intercourse. But the moment we have done this we set about undoing it, by enacting protective and prohibitory tariffs, which are equivalent to breaking up the railroad or burning the steamship, or at least the equivalent of a serious diminution of their utility. But when we build a railroad or a steamship we know that these beneficent instruments, like most others, may be perverted to pernicious uses. They are excellent for carrying passengers ; but it does not follow that they should be used by every passenger. A thief, a spy, a murderer, a person afflicted with the small-pox, may surely be refused a passage, without subjecting the directors to a charge of absurdity. They are also excellent for carrying freight ; but they do not become any less excellent when their managers forbid infectious or dangerous or injurious commodities being conveyed by them.

We form these instruments of locomotion to promote such commerce as for good and sufficient reasons we deem advantageous, and the multiplication of railroads and steamships and their good dividends bear witness to the fact that there is plenty for them to do, in spite of the wicked and absurd protective laws. Men have not yet found reason to adopt the general proposition, that Whatever traffic is carried on by railroads or steamships is *ipso facto* and necessarily beneficial !

Nor yet this other general proposition, To forbid any traffic which is carried on by means of a railroad or steamship is absurd and ridiculous. Such arguments, when stripped of the wit and rhetoric by which Bastiat and his imitators have covered them up, need no refutation. To show them as they are is sufficient.

One who reads Bastiat's admirable chapter upon Capital and Interest is filled with wonder at the venerable blunders found in other parts of his work. As one example, he says:

"On what depends the demand for labor? On the quantity of disposable national capital. And the law which says, ' Such or such an article shall be limited to home production and no longer imported from foreign countries,' can it in any degree increase this capital? Not in the least. This law may withdraw it from one course and transfer it to another, but cannot increase it one penny. Then it cannot increase the demand for labor."

Let us see. A nation is, as before supposed, producing annually commodities worth $6,000,000,000, and it has normally in stock $1,000,000,000, being commodities in the hands of producers or dealers and advanced upon by banks or moneyed men.

Now the law steps in and says: There is an article (say woollen goods) for which there is a large demand in the country, but which has hitherto been brought from abroad. We are under no disability as to climate. When we have acquired the requisite skill, we can produce with as little cost (in labor and abstinence) as any other country. Let there be a duty placed upon importations sufficient to amply protect the new industry.

Under these encouragements capitalists all over the country subscribe to establish woollen mills, to build the mills and furnish the floating capital, and then to proceed to work. Let the movement be of large dimensions, say to the extent of $300,000,000 the first year paid away to workmen. The $1,000,000,000 of unemployed capital is ample without disturbing any previous industry. It is more than three times what is ample. So far, so good! But the money paid out for labor will nearly all be spent by the laborers — for what? For the very commodities which constitute the unemployed capital. The producers of these, finding an extra demand to the extent of nearly a third of their stocks, are all along in condition to increase their production by employing more labor and paying more wages. They may do this to nearly the extent of $300,000,000, with the result of producing commodities worth more than twice the wages disbursed. Here, then, the community at the end of the year finds its floating capital about the same as at the beginning, and its fixed capital increased $300,000,000 ; and its laborers have had and used during the year $600,000,000 more than they would have had without the law. But M. Bastiat, as we have seen above, lays it down as the indubitable teaching of his science, that the law cannot increase the capital disposable for the payment of wages a single penny. This is the patriarch of free-trade sophisms or blunders, having been born in the house of Adam Smith more than a hundred years ago.

As another example of venerable blunders, take the following. He says : —

" France, according to our supposition, manufactures 10,000,000 of hats at fifteen francs each. Let us now suppose that a foreign producer brings them into our market at ten francs. I maintain that *national labor* is thus in no wise diminished. It will be obliged to produce the equivalent of the 100,000,000 francs which go to pay for the 10,000,000 of hats at ten francs, and then there remains to each buyer five francs, saved on the purchase of his hat, or, in total, 50,-000,000 francs, which serve for the acquisition of other comforts and the encouragement of other labor."

Let us see. France, according to his first supposition, produced 10,000,000 of hats selling for 150,000,000 francs ; but the recipients of these 150,000,000 francs did not eat or drink or live in them. They exchanged them for other 150,000,000 francs of products. Here, then, were 300,000,000 francs of French products, every franc of which (see M. J. B. Say) was net income to some Frenchman. Total net income, then, under this supposition, 300,000,000 francs.

Under the other supposition, foreigners bring in 10,000,000 hats and receive French products worth 100,000,000 francs. The French consumers get their hats the same as before ; and, if they spend the whole of the 50,000,000 francs saved by the change to a foreign producer, there will be an additional demand for 50,000,000 francs of varied products. The total French product, then, under this supposition, will be 150,000,000 francs, every franc of which will be net individual income to somebody. Total net income, then, under this supposition, 150,000,000 francs. The aggregate of the French incomes, then, has been reduced 150,000,000 francs by the change from a French to a foreign producer.

But the hat-makers, you may say, will do something else. But in saying this you introduce a new element into the question ; and, moreover, you are by no means warranted in your assumption. Mr. John Stuart Mill ought to be a good enough authority for free-traders, and he says, in regard to a similar case (see book i. chap. v. sec. 9) : —

"The very sum which the consumer now employs in buying velvet (for velvet, read English hats) formerly passed into the hands of journeymen bricklayers (for journeymen bricklayers, read French hat-makers), who expended it in food and necessaries, which they now either go without or *squeeze, by their competition, from the shares* of other laborers."

The change of the demand for hats from France to, say, England does not increase the demand for other French products a single franc, even on the supposition that the hat consumers spend all they save in the price of hats upon other products. If they capitalize any of their savings, the gross demand for other French products will be less than before. The hypothesis, then, finds no funds for the support of the displaced French hat-makers. They must starve, or squeeze a living (by competition) out of the remuneration of other laborers.

This is not only a venerable blunder ; but worse still, it is a dead blunder. It was killed by Sir John Barnard Byles in the " Sophisms of Free-Trade," in 1849, and witness was borne to its peaceful interment by William Lucas Sargant in the "Science of Social Opulence," a work favoring free trade, published in 1856. But this ghost of a blunder so long buried was produced afresh as a valid argument in M. Bastiat's "Sophisms of Protection," translated for the instruction of the American public under the auspices of " The American Free-Trade League."

A large proportion, however, of American converts to free trade become so really through influences which are quite natural and amiable, but which are perfectly innocent of logic. A vast host of wealthy and cultivated persons every year visit Great Britain, where they find almost every man, woman, and child a free-trade missionary, ready to tenderly influence and instruct their less fortunate cousins from the western side of the Atlantic. Every man, woman, and child is completely possessed with the conviction that political economy is already a science, but one, alas! only understood in England. Our ignorance is gently forgiven, our wayward perversity is borne with, any wavering in our convictions is greeted with encouragement and suitable applause, any symptoms of actual conversion are received with unmeasured caresses. The stateliest doors fly open to the truly repentant protectionist; and the highest talent of the land can find time to pause approvingly and to recognize that the individual who, having been born in utter darkness, can still thus bare his eyes to the almost overpowering glare of truth, must possess not only a good heart, but also a commanding intellect! A large portion of the beliefs and opinions of men are rather, as it were, inhaled or absorbed from the social atmosphere around them, than arrived at by any process of reason. We find it easy and pleasant to agree with those who treat us with delicacy and attention, and almost anything seems logical which brings us into accord with the great, the wise, and the good. We do not reflect that Bacon, in his time, could not easily have avoided believing in witchcraft ; that Samuel Johnson was ready to be scared out of his wits by reports of a ghost ; and that the present opinion of Mr. Gladstone or other great thinkers and scholars in favor of free trade has intrinsically no more value than had theirs in favor of the beliefs which the world has now so entirely outgrown. The universality of an opinion is so far from being proof of its correctness, that it should rather inspire a fear of error, — a fear that only one side of the question had been heard.

It is really curious to observe the unanimity with which our English cousins believe themselves masters of political economy; but one of themselves, an author who has made valuable additions to the materials of political economy, declares, in reference to Great Britain, that

" Political economy is little understood, even by educated men. A few of its doctrines, indeed, — those, for example, relating to the division of labor and free trade, — have taken their place in the familiar philosophy of Western Europe. Men learn them, however, by rote, not by study."

But the traveller is not aware of this. He is in contact continually with free-trade opinions, and gradually acquires them by contact or by infection, just as he would catch the small-pox or a malarial fever; and, in this condition of mind, he returns, to be vexed and worried and made to pay out money by the custom-house authorities. Here personal irritation comes in to complete the conversion. He sees very clearly what he has to pay; he does not see by any means so clearly that the ample income which made his travels possible had sprung from the system of which the custom-house annoyances were a necessary portion. He becomes a hater of all tariffs, as obstructions to intercourse, and a ready listener to such sophistries as the following, put forth by Mr. David A. Wells since his conversion to free trade during a visit to England. He says, in his " Creed of Free-Trade : " —

" The highest right of property is the right to freely exchange it for other property. Any system of laws which denies or restricts this right. for the purpose of subserving private or class interests, reaffirms in effect the principle of slavery. Whatever facilitates or cheapens the interchange of commodities or services — good roads, the locomotive, the steamship, or the telegraph — promotes abundance, and consequently the aggregate of human comfort and happiness. Whatever, on the other hand, restricts or makes costly the exchange of commodities or services — be it in the nature of bad roads, high mountains, tempestuous oceans, swamps, deserts, or restrictive laws — increases scarcity, and consequently the aggregate of human poverty and discomfort."

This seems admirable reasoning to one whose preconceived opinions are all in favor of free trade. Let us see whether it is so.

The first sentence contains a proposition altogether foreign to political economy, which concerns itself solely with questions relating to social opulence. This proposition belongs to the domain of law and to the domain of social science, of which political economy is only a portion, a portion in which this question has no place. That it is dragged into a discussion regarding free trade shows a consciousness of weakness. But a lawyer or a professor of social science would meet with a smile the assertion that " the right of every possessor of property to exchange it for other property is so full, universal, and sacred, that the whole community must abstain from any regulation thereof " !

Even if the pecuniary interests of some individuals were *injured*, these ought to give way to the interests of the whole community ; and to liken such pecuniary interests or rights to the rights to life and liberty invaded by slavery, is a monstrous sophism. The insinuation that the restriction of the right of exchange by protection is made in order to subserve private or class interests, is to carry the discussion entirely out of the domain of truth, as the whole aim and object of protection is to increase the total annual product for the benefit of the community as a whole. That good roads, the locomotive, the steamship, and the telegraph promote abundance in all cases is not true. They promote abundance when they are restricted to beneficent exchanges ; they promote scarcity when used to carry on a commerce which, after destroying our means of helping ourselves, can only give us a fifth or a tenth of what we enjoyed before. We have a natural advantage in producing cotton, tobacco, wheat, and a few other products which are salable abroad ; but the market for these products is not sufficiently great, nor can it become sufficiently great, to warrant the employing upon them one-half our present or a fourth of the population we shall have in 1905. To endeavor to confine ourselves to these would be to transfer the whole of our natural advantages to the foreigner, and to reduce ourselves to the condition of Ireland, Turkey, India, and other countries which are prevented from helping themselves and compelled to look to England for mechanical and manufactured products. This is an eminently practical question, upon which the rhetorical sentences quoted from Mr. Wells have no bearing whatsoever. The following is equally irrelevant. He says: —

"In the absence of all freedom of exchange between man and man, civilization would obviously be impossible ; and it would seem to stand to reason that to the degree in which we impede or obstruct the freedom of exchange, — or, what is the same thing, commercial intercourse, — to that same degree we oppose the development of civilization."

But this is reasoning from a " particular " proposition as if it were universal. *Some* exchanges are necessary conditions of civilization, but others may be highly prejudicial to civilization ; there may be many exchanges which must be *suppressed* in order to reach the highest civilization. The suppression of some foreign exchanges may bring into existence many times the number of more advantageous exchanges at home.

Mr. Wells thinks it strange that the American people, who insist upon free trade among themselves, should object to free trade with foreign countries, and thinks that "foreign trade presents no element peculiar to itself."

This is a strange assertion. It would seem that foreign trade is subject to foreign legislation, and not to domestic legislation ; that foreign trade is especially liable to interruption from war; that foreign trade (especially with England and Europe) is more distant as to markets; that foreign trade is carried on with nations having very different conditions of production, and having both the will and the ability to greatly injure and even crush our industries by selling products at a loss, for the very purpose of driving us from our own markets and then making us pay high prices. It would seem that an exchange with the foreigner provokes only one production, where a domestic exchange provokes two ; and that this alone is of supreme importance, inasmuch as the *whole* price of everything produced constitutes net individual income to somebody, as is proved by J. B. Say.

Volumes could be filled with examples of the errors committed by economists of the English school in their deductive reasoning. We have seen that Mr. J. S. Mill, who gave the world an admirable treatise upon the science of logic, could yet amaze his own scholars by giving them one of the best possible specimens of the fallacy called " Changing the Premises," and thus arrive at a false conclusion upon a vital question in political economy. Both he and Professor Cairnes, we have seen, apply to commodities the argumentation which is only true with respect to all values, of which commodities form only a small portion. By this error they come to the conclusion that a glut is impossible, — a conclusion which is contrary to fact, and contradicted by all correct deductive reasoning. Every economist of the English school enjoins upon us to buy in the cheapest market with some portion of our own products in raising which we have an advantage. We reply, that the products in which we have an advantage are not salable abroad to an extent which would pay for one-third part of the other products that we now make for ourselves. We are 50,000,000, we say, and require, and actually obtain and enjoy, annually, commodities produced by the mechanical and manufacturing arts of the value of at least $4,000,000,000. In twenty-five years we shall be 100,000,000.; and, if we continue the protective policy, we shall no doubt then annually obtain and enjoy similar commodities to the value of $10,000,000,000, — a sum equal to about three times the total annual consumption of the British Islands, of which consumption, be it noted, only a small fraction could, under any possible circumstances, be taken from the United States. Great Britain cannot supply our wants ; but she can, and, if we will allow her to do so, she will, prevent our supplying them by our own industry. She would give us a comparatively small quantity cheap, and we could go without the balance. This is the only kind of abundance (!) which free trade ever can produce for the United States.

This is the abundance which free trade gives to India. In that country are to be found 200,000,000 of people of a highly acute and industrious race. To be on a par with the United States, their annual product should be about $25,000,000,000 in value. It is in reality far less than a tenth of that sum ; and every few years there is (now in this, then in that province) a famine that carries off from one to two millions of human creatures. And what advantage does Great Britain obtain from this deplorable condition of affairs? The pitiful advantage of selling in India some $120,000,000 worth of English products, and making thereon perhaps a profit of $25,000,000. Where England profits a dollar, India foregoes producing a thousand.

Similar has been the effect of English free trade upon Ireland, Portugal, and Turkey, and upon her own colonies. Deductive reasoning leads directly to the conclusion that the only way in which the British Islands, with 30,000,000 of people, can be the workshop of the world, is by preventing the world from helping itself; and, on the other hand, the imagination would fail to picture the magnificence of her empire after a period of fifty years, should she set herself resolutely to the task of developing in Ireland, in India, and in the colonies the arts and sciences which she herself possesses. She has a heart large enough to adopt so beneficent a policy. She does not do so, because sophistical arguments have fixed upon her a belief which future ages will wonder at, as we now wonder at her once equally unanimous belief in the existence of witchcraft.

REVIEW

OF

BASTIAT'S SOPHISMS OF PROTECTION.

THE preface tells us that " the primary object of the League is to educate public opinion, to convince the people of the United States of the folly and wrongfulness of the protective system." It quotes Senator Morrill as saying that " the year 1860 was a year of as large production and as much general prosperity as any, perhaps, in our history "; but these words would probably bear a different aspect if read with the context, as the condition of that year was very differently described by H. C. Carey as follows : —

" What it is which may be *positively affirmed* in reference to that *fluctuation of policy* which struck down the great iron manufacture, at the moment at which it had just begun to exhibit its power for good, would seem to be this: that in the British monopoly system which thereafter followed, we added something less than forty per cent. to our population ; seventy, to our machinery for water transportation; and five hundred, to that required for transportation by land ; meanwhile materially *diminishing* the quantity of iron applied to works of production. When you shall have carefully studied all this, you may perhaps find yourself enabled to account for the facts, that in the closing year of the free trade period, railroad property that had cost more than a thousand millions could not have been sold for three hundred and fifty ; that ships had become ruinous to nearly all their owners ; that factories, furnaces, mills, mines, and workshops had been everywhere deserted ; that hundreds of thousands of working men had been everywhere seeking, and vainly seeking, to sell their labor; that immigration had heavily declined ; that pauperism had existed to an extent wholly unknown since the great free trade crisis of 1842 ; that bankruptcies had become general throughout the Union; that power to contribute to the public revenue had greatly diminished ; and finally, that the slave power had felt itself to have become so greatly strengthened as to warrant it in entering on the Great Rebellion."

So much for one of the premises of the preface. Another of the premises is a quotation from Miss Martineau made to show that the superiority of Great Britain in manufactures was not attained by means of protection, but that protection had brought Great Britain to the verge of ruin in 1842.

But the superiority of Great Britain was gained long before 1842. The troubles at that time were the result of over-trading, of over-pushing of the manufacturing industries. Sir Robert Peel afterwards lost his head, and yielded to the Free Trade League, who were waging war upon the land-owners, and seeking to make the prosperity of England hang, as Carlyle forcibly said, upon being able to manufacture cottons a farthing a yard cheaper than other people. The millocracy triumphed over the landowners, and, fortunately for England, the gold of California and Australia brought about a general improvement in trade, which postponed the consequences for a long period. But they are seen now in Ireland, and may soon be seen in England. Meanwhile free trade has not prevented scenes in England quite equal to those pictured by Miss Martineau. They occurred from 1866 to 1870 ; but quotations would needlessly swell this article.

The preface adds,—

"Again, it is said there is need of diversifying our industries, as though industry would not diversify itself sufficiently through the diverse tastes and predilections of individuals,— as though it was necessary to supplement the work of the Creator in this behalf by human enactments founded upon reciprocal rapine."

The " work of the Creator " and " reciprocal rapine " are good rhetoric : they are not logic. They take for granted the question which is to be proved. The pretty alliteration might delight a *doctrinaire:* it would produce no effect upon the masculine judgment of a Napoleon, against whom Bastiat modestly puts himself.

We come now to Chapter I., entitled, "Abundance,— Scarcity."

Throughout this chapter M. Bastiat supposes that abundance and cheapness are necessarily coexistent. He does not know, or he does not appear to know, that a low price is perfectly compatible with great scarcity; that abundance exists only where a large supply is co-existent with a large effective demand; that it is in vain to offer things for a little money to one who has *no* money, and no work by which to earn money. At the end he says:—

"But it is answered, if we are inundated with foreign goods and produce, our coin will leave the country. . . . . Well, and what matters that? Man is not fed with coin. He does not dress in gold, nor warm himself with silver. What difference does it make whether there be more or less coin in the country, provided there be more bread in the cupboard, more meat in the larder, more clothing in the press, and more wood in the cellar?"

Yes! *provided;* but how would it be *provided* there was much less of all these things?

Did not M. Bastiat know that the very fact of the coin leaving the country proved that the home industries were not adequate to pay for the importations, and that these must therefore cease as soon as the coin was exhausted? A country has perchance four thousand millions of mechanical and manufactured products, the result of its own industry. It hankers after cheapness, and opens its ports. It is deluged. It gets products at first more cheaply. But the industries in which it has an advantage furnish only, or can be taken only to the extent of, one thousand millions. When its treasure is gone, it must satisfy itself with one thousand millions. These it may or may not thereafter get cheaply. Probably it will get them very dearly by reason of the low price at which it will have to sell what previously, with a fully employed population, it could use itself. But whether

it gets its small pittance cheaply or dearly, it must go without
the other three thousand millions.   This is what it will get
for mistaking cheapness for abundance.

Bastiat concludes as follows:—

"To restrictive laws I offer this dilemma,— Either you allow that
you produce scarcity, or you do not allow it.   If you allow it, you
confess at once that your end is to injure the people as much as
possible.   If you do not allow it, then you deny your power to diminish the supply, to raise the price, and consequently you deny having
favored the producer.   You are either injurious or inefficient.   You
can never be useful."

M. Bastiat evidently thought he had used brilliant logic.
But restrictive laws have for their object to produce abundance, and they effect their object: if they raise the price,
they increase in a much greater degree the effective demand,
— the ability to pay the price.   The limitation of the foreign market makes it simply impossible to employ the whole
working force of the United States upon those industries
in which it has a decided advantage.   The rest must be
employed upon fields, less advantageous perhaps, but infinitely more advantageous than living in the poorhouse or
helping somebody do what he can perfectly well do alone.

Napoleon hit the mark when he said that "if an empire
were made of adamant, the economists would grind it to
powder."

Bastiat desires the consumer to have everything offered to
him at a cheap rate; he is entirely indifferent about his
having or not having the means of buying.   In fact, the
consumer of the free trader was described by Homer, under
the name of Tantalus:—

"Then Tantalus along the Stygian bounds;
Pours out deep groans; with groans all hell resounds.
From circling floods in vain refreshment craves,
And pines with thirst amidst a sea of waves;
When to the water he his lip applies,
Back from his lip the treacherous water flies.

Above, beneath, around his hapless head,
Trees of all kinds delicious fruitage spread ;
There figs, sky-dyed, a purple hue disclose ;
Green looks the olive, the pomegranate glows ;
There dangling pears exalted scents unfold,
And yellow apples ripen into gold.
The fruit he strives to seize ; but blasts arise,
Toss it on high, and whirl it to the skies."—*Pope's Odyssey.*

For nineteen twentieths, nay the whole of the community, production is the condition precedent of consumption. That which a nation can consume in a year is its annual product. Strike to the earth a third part of its industries, and you by the very act strike off a third of the average individual income. The economist who is not aware of these things has studied to little purpose either Adam Smith or J. B. Say : he has gathered in their chaff, and left the wheat untouched. Abundance is impossible to the man of the empty purse.

After the Bastiat fashion, I will offer a dilemma to the free-traders. Either they know the above, or they do not know it. If they know it, they must cease preaching free-trade ; if they do not know it, they should come to the people of the United States to learn, but not to teach, political economy.

Chapter II. is entitled " Obstacle — Cause."
In this chapter Bastiat misses entirely the perception of the protectionist doctrine, which is *not* that wants are riches, or that labor is riches, but that the ability to satisfy wants is riches. The gross annual product of the nation being A, will not be diminished by the introduction of machinery. It will be diminished by substituting a foreign for a domestic product, unless the foreign product is so much cheaper as to immensely increase consumption in spite of the diminished means of purchase, and unless also the relations of the two nations financially are such that the imports will be paid for by exports : and even then the new arrangement leaves the country less independent ; withdraws from it the possi-

bility — nay, probability — of afterwards reducing the cost by increased skill and by invention; lessens the diversification of industries; and takes from the nation the incidental advantages which often spring from the stimulating effect of one industry upon others. Who can measure the effect in the United States of the introduction of the cotton manufacture upon the other industries in which machinery assists labor? If we had never had the cotton manufacture, it is not likely that even our agriculture would have reached anything like its present efficiency; and many other arts would probably not have been acquired at all up to the present day.

In this chapter Bastiat says, with italics, that "*labor is never without employment.*" This is flying in the face of facts with a vengeance. What can be the value of the method of reasoning which conducts a clever man to such a conclusion in spite of his eyes and ears?

Chapter III. is entitled "Effort — Result."

In this chapter Bastiat quotes a number of French legislators; and if he quotes them correctly, the reasons they gave for their votes or measures were not very wise, and furnished an opportunity for an easy victory. But it often happens that practical men are not introspective, not accustomed to put into words the real reasons which underlie their actions. When called upon to do so, they fumble about in their minds, and end in producing, not their real reason, but some very inadequate substitute of it. A "smart" writer like M. Bastiat at once falls upon their alleged reasons, demolishes them, and concludes that their authors were fools, when very likely they were in reality far wiser than he who felt himself entitled to sit in judgment. It may well be, taking all things into consideration, that the opulence of France, altogether, is increased rather than diminished by herself producing iron at sixteen francs which she could buy of England at eight: her safety and independence are certainly promoted.

Chapter IV. is entitled "Equalizing of the Facilities of Production."

M. Bastiat first quarrels with the phrase, which has not certainly mathematical exactitude, but which can easily enough be understood by any one whose object is to get at ideas, and not to triumph over words. It means that where one nation has an advantage over another *as to cheapness of production*, — such as Great Britain has over the United States by reason of cheaper labor, not yet compensated by greater skill upon our part, — she can beat down and annihilate our efforts to help ourselves and to acquire greater skill. She has been prevented from doing this by our protective duties ; and in many articles we have already acquired a skill sufficient to give us here at home the articles, even at a cheaper monied price than we could import them. In some we have not succeeded as yet so well ; and in some we probably never shall, so long as we strive to keep up among us that higher rate of real wages which is our chief hope for the future. But the higher price will be much more than compensated to the nation by the double production provoked by a home exchange, as against the single production provoked by a foreign exchange ; as also by our greater security both in peace and in war, and also by the incidental stimulus which one industry gives to others.

Bastiat says that in this case, as in all, " the protectionists favor the producer, while the *poor consumer* seems entirely to have escaped their attention." He seems to forget that nearly all of the *poor consumers* are consumers only in consequence of their being able to produce ; and that those few who do not produce themselves are dependent upon the profits of productive instruments, which would cease to yield a profit if the producing consumers could not produce, and therefore could not consume. If the consumers' means of buying were rained down miraculously from the sky, the Bastiat philosophy might be excellent ; but as long as their means of buying are entirely dependent upon their first *producing*, it would seem that the individual should be considered in both relations.

Bastiat contends, first, that equalizing the facilities of production is to attack the foundations of all trade.

To attempt to equalize all facilities — say, rather, to counter balance all advantages — might be open to his objection. But the American protectionist, for whose conversion the volume under review was published, does not propose to compensate great differences growing out of soil and climate. He does not propose to grow pineapples under glass at ten times the cost of importation, nor to do any other of the like absurdities imagined by Bastiat. What he does propose is, to balance the altogether artificial advantages arising out of accidental superiority in skill until we can ourselves acquire the like skill ; to balance the difference arising out of our dearer labor and capital ; and to protect our industries from the mischievous attacks in which products are sold under cost for the very object of destroying competitors. We have full faith that the competition of fifty millions of people will suffice to bring as low prices and as much skill as are possible under the circumstances ; and that the result will be that we shall produce everything which our climate and soil permit at considerably less sacrifice of labor and abstinence than the same things cost when brought from abroad.

M. Bastiat says, second, that it is not true that the labor of one country can be crushed by the competition of more favored climates.

But it is quite true that domestic arts and manufactures, which are most important to possess, can be crushed by the competition of countries having cheaper labor and equal or greater skill. If he meant his No. 2 to assert or insinuate the contrary, the hardihood of the assertion or insinuation would hardly require an answer. Deductive reasoning shows that it can, and history shows that it does.

He says, third, that protective duties cannot equalize the facilities of production ; fourth, that freedom of trade equalizes these conditions as much as possible ; and, fifth, that the countries which are the least favored by nature are those which profit most by freedom of trade.

In all this he chooses to misunderstand what is meant by equalizing the facilities of production. This is simple trifling. Next he exemplifies his position by supposing a case of Parisian speculators producing oranges at ten times the cost of importing them from Portugal, and being protected by a duty of nine hundred per cent. This is also trifling: it has nothing to do whatever with any actual question as to protection. Then follow several excellent paragraphs, showing how any improvement in production spreads itself to the advantage of the whole community, and showing how natural advantages, and also, finally, the advantages arising from inventions, come to be enjoyed by consumers gratis, they paying only the necessary wages of labor and abstinence. But after all those excellent and really eloquent paragraphs comes this : —

"Hence we see the enormous absurdity of the consuming country, which rejects produce precisely because it is cheap. It is as though we should say, 'We will have nothing of that which Nature gives you. You ask of us an effort equal to two, in order to furnish ourselves with articles only attainable at home by an effort equal to four. You can do it because with you Nature does half the work. But we will have nothing to do with it; we will wait till your climate, becoming more inclement, forces you to ask of us a labor equal to four, and then we can treat with you *upon an equal footing.*'"

This is one of Bastiat's extreme cases, but under certain circumstances it would not be altogether so absurd as he appears to imagine, *e. g.* : —

The products in which the United States have an advantage are agricultural. They can produce enough for themselves and as much more. Call the possible product 2 A. Suppose that what they cannot produce except at a double effort are mechanical and manufactured products. Call these M. There is a foreign demand for $\frac{1}{2}$ A. Under free trade there can be produced and imported $1\frac{1}{2}$ A; M imported being equal to $\frac{1}{2}$ A; and the country will have for consumption A + M. Now remove one half of the population from agriculture to the mechanical and manufacturing arts. The half who are left can still produce 1 A, or enough agricultural products for the whole population ; and the other half can produce M by a double effort. There will then be for consumption A + M, notwithstanding the double effort. But suppose the required effort not double, but $1\frac{1}{2}$.   The product will then be $A + \frac{4}{3} M$.   The whole population, both agricultural and mechanical and manufacturing, will then have one third more of M under protection than under free trade, even if the effort necessary be 50 per cent greater to produce M.   If the effort (measured by labor and abstinence) be the same, then the product under protection will be $A + 2 M$.

The mechanical and manufacturing arts then which are introduced under a duty of 50 per cent in such circumstances, will at once give the whole country one third more of their products than can be had under free trade ; and, as skill increases, they will give more and more ; and their skill will react upon agriculture, rendering its processes more effectual, and enabling a still greater withdrawal of men from agriculture to the arts.   And the home market will be always safe against war and against excessive foreign crops ; and, moreover, it will grow step by step with the population, which the foreign market never can.

M. Bastiat makes a great friend of *Nature :* but it is not against *Nature* that the American protectionist raises his bulwarks.   He imports many tropical products free of duty, but he intrenches against the foreign skill which is not *natural* but purely artificial, and which is speedily overtaken by our own ; and he intrenches against the lower wages current abroad, which we do not wish to imitate here.   In spite of a 50 per cent duty, the whole country is richer immediately, and gains more and more as skill is acquired.

M. Bastiat says that we call the free traders theorists, and he retorts the accusation ; but he mistakes us.   We do not complain of them for being theorists, but for being bad theorists, blundering theorists, theorists who use arguments in every case which are only applicable in one of all possible cases, to wit. in the case where the whole population can be fully occupied in those industries in which it has an advantage, and where, *also,* their whole surplus can find steady, sure, uninterrupted markets.   In this very exceptional case, to buy in the cheapest market is best in a purely financial aspect.   Their proposition is not universal, not one of even frequent application. To argue from it as if it were a universal proposition, as the free traders do, is to violate one of the fundamental maxims of logic.

Chapter V, — "Our Productions are overloaded with Taxes."

Here is more bad theory. We are taxed heavily, he says. How absurd, then, to add another tax which makes France pay twelve francs for iron which it can get from England for eight. The blunder here consists in not perceiving that, although the extra price of iron may in a certain sense be called a tax, yet it is of an entirely different nature from the other things called by the same name. Suppose, for instance, that France is using 2,000,000 of tons of iron produced in France and costing twelve dollars a ton. Here are $24,000,000 of products which are paid for by other $24,000,000 of various French products. The result is commodities worth $48,000,000, every dollar of which is net individual income to some French citizen, as has been well shown by J. B. Say. The totality of French industries is in equilibrium. Each employs all the capital and all the industry it can, and carries along its normal surplus stock. The expansion of each industry, both as to capital and quantity of labor employed, is limited by the extent of the market. Now open the ports and bring in the 2,000,000 tons of English iron at eight dollars. The immediate effect upon the consumers of iron is that they save $8,000,000: but the general demand for French products is diminished $32,000,000. The importation of iron selling for $16,000,000 provokes a French production of $16,000,000. The home production of the iron, on the contrary, gave a total home product of $48,000,000, — a difference of $32,000,000. It is true that the community saves $8,000,000 in the price of the iron, but on the other hand its aggregate ability to consume is reduced $32,000,000; and under these circumstances it may well happen that its ability to consume imported iron at eight dollars will be less than its ability to consume homemade iron at twelve dollars. The free-traders call the sums collected to pay the interest on the national debt and the expenses of government *taxes*, and they call the extra price (when there is an extra price) paid for home-made products also *taxes*. But they are entirely different; almost as different as the files of a carpenter and the files of a regiment. The tax arising out of protective laws, in the instance under examination, takes from the French consumers four dollars a ton; but it gives them twelve: the net result is that they are better off by eight, or twice the amount of the so-called tax. This flows inevitably from Say's proposition that the *whole* price of everything produced in a country is net individual income to some citizen of that country. If the free-traders would make the other " taxes " produce a similar result, we would all clamor for more taxes.

Chapter VI. is called "Balance of Trade." He begins as follows: —

"Our adversaries have adopted a system of tactics which embarrasses us not a little. Do we prove our doctrine? They admit the truth of it in the most respectful manner. Do we attack their principles? They abandon them with the best possible grace. They only ask that our doctrine, which they acknowledge to be true, should be confined to books; and that their principles, which they allow to be false, should be established in practice. If we will give up to them the regulation of our tariffs, they will leave us triumphant in the domain of theory."

M. Bastiat was in error as to the attitude of protectionists generally. They do *not* admit that the theory of the free-traders is correct, nor their own practice wrong; but when worried by much beating of gongs — represented to be logical instruments — and by much assumption of superiority in reasoning, they have often been inclined to reply: " You puzzle us with sophistical riddles. We feel them to be wrong, but have not the time, perhaps not the ability, to show wherein they are wrong. We have seen your own chiefs perplexed with the fallacy of Achilles and the tortoise, and some of them declaring it to be insoluble, — that being an argument known to be erroneous, but one of which no one has ever yet given a wholly satisfactory explanation. Now, we feel that your arguments are sophistical; we are so sure of it that we are ready to risk our fortunes upon the belief. We are not able to talk you down, and are willing you should theorize to your hearts' content, so long as you will confine yourselves to theory." Such is the feeling of many. It is not the feeling of the writer. It is as absurd as anything well can be to say, "So and so may be very well in theory, but it will not do in practice." If it will not do in practice, . it most assuredly is not good in theory. It may be good in pseudo-theory; but true theory must explain practice, or be in accord with it. Sound theory and sound practice are Siamese twins. As was said before, we do not, as you have the presumption to say, object to you as theorists: we only object to you as bad theorists.

M. Bastiat gives us examples in which every merchant will find errors; upon which, however, it is not worth while to expend time. and patience, — the main object of the chapter being to show, what everybody knew before, namely, that an unusually successful voyage brings into a country a much larger value than it takes out. But there are also very unsuccessful voyages, which bring in much less than they take out; and everybody who knows anything of commerce is aware that the average result is cost, expenses, — and a profit not greater than what is usual in other kinds of business. This is fact; and this also is the result which the reasoning of all respectable economists, from Adam Smith down, points out as what must necessarily be fact. The balance of trade in our days is so complicated by the transfer of securities, and by the remittances of the profits upon foreign investments, that no certain conclusion can be drawn from custom-house statistics; but for all that, an exportation of treasure, exceeding greatly the product of the country, indicates an adverse balance of trade, which cannot exist many years without financial convulsion.

Chapter VII. is entitled "Petition from the Manufacturers of Candles, Wax-lights, Lamps, Chandeliers, Reflectors,

Snuffers, Extinguishers; and from the Producers of Tallow, Oil, Resin, Alcohol, and generally of Everything used for Lights."

This is a petition against sunshine, and regarded as persiflage, it is excellent. Considered as an economical argument, it can impose upon no one who has the least common-sense, or the least logic, which is only common sense put into a formula. As the sun does not give us light, through the twenty-four hours, artificial light must be had and can be had only through labor. If the circumstances are such that by procuring it from abroad the gross annual product is greater than it is by producing it at home, then, financially considered, it is better to procure it from abroad. But this case seldom occurs, as has already been sufficiently shown.

Chapter VIII. is entitled "Discriminating Duties."

This is a particular case, made up with just such circumstances as might lead a poor wine-grower to draw from it illegitimately an universal conclusion. As rhetoric, intended to deceive, it is very good. It is entirely unworthy of one who is seriously investigating national interests.

Chapter IX. is entitled "Wonderful Discovery."

In this, M. Bastiat discovers that a railroad has been made between Paris and Brussels in order to obviate or overcome natural obstacles to trade, but that the duty on goods between the two places was an artificial obstacle, and consequently absurd. The answer is, that the railroad was built with the intention of removing obstacles from desirable and beneficent communication. It was not built to facilitate the passage of foreign soldiers to Paris, nor to facilitate the invasion of the markets of France by produce that is not desirable. Whether the introduction of the produce be desirable or not, must be determined by other reasons than the fact that a railroad exists by which it can be conveyed. Distance is an obstacle to every sort of communication. That we take measures to overcome the obstacle does not prove that every sort of communication is productive of opulence.

M. Bastiat says: —

"Frankly, is it not humiliating to the nineteenth century that it should be destined to transmit to future ages the example of such puerilities seriously and gravely practised?"

We reply, Frankly, it *will be* humiliating to the nineteenth century to have to transmit to future ages Bastiat's puerilities in reasoning as examples of what could be thought worthy of being presented to France, England, and the United States by a person claiming to be, and by many even highly educated persons held out to be, an eminent logician.

Chapter X., entitled "Reciprocity," is in the same vein. A swamp, a bog, a rut, a steep hill, stormy oceans, etc. are veritable protective tariffs. By the railroad, the steamship, etc. we do all we can to remove the other obstacles; but the artificial obstacle, which it will cost nothing to remove, we suffer to remain. Why do we suffer it to remain? Because we believe that this particular obstacle to intercourse is not an obstacle, but an aid, to acquiring opulence. Whether it is or is not so cannot be determined by giving it the same name, putting it in the same class, with other things which we recognize as pernicious. If there were a tunnel formed between England and France, it would not be absurd to take such measures as would prevent its being used for the passage of hostile forces. When we build railroads and steamships, we do not logically bind ourselves to allow them to be used for every conceivable purpose, whether useful or pernicious; and the fact that the railroad or the steamship may be made to subserve a certain purpose, affords no ground for inferring that such purpose is or is not desirable. This must be ascertained by quite another sort of logic. Opium and rum, the smallpox and the yellow fever, are not necessarily beneficial because distributed by steamships and railroads.

Chapter XI. is entitled "Absolute Prices." He says: —

"If we wish to judge between freedom of trade and protection, to calculate the probable effect of any political phenomenon, we should notice how far its influence tends to the production of *abundance* or *scarcity*. We must beware of trusting to absolute prices; it would lead to inextricable confusion."

He assumes throughout the chapter that protection produces scarcity, and free-trade abundance. Cases might exist where it would do so. Generally it does the reverse, and it is notably so in the United States. Why is this? Because, when the population is fully occupied, much is produced; there is much to divide. When a considerable proportion is unoccupied, little comparatively is produced; there is less to divide. We saw the latter from 1873 to 1879: wages and profits were both low. We see the former now in 1881: the people are more fully occupied, and both wages and profits are higher. But the tariff also is higher. The difference has arisen from the abandonment in 1873 of the active formation of instruments, and from the resumption of the movement in 1880. But the larger production is concomitant with high prices, and the smaller production was concomitant with low prices. Cheapness, then, may exist without abundance, and abundance may exist without cheapness, however much this may astonish the free-trader.

Chapter XII. is entitled, " Does Protection raise the Rate of Wages ? "

M. Bastiat says to the working-man : —

" But *justice*, simple *justice*, — nobody thinks of rendering you this. For would it not be *just* that after a long day's labor, when you have received your little wages, you should be permitted to exchange them for the largest possible sum of comforts that you can obtain voluntarily from any man whatsoever upon the face of the earth.?"

M. Bastiat put himself forward as a logician, and also as a sincere expositor of truth. He desired and intended, so he implied, to teach the truth, *the whole truth*, and nothing but the truth ; and yet we here have him commencing his argument from the middle of the economical fact he was examining. He commences with the poor laborer when he has *got* his little wages : then, truly, it would be well for him to get as much in exchange for them as possible. But M. Bastiat carefully keeps out of sight that it is the protective policy which has given the man his employment, and consequently his wages. M. Bastiat may have believed that the man would get as good or better employment under a *régime* of free-trade ; but if so, that was the point at issue. To assume it would seem to show M. Bastiat to have been more anxious to gain his point than to ascertain the truth.

M. Bastiat continues :—

"Is it true that protection, which avowedly raises prices, and thus injures you, raises proportionately the rate of wages ?"

Here is the same rhetorical trick repeated. It is *assumed* that the man will get work under free trade the same as under a protective policy. To *assume* this is to take the whole free-trade theory for granted, without any proof or argument. M. Bastiat, however, to give everyone his due, seems really to believe he is right; and he sometimes does argue the question effectively from the premises which he assumes. These, however (unfortunately for free-trade philosophy), are simple blunders. They are venerable blunders, it is true, as they can claim the respectable paternity of Adam Smith more than a hundred years ago ; but they are very evident blunders for all that. We may borrow here Quinctilian's charitable remark about Homer, and say, "Sometimes the good Adam Smith nods." Unfortunately, he nodded at a very important point ; and he did the sleeping scene so naturally and effectively in his pages that every free-trade economist for a century and over has fallen into a slumber just where he did.

Bastiat says :—

"The rate of wages depends upon the proportion which the supply of labor bears to the demand."

Very true. He continues thus :—

"On what depends the demand for labor? On the quantity of disposable national capital. And the law which says ' Such or such an article shall be limited to home production, and no longer imported from foreign countries,' can it in any way increase that capital? Not in the least. The law may withdraw it from one course, and transfer it to another; but cannot increase it one penny. Then it cannot increase the demand for labor."

This is the fundamental position of the free traders. It was taken by Adam Smith more than a hundred years ago, was repeated by Mr. John Stuart Mill some thirty years ago, again repeated by M. Bastiat, and is now presented to the American people by the Free Trade League of New York in the translation of M. Bastiat's "Sophisms of Protection" now under review. If this position can be maintained, the free-trade doctrine stands. If it cannot be maintained, the free-trade doctrine falls. It has been already examined as presented by Adam Smith, and again examined as presented by Mr. Mill. Let us now examine it as put forward by M. Bastiat. He, of course, uses the word "capital" in the French sense, as signifying everything which can be used to assist or support labor; and his proposition is therefore somewhat broader than that of the English authors, who limited the words to the funds set apart for the support of *productive* labor.

To get at the bottom of this question, we must see what is the normal condition of an industrial community. Evidently it must be possessed of certain industries, A, B, C, D, etc. Let us examine industry A. It was commenced for the sake of profit. The same motive led to its increase continually, so long as the satisfactory profit was attainable; but, finally, it over-ran the market, as was evidenced by a portion of its products remaining unsold (or a portion of its materials remaining unconverted into finished products) by reason of a lack of demand. The producers then find a portion of their capital locked up, either in finished products or in unconverted material, or in both, and are compelled to cease augmenting their production. Some stock they find it, upon the whole, convenient to carry rather than be unprepared for fluctuations in the demand ; and they naturally carry as large a stock as they can without reducing profits below the point which satisfies the existing "effective demand for accumulation." Industry A, then, normally carries on a certain stock of products, and this stock locks up a portion of the capital employed in the industry. This stock is unemployed capital, and is recognized as such by Mr. John Stuart Mill, who, however, failed to observe the significance of the fact, or its important bearing upon economical reasoning. What is true of industry A is true of B, C, D, and all the others acquired by the community, which thus is seen to contain a multitude of industries, whose aggregate stocks of finished products and materials compose the aggregate unemployed capital of the community. It is the function of this unemployed capital to regulate the movement of industry. When the stocks increase, they enforce a slower movement ; when they are diminished, prices rise, and the industrial movement is stimulated to greater activity. We come, then, inevitably to the conclusion that in an industrial community the increase of industry is not limited by capital, but that the increase of both industry *and* capital is limited by the " field of employment."

But what limits the field of employment? Evidently, the limits which exist to effective demand. Let us confine our attention to a single industry, say the shoe manufacture. The desire of men for shoes is in itself limited. If they could be had without effort or sacrifice, a certain number of human beings would use only a certain number of shoes. Interpose a difficulty of attainment, the necessity for effort or sacrifice, and less will be used. There is, then, a limit to the shoe manufacture, even in a community where every person could find a sale for his labor if he desired to find one ; and the field is narrowed still further if a portion of the community is not able to find employment. Evidently, only a certain number of shoes can be profitably made at any cost you choose to fix upon. Reduce profits ever so low, and still the manufacture has its limits. Increase now the aggregate means of the community for the purchase of

shoes, whether by increasing the population or by increasing
the proportion of the population which can find a sale for its
labor, and the demand for shoes will increase, their exchangeable value will rise, the profits of the manufacture will
augment, and it will be enlarged to meet the changed conditions.   It will find its new limits in the production which
again reduces the exchangeable value of shoes to that point
where the profits fall to the rate usual in the community.
The moment profits are such as to enable the manufacturers
to save, and add to their capital an annual percentage,
greater than that by which the population increases, they
will increase their production faster than the population
increases; when profits are less, they will allow the population to gain upon the production.   There is, evidently, a
limit to the field of employment open to this industry.   It
will be wider under certain circumstances, narrower under
others.   But it is this limit,—the limit of the field of employment,— which regulates both the quantity of labor and the
quantity of capital which will be employed in it.   But what is
true of shoes is true of every other commodity, and of every
service known to the community.   It would seem, then, that
the normal condition of an improving community was this.
Skill, dexterity, judgment, machinery are constantly diminishing the sacrifice at which men can procure the commodities
produced by its industries; but they are also constantly increasing the mass of unemployed capital, and forcing it to
search for new commodities and new services, which may
tempt the capitalists, great and small, to increase their consumption, so as to keep pace with the increasing capacity for
production.   Each new commodity, convenience, and amusement furnishes a new market for the existing industries, and
enlarges the effective demand.   The field of employment is
increased, the people are more fully occupied, the gross
annual product is augmented, and the purposes to which an
additional fixed and floating capital can be applied are multiplied.   This is a society in which the introduction of a new
industry finds ample unemployed capital for its development,
and in which its products immediately enlarge the market

for the products of the old industries, and enable them to increase their production and the capital employed by them.

The normal condition of the society imagined by Adam Smith, and by John Stuart Mill in his first volume, and by Bastiat, is one where the field of employment is checked by the want of capital. Deductive reasoning leads us to the conviction that they put the cart before the horse ; to the conviction that, on the contrary, it is capital which is limited by the limitation of the field of employment. Introduce the new industry, and the capital necessary for its development will be found waiting for the work, and will be rapidly repro-. duced and more than reproduced by the augmented activity of the previously acquired industries. There will be a demand for more labor, and the increased annual product will reward the labor with higher wages.

Pure reasoning would have led to the conclusion that in a community possessed of a considerable variety of industries there must be an enormous aggregate of commodities unsold or unconverted, or, in other words, of unemployed capital; and an inquiry in Wall Street or State Street would have revealed that such was the fact. The free traders missed the fact, because they did not stop to reason, but preferred to jump at conclusions.

M. Bastiat's assertion, then, that a protective. law, which says such or such an article shall be limited to home production, cannot increase disposable capital a single penny is simply a blunder. It can increase it in the United States many hundred millions of dollars a year. The surplus stocks of the existing industries will immediately supply the capital required, and will be replaced in an exceedingly short time by the stimulated activity of those industries ; and, meanwhile, the people will have had paid to them for labor about twice the amount of capital invested in the new industry. Take the following as an illustration. Let us suppose that a country exists (call it, if you please, the United States) where the annual product is six thousand millions of dollars, and the normal surplus stock of commodities is equal to a consumption of sixty days, — a value of about one thousand millions.

We will suppose that it uses largely of woollen goods procured from abroad. The people, looking round, perceive that the climate is in no way unfavorable to the woollen industry; that they themselves are by no means wanting in general aptitude to mechanical and manufacturing industries; that there is every reason to suppose the requisite skill can be attained; and that well-directed efforts to import the industry will end in our producing, here, close at hand, as good or better cloths at a somewhat lower cost *of labor and abstinence* than they cost when imported from abroad. Accordingly the people say, let a law be passed giving a protection of say fifty per cent to woollens. The law is passed, and here and there all over the country woollen mills are commenced by the combined capital of a multitude of individuals. Gradually, as the mills are built, they pay in their subscriptions. Some draw out of the savings banks, which hold over a thousand millions; some have money with other banks or bankers, the deposits with whom exceed another thousand millions; some sell stocks or property. Twenty millions a month over the whole country will not make a ripple in the money market. Suppose, then, the operations are to the extent of twenty millions a month. As soon as gathered in they are paid out for labor and spent by labor in buying commodities. The producers of commodities now find their stocks diminishing, — that is, a part of their unemployed capital is set free. They will know this if the free-trade philosophers do not, and they will employ more labor to meet the increased demand for commodities. They will be able to pay out twenty millions a month more for labor, and this will bring about an additional production of more than forty millions, — more than sufficient to pay for the additional labor and the construction of the woollen mills besides. This is warranted by the facts given in the United States Census for 1870, which showed that the mechanical and manufacturing industries in the United States added $1,744,000,000 to the value of the material used, and that of this $776,000,000 went to labor. It would seem, then, that $240,000,000 a year would be invested in woollen mills in the year without diminishing the floating capital of the country a cent. At the end of the year the country will have woollen mills which cost $240,000,000 as an addition to its fixed capital, and the laboring classes will have had $480,000,000 additional to spend. The investors in mills will have withdrawn $240,000,000 from the monied reserves, but the master mechanics and manufacturers will have added an equal or somewhat larger amount. The nation altogether will be richer by $240,000,000 in the shape of woollen mills, although it has had and spent $480,000,000 more within the year; and this is the result of giving fuller occupation to the people. More commodities are made and there are more consumed.

This is the effect of the law which Bastiat says cannot add a single cent to the wages of labor. Let business men, who understand accounts, examine the above theory of the protectionists, and compare it with the theory of the free-traders, and then decide which represents and explains the actual course of financial affairs as they go on continually before our eyes, and which ought to be taught to young men who are preparing for practical life.

Bastiat says that " when a nation isolates itself by the prohibitive system, its *number* of industrial pursuits is certainly multiplied, but their importance is diminished. In proportion to their number they become less productive, *for the same capital and* same skill are obliged to meet a greater number of difficulties. The fixed capital absorbs a greater part of the circulating capital; that is to say, a greater part of the funds destined to the payment of wages.

Was this a man capable of teaching the people of the United States? "*Isolate*" is a good piece of rhetoric. The abominable, absurd, suicidal, ridiculous, impoverishing tariff of the United States has so "isolated" the nation that it sends abroad for sale an annual value of about nine hundred millions, and keeps five or six times as much at home. It is so poor that its average annual individual income exceeds that of any other country in the world, not even excepting Great Britain. It has on its hands no starving Ireland, no starving Orissa, no starving Behar; nor would it have were those countries transferred to its dominion. For "starving" would then have to be substituted in every case the words "flourishing," "contented," "prosperous;" for they would be protected from hostile industries as much as from hostile armies.

M. Bastiat imagined that a new industry would be established by capital drawn from the old industries, which would be thus cramped and diminished, whereas the new industry would be established and equipped by capital already existing, and replaced during the period of its introduction by labor which would otherwise have been unemployed; and its products, when established, constitute an additional market for the products of the old industries, enabling them all to increase their production.

Chapter XIII. is called "Theory — Practice."

In this chapter M. Bastiat claims for each individual the "*free disposition of his own property.*"

This is a proposition in law or in social science. It has nothing to do with political economy, which is an inquiry into the means of increasing national opulence. If it were shown that protection was one means, it would be no answer to say that protection invaded natural rights. Either legal or social science would laugh at any such pretension.[1] A certain society has come to the belief that the opulence of all and each of its members will be promoted by a regulation that while A is employed by B, C, D, etc., he shall in turn use the products of B, C, D, etc. A does not like the regulation. His particular industry is such that B, C, D, etc., must employ him, while he has discovered that D's product can be got a little cheaper outside the society. A would like to work for the society and enjoy all the advantages of their custom; but he would prefer not to give any custom in return. He maintains that by an opposite arrangement the society altogether will grow rich. B, C, D, etc., reply that if the industry of D be abolished, D will have to be supported by the rest; and that in the particular circumstances of their society it is vastly cheaper to get the products through D than

---

[1] See note 1, page 79.

to get them from abroad and let D sit idle. "But D is a monopolist!" cries A. "No;" reply the rest of the alphabet, "D is faithfully working in his special field, and he is gaining skill yearly. It is our will that his field, although not the most fertile the society possesses, shall be cultivated. We believe that in this way we shall altogether be a wealthier society than if we follow A's suggestion. Let A convince us to the contrary, and we will do as A proposes; but calling D a monopolist does not seem to us to have any bearing upon the calculation. It is simply the throwing of mud. It would seem that A's arguments must be weak and few, if he finds himself reduced to such expedients." "But," says A, "it is the natural right of every man to do what he pleases with his own property." Again reply B, C, D, etc., "This is not the question before us. The question is, How shall we all enjoy the greatest abundance? If you fly away from the question we shall conclude that you have nothing relevant to offer." "But," rejoins A, "political economy and common sense tell us that to secure the greatest abundance we have only to buy in the cheapest market. It is absurd to buy of D at four dollars what you can have from abroad for three dollars." "This," say B, C, D, etc., "may be your political economy and your common sense; but it is not ours. D will take payment in that which we have to give; he pays his landlord, his butcher, his baker, his tailor, his clergyman, his lawyer, his physician, his laborers, with our products, or with money which is expended for our products; whereas, the foreign producer of D's commodity can consume, or cause to be consumed, only a tenth part as much of our products. We can, therefore, have from D more of his products than we can have from D's foreign competitor, and we enable D to support himself; whereas, in the other case, he must be supported by us. D is not producing pineapples under glass, nor doing any other absurdity: he is only producing something which nominally costs perhaps a third more than it is offered at by your foreign friends, but which really, taking all things into account, costs less, and will cost a great deal less when D has acquired greater skill. This is our political economy. Convince us that we are wrong and we

will act accordingly; but you will never convince us we are
wrong by calling D a monopolist, a robber, a thief, a liver
upon public charity, a man actuated by the spirit of a slave-
holder, etc.; nor will you convince us by talking about the
shame of preventing our poor laborers from spending their
hardly earned wages as they please. We recognize all such
twistings and turnings as the tricks of the rhetorician. If
you cannot convince us by good sound logic and common
sense, you are at liberty to depart out of our prosperous
society. There are plenty of people who will be glad to buy
you out."

M. Bastiat writes: —

"You, Messrs. Monopolists, maintain that *facts* are for you, and
that we, on our side, have only *theory*. You even flatter yourselves
that this long series of public acts, this old experience of Europe
which you invoke, appeared imposing to M. Say; and I confess that
he has not refuted you with his usual sagacity.

"I, for my part, cannot consent to give up to you the domain of
facts; for, while on your side you can advance only limited and special
facts, we can oppose to them universal facts, the free and voluntary
acts of all men.

"What do *we* maintain? And what do *you* maintain?

"*We* maintain that 'it is best to buy from others what we can ourselves produce only at a higher price.'

"*You* maintain that 'it is best to make for ourselves, even though
it should cost us more than to buy from others.'

"Now, gentlemen, putting aside theory, demonstration, reasoning
(things which seem to nauseate you), which of these assertions is
sanctioned by universal practice?"

M. Bastiat was in error. Nothing would delight us more
than sound theory and reasoning; nothing more than a real
demonstration; but theory which is built up by drawing universal conclusions from particular premises, reasoning which
violates every canon of logic, a demonstration drawn from an
identical proposition, — these certainly do turn our stomachs.

We deny that "it is always best to buy from others what
we can ourselves produce only at a higher price." The distribution of the individuals in a community, under the *régime*

of the division of occupations, is not found to be so perfect
that each person finds employment all the time in his peculiar
calling.   Many find themselves out of work much of the
time ; and this leisure those who are thrifty employ to the
best advantage they can.   The product, if sold in the market,
might not net more than half as much per day as they earn
at their occupations when they are at work ; but it is clear
gain.   They are good economists in so employing themselves
rather than sit idle and repine at the want of work.

We protectionists do *not* maintain the general proposition
which you thrust upon us.   We do not maintain that " it
is best to make for ourselves, even though it should cost us
more than to buy of others."   The proposition, by an artful
misuse of words, begs the whole question.   *Costs* us more
than to buy of others !   What does this mean ?   What is the
cost to an individual of a piece of work done when he would
otherwise have done nothing ?   What is the *cost* to a nation
of work done by labor otherwise unoccupied assisted by capital otherwise unemployed ?   What we do maintain is, that
for an individual it is best to do something for himself or
others during the·days when his special trade or art leaves
him unoccupied ; and that, for a nation, it is best to promote
that distribution of labor and capital which evolves the
greatest gross annual product ; for the gross annual product
is the sum of the net individual incomes, as has been recognized both by Adam Smith and J. B. Say.   The individual
must be left, in his local position, to find out what is best for
him to do.   He will do one thing under free trade — quite
another thing under protective laws.   What he does under
one system affords no evidence of the goodness or badness
of the other ; nor can the fact that he does this or that afford
any evidence that this or that will promote the general interest.   Adam Smith, indeed, after adducing a few instances
in which he thought individuals acting solely with a view to
their own interests would, nevertheless, unintentionally promote that of the society, added the words, — " and he (the
individual) is in this, as in many other cases, led by an invisible hand to promote an end which was no part of his

intention ; " but it will be observed that Adam Smith had not
the folly to put this forth as a true induction.   He threw it
out as a rhetorical flourish, knowing well that a thoughtless
crowd *would* seize upon it as a general proposition revealing
the deep plans of Providence ; and that, having so seized upon
it, they would be too innocent of logic to be shaken in their
faith by any number of negative instances.   But fortunately
all men are not imposed upon by a rhetorical flourish.   Indeed,
Adam Smith did not thus impose upon himself, for he advo-
cated government restraints upon the issues of banks, and
defended it in Book II., Chapter II., of the " Wealth of Nations " (towards the end), in the following words : —

" To restrain private people, it may be said, from receiving in payment the promissory notes of a banker, for any sum, whether great or
small, when they themselves are willing to receive them ; or to
restrain a banker from issuing such notes, when all his neighbors are
willing to accept them, is a manifest violation of that natural liberty
which it is the proper business of law, not to infringe, but to support. Such regulations may, no doubt, be considered as in some
respect a violation of natural liberty. But those exertions of the
natural liberty of a few individuals, which might endanger the security
of the whole society, are, and ought to be, restrained by the laws of
all governments, — of the most free as well as of the most despotical.
The obligation of building party walls, in order to prevent communication of fire, is a violation of natural liberty, exactly of the same
kind with the regulations of the banking trade which are here
proposed."

But if it did not impose upon Adam Smith himself, it did
upon many others, as may be inferred from the following
extract from Mr. John Stuart Mill's " Political Economy,"
Book V., Chapter XI., paragraph 12 : —

" Mr. Wakefield therefore proposed to check the premature occupation of land, and dispersion of the people, by putting upon all unap-
propriated lands a rather high price, the proceeds of which were to be
expended in conveying emigrant laborers from the mother country.

" This salutary provision, however, has been objected to, in the
name and on the authority of what was represented as the great principle of political economy, that individuals are the best judges of their

own interest. It was said that when things are left to themselves, land is appropriated and occupied by the spontaneous choice of individuals, in the quantities and at the times most advantageous to each person, and therefore to the community generally ; and that to interpose artificial obstacles to their obtaining land is to prevent them from adopting the course which, in their own judgment, is most beneficial to them, from a self-conceited notion of the legislator, that he knows what is most for their interests, better than they do themselves. Now this is a complete misunderstanding, either of the system itself, or of the principle with which it is alleged to conflict. The oversight is similar to that which we have just seen exemplified on the subject of hours of labor. However beneficial it might be to the colony in the aggregate, and to each individual composing it, that no one should occupy more land than he can properly cultivate, nor become a proprietor until there are other laborers ready to take his place in working for hire, it can never be the interest of an individual to exercise this forbearance, unless he is assured that others will do so too. Surrounded by settlers who have each their thousand acres, how is he benefited by restricting himself to fifty ? or what does he gain by deferring the acquisition for a few years, if all other laborers rush to convert their first earnings into estates in the wilderness, several miles apart from one another ? If they, by seizing on land, prevent the formation of a class of laborers for wages, he will not, by postponing the time of his becoming a proprietor, be enabled to employ the land to any greater advantage when he does obtain it ; to what end should he place himself in what will appear to him and others a position of inferiority, by remaining a laborer when all around him are proprietors? It is the interest of each to do what is good for all, but only if others will do likewise.

" The principle that each is the best judge of his own interest, understood as these objectors understand it, would prove that governments ought not to fulfil any of their acknowledged duties, — ought not, in fact, to exist at all. It is greatly the interest of the community, collectively and individually, not to rob or defraud one another ; but there is not the less necessity for laws to punish robbery and fraud ; because, although it is the interest of each that nobody should rob or cheat, it cannot be any one's interest to refrain from robbing and cheating others when all others are permitted to rob and cheat him. Penal laws exist at all, chiefly for this reason, because an even unanimous opinion that a certain line of conduct is for the general interest, does not make it people's individual interest to adhere to that line of conduct."

By parity of reasoning, we must say that when it is the interest of the community, collectively and individually, to build up a home market by buying " each of the other," there is not the less necessity for protective laws ; because although it is the interest of each that nobody should buy some article abroad, it cannot be any one's interest to refrain from buying abroad when all others are permitted to do so.

It will be seen that both Adam Smith and Mr. Mill take the pretty little dream of the invisible hand, and the doctrine that individuals can judge best about their own interests, at their true value. They may be used to support a position which they wish to establish ; but they are really of no importance. They neither of them put forward Bastiat's absurdity that each individual by the right of property is invested with power to veto the action of the whole community.

M. Bastiat continues : —

" You are not then sustained by *practice*, since it would be impossible, were you to search the world, to show us a single man who acts according to your principle."

As we have seen that every prudent and thrifty individual acts contrary to the principles laid down by M. Bastiat as those of free trade, and in accordance with the real principles of the protective theory, the intrepidity of the above assertion is marvellous.

The rest of the chapter is full of similar intrepidity ; imputing admissions and arguments which protectionists never make, and then securing to himself an easy victory over his men of straw.   He concludes as follows : —

" And all this for what ?   To prove to us that we consumers, — we are your property ; that we belong to you, soul and body ; that you have an exclusive right on our stomachs and our limbs ; that it is your right to feed and dress us at your own price, however great your ignorance, your rapacity, or the inferiority of your work !   Truly, then, your system is one not founded upon practice ; it is one of abstraction — of extortion."

Pray who are these obstreperous consumers, in whose name M. Bastiat presumes to speak? Nineteen twentieths of the consumers, as already shown, are also producers, either of commodities or services, with whom the only means of purchase are their products; with whom to produce is the condition precedent of consumption. He certainly had no reason to speak for them. Nor is the case any better with the remaining twentieth. The gross annual product of commodities must be consumed or there will ensue immediate glut and stagnation. In the long run and upon an average of years it is consumed; being distributed in wages, profits, and rent, in proportion to the relative importance to the community of the labor and the capital which each brings to the service of the community. An augmented annual production must then issue in an augmented recompense to both labor and capital. The totality of consumers is benefited; and each is benefited in proportion to the importance the contribution which his labor or his capital makes to the gross product which has to be divided. The manufacturer, then, who, in these United States, is secretly sighing for a reduction of wages which will enable him to compete in the "great market of the world" with Great Britain, is in reality sighing for a gain which must bring with it a much greater loss in the diminution of the vastly more extensive home market; and the clergyman, lawyer, physician, literary man, and all receivers of salaries, etc., labor under a similar hallucination, when they long for the cheaper products of cheaper labor from across the Atlantic; for with such cheaper products must come less employment for the home population, and a diminution in the gross annual product which pays not only all labor but all salaries, all fees, all incomes. This might not be true if the whole of our productive population (actual and potential) could be employed upon the branches of production in which we have an advantage, and employed without overstocking the markets of the world; but it appears to be indubitably true in the actual situation in which the United States and other nations are now placed.

Possibly a world might exist where it would promote the

opulence of each nation, and of all nations, were each to confine itself to those fields of production in which it has an
advantage ; but we are only concerned with the world as it is ;
and in this neither inductive nor deductive reasoning leads to
the conviction that the best possible arrangement springs
" naturally " from the unregulated strife of individual competition, — the clash of chaotic cupidities.   The laws of
nature are manifold.   Man studies them ; and, by artificial
collocation of materials and forces, brings those into play
which promote his ends.   He does this in every other department.   Why should he not do it in the department which
aims at social opulence, at abundance ?   He sees in other
nations arts which give a prodigious power over nature ; why
should he not seek to acquire them ?   Nature invites and rewards study with a most liberal hand in all other fields ; has
she forbidden him to study this ?   No ; it is not nature that has
forbidden him, but only Adam Smith ! — a very sagacious and
eminent author indeed, but one hardly justified in warning off
the human mind from a most important field of investigation,
— perhaps, indeed, *the* most important so far as material well-
being is concerned.   That individual interest can rarely lead
to the acquirement of those arts has been admirably shown
by John Ray in a work which the writer has just referred to
with delight and instruction.   That is the work of a philosopher and seeker after truth : everywhere cool logic, veracity,
dignity ; earnestness, indeed, but earnestness to discover what
is right, not earnestness to prove this or that preconcep-
tion to be right.   There is no appeal to the passions, to anger,
to pity, to envy, to greed, nor even to religious prejudices.
He never misrepresents the arguments or ideas of Adam
Smith, with whom he differs ; never puts into his mouth what
he did not say ; never bursts into passionate rhetorical spasms,
like Bastiat.   He neither disgraces himself nor affronts his
readers by the exercise of any such arts.   If a similar work
is to be found upon the free-trade side of political economy,
it is a pity the League should have paid so poor a compliment
to the good sense of the American people as to have preferred
presenting them with the " Sophisms " of Bastiat.

Chapter XIV. is entitled " Conflicting Principles."
In this M. Bastiat starts from this premise: —

" The disposing by law of consumers, forcing them to the support of home industry, is an encroachment upon their liberty, the forbidding of an action (mutual exchange) which is in no way opposed to morality. In a word, it is an act of *injustice*."

Under the *régime* of the division of employments, each individual produces a certain article or articles with which to buy whatever he requires. The greater the value of what he produces, the greater the amount that he can consume. If by buying of A he gets more than by buying of B, he does so. His interests as a consumer are identical with his interests as a producer.

But has a nation no rights? There is a nation called the United States: fifty millions of persons, soon to be a hundred millions. It possesses vast resources still undeveloped. It says to all the world, " Come over and share our prosperity. All we ask is that you should live like men as we do; and that, being furnished with work by us, we taking your products and services, you shall in turn consume the products and services of others among us so far as our laws and customs require. We have become convinced that this system promotes the general good, and that under it you will yourselves enjoy a greater abundance than under any other." " But," says A, " this is not what I desire. I would like to have you give me high wages; but, when I have got them, I have a right to buy of whomsoever I please; and C, across the Atlantic, being willing to live a great deal cheaper than B, can give me considerably more for my wages than B will." The United States might reply: " If you have any such right, then one individual can veto the action of fifty millions, making their interests give way to what he supposes to be his, but which we are satisfied are not his, because if A is to be allowed to act in this way every other citizen must be allowed to do so; and then, a large proportion of our industries being transferred abroad, high wages will disappear, and with them the ability to buy the cheap foreign goods." " But this is not so," cries A. " Adam Smith and all the illustrious and learned foreign economists down to M. Bastiat agree that it is best to allow every man to buy where he can buy cheapest. They assure me that they have demonstrated the doctrine, and that none but ignorant people have any doubt upon the subject." The fifty millions might reply : " Protectionist writers have gone over those reasonings and pointed out gross blunders in them ; blunders that would ruin the reputation of any of us ignorant people. Moreover, we see clearly enough that where much is produced there is much to consume. If half of us, working in the industries where we have a decided advantage, can produce as much as we all require, and as much as can find a good market abroad, it needs no philosopher to see that the other half of the population had better be employed, even upon less productive fields. This is our theory ; and under it we have always prospered, except during the years 1873–1879, when other sufficient causes produced depression?[1] Whenever we have faltered in this policy we have suffered, even during the years following 1849, when Australian and Californian gold favored prosperity everywhere. We believe that both inductive and deductive reasoning warrant our practice ; and if A does not think so he had better go to England and stay there. To allow him to remain and do as he likes, to the detriment of the community which gives him his opportunity of gaining a living, — *this*, indeed, would be an injustice. His demand *is* opposed to morality. Every moral teacher from Socrates down would so declare it."

There is no ground then for M. Bastiat's deduction that according to protectionist reasoning *utility* is incompatible with the internal administration of justice or incompatible with the maintenance of external peace. These are M. Bastiat's conclusions, indeed, but they cannot be worked out from any sound premises. As to the foreign consumer, we have no charge of his interests. By looking after those of the United States we shall do all we have any title to do. By taking good care of our own affairs, we may very likely promote those of the rest of the world as effectually as if we assumed

[1] See note 2, page 79.

the *rôle* of general philanthropist. A multitude of opulent nations would still have a vast international trade, — probably much larger in actual volume (though less, perhaps, in proportion to the total annual products) than can be supported between the same nations impoverished by free trade.

There is no call, then, for M. Bastiat's rhapsodies and declamations about horrible blasphemy, liberty, utility, justice, peace, and the manifestation of the wisdom of God as shown in the sublime harmony of material creation. The sober and clear-headed American people are not likely to be fooled in this way.

Chapter XV. is entitled " Reciprocity Again."

This chapter argues that an individual in a nation having no external relations sells his product for money, " casts his product into the national circulation," and by means of money withdraws a like value; that if thereafter the exchanges of the nation be opened — made free — with other nations, the individual will in like manner cast his product into the larger market, that of the world.

But induction from facts and deductive reasoning alike show that the individual may find the universal market smaller than the national. The farmer may have an advantage not only in growing wheat, cotton, and tobacco, but also in growing green crops and market products not susceptible of distant conveyance. He wishes to exchange *these* for manufactured goods which can be brought from the ends of the earth. He throws them into the market of the world ; but the world market for *them* is bounded by a radius of a few tens of miles. He can produce of them (his most profitable crops) only what can be taken by the population occupying the limited area. Put a cotton or woollen mill or any other manufacturing establishment near the farmer and his possible production of salable articles, and consequently his possible consumption is increased greatly. The *laissez-faire* system produces here a smaller product for the individual, for his immediate vicinity, for his nation, and for the world. If he buys that which comes from a great distance, he must raise

that which can be carried to a great distance, — that is, a few
articles, for which the distant markets are very limited.

Bastiat next reasons from individual action to national,
forgetting that nations are few and individuals many. A
casts his individual product into the national market, and sells
it. Innumerable producers compete to supply him with what
he needs. Frequent combinations among them to fleece him
are beyond the range of probability ; and any occurrence which
should stop his supply is scarcely possible. It is not so with
nations. They are few, and the possible events which might
stop a foreign supply are very many.

Finally, Bastiat says that if the supply and demand from
abroad should stop, we should only be forced upon *isolation*,
to reach which is the ideal of the protective system.

But it has been already observed that protection does not
aim at nor tend to *isolation*. It aims at and accomplishes a
comparative independence as to the great necessaries of life,
and brings about a great increase of opulence, from which
springs the ability to enjoy a thousand luxuries which can
really be got to better advantage elsewhere. The products
which the United States throws into the market of the world
are thirty times greater (per head) than free-trade India
throws; they are many times greater than those of Portugal,
Turkey, Ireland, and nearly equal to those of Great Britain's
American colonies, being $16.70 per head to $19.04 per head.
This last is a remarkable fact. The United States makes for
herself vastly more, per head, than those colonies consume,
and still sells in the market of the world a surplus as great,
or nearly as great, as theirs under free trade.

We say that this is a fact. You cannot deny it. But you
deny that the fact has any connection with protection. We
reply that by deductive reasoning we show that such a fact
ought to occur under protection; and by observations which
you cannot and do not deny, we show that it does occur.
You reply that you have shown by deductive reasoning that
no such fact could follow such a cause. We answer, in turn,
that we have pointed out errors in your deductions, errors
which absolutely annihilate them; while you have not found

any errors in our deductions, but answer them only by a repetition of your own (just as if they had never been confuted), and by a vast amount of declamation and rhetoric. You do not prove the contradictory of our propositions, but only the contradictory of some other propositions, which you put into our mouths, but which we ourselves never dreamed of.

Chapter XVI., — "Obstructed Rivers pleading for the Prohibitionists."

This is the case of the Douro, which, according to M. Bastiat, neither Spain nor Portugal was willing to improve, for fear that grain would pass between the two countries. The chapter does not give sufficient facts to enable a protectionist to decide whether, under the circumstances, it was or was not desirable to expend money in removing the obstructions. To M. Bastiat the case appeared simple. He was for removing all obstructions to individual action. To protectionists, who do not believe that individual action necessarily leads to the best result for a community, the case is not so clear. We believe that Adam Smith was right in advocating the regulation by the society of individual action regarding the currency, and that Mr. John Stuart Mill was right in advocating similar regulations regarding a variety of matters touching the general good. We believe that *laissez faire* and giving perfect freedom to individual action is not good in theory, and has never yet anywhere been adopted in practice.

Chapter XVII. is entitled " A Negative Railroad."

This chapter is a good specimen of M. Bastiat's reasoning. By diligent search or lively invention, he produces an absurd proposal that a railroad should have a break or terminus at Bordeaux, in order that goods and passengers should be thus forced to contribute to the profits of the boatmen, porters, commission-merchants, hotel-keepers, etc. He then argues that if such profit be conformable to the public interest, there ought to be similar breaks elsewhere, and these too would be for the general good, and for the interest of national labor.

" For it is certain that in proportion to the number of these breaks or termini will be the increase in consignments, commissions, lading, unlading, etc." A protectionist would say at once that the first break was detrimental, and that many would utterly prevent all consignments, commissions, etc., coming thus to a conclusion the opposite of that which M. Bastiat says is certain, — a conclusion, by the way, which would *not* be certain, even *if* the premises were sound. M. Bastiat, however, insists —

" that the *restrictive principle* is identical with that which would maintain this system of breaks ; it is the sacrifice of the consumer to the producer, — of the end to the means."

This shows, out of M. Bastiat's own mouth, that he had no conception of what protection does actually aim at. It aims at the greatest possible consumption, but recognizes (what M. Bastiat apparently did not) that, before an individual or a nation can consume largely, he or it must produce. Protectionists are as anxious as free-traders — more anxious than free-traders — to remove obstacles, to improve machinery, to improve tools, to improve the arrangement and organization of society. It aims at whatever will increase the gross annual product. Evidently M. Bastiat never learned such a doctrine; but he might have deduced it by easy economical reasoning from the sound parts of Adam Smith and J. B. Say. The trouble with him was that he gathered in their errors, and passed by their sound reasoning ; that he took in sober earnest, and as universal generalizations, what they threw out as rhetorical flourishes. Tinsel caught his eye quicker than solid gold. So he swallowed *laissez faire*, and thought to build a science upon a proposition drawn from a few and uncertain instances, and forbidden by innumerable negative instances. M. Bastiat certainly profited little from the " Novum Organum," or from Mr. John Stuart Mill's " Logic."

Chapter XVIII., — " There are no Absolute Principles."

M. Bastiat scoffs at the idea that there are in political economy no absolute principles, and reaffirms that the freedom of exchanges is an absolute principle. He deduces this from the provisioning of a great city. He says : —

" Contemplating this great city of Paris, I have thought to myself : Here are a million of human beings, who would die in a few days if provisions of every kind did not flow towards this vast metropolis. The imagination is unable to contemplate the multiplicity of objects which to-morrow must enter its gates, to prevent the life of its inhabitants terminating in famine, riot, or pillage. And yet, at this moment all are asleep, without feeling one moment's uneasiness from the contemplation of this frightful possibility. On the other side, we see eighty departments who have this day labored, without concert, without mutual understanding, for the victualling of Paris. How can each day bring just what is necessary, nothing less, nothing more, to this gigantic market ? What is the ingenious and secret power which presides over the astonishing regularity of such complicated movements, — a regularity in which we all have so implicit, though thoughtless, a faith ; on which our comfort, our very existence depends ? This power is an absolute principle, the principle of freedom in exchanges. We have faith in that inner light which Providence has placed in the hearts of all men, confiding to it the preservation and amelioration of our species, — interest, since we must give its name, so vigilant, so active, having so much forecast, when allowed its free action."

M. Bastiat then declares that no minister, however superior his abilities, could arrange things so well, and that if he should attempt it, the actually existing misery would be infinitely increased, etc., etc.

This chapter may be good, considered as declamation or rhetoric, but we fear it would hardly stand a test by Mr. Mill's canons of inductive logic. What M. Bastiat undertook to prove was that in political economy it was an absolute (by which he must have meant a universal) proposition that freedom in exchanges is, in every case, promotive of opulence ; or that every constraint put upon the freedom of exchanges is unfavorable to progress in opulence.

His method of proof was to present the case of a great city provisioned regularly without any supervision. He represents that there is never too much, never too little, etc., statements which it would be necessary to verify, and which could not be verified. On the contrary, it would be found that at times there are short, and at times excessive, supplies; that much food perishes unused almost in the sight, nay, quite in the sight, of hungry crowds; that much clothing wears out on the shop shelves in the sight of shivering myriads. M. Bastiat alleges that matters would be much worse under the management of a single head with suitable assistants, but he does not prove this; and a general proposition intended to be the basis of an important science should not rest upon opinion. As there is great irregularity of supply, so great that some 90 per cent of the mercantile classes (who undertake the management of such matters) fail and become bankrupts, the results of free competition are evidently far from perfect. Whether they could or could not be better managed by a government bureau is a matter of opinion, not a matter of certainty. To establish M. Bastiat's proposition inductively, it is necessary to find not only instances in which opulence attends freedom of exchange, but also to show that poverty never attends it. How then about Ireland, Turkey, Portugal, India; and, to a minor extent, but still to a very observable extent, all the American colonies of Great Britain? Freedom of exchange has not prevented millions from starving in Ireland and India in the midst of all the possibilities of plenty. These are negative instances, any one of which would be sufficient to forbid the proposed generalization. If, then, it is to be proved that freedom of exchange is even one among many causes of opulence, it must be proved deductively. It cannot be proved *a posteriori* in the face of numerous negative instances. Let us then try the case deductively, and first with regard to an individual. A produces something. Free trade says, Stick to your particular business, and buy with your products, in which you have an advantage, the other things you desire which are produced by persons who have an advantage over you in their production. Yes; certainly, *if* A has occupation all the time. But if he has occupation for only four days out of six, then most certainly let him do something else during the two unoccupied days, rather than call in a skilled artist to do it for him. He may

not do it as well or easily at first, but he will do it after a
fashion, and better and better every time he tries ; and he
will save a portion of his four days' earnings, which would
otherwise be paid out for the work he now does for himself.
If he be thrifty he will do this of his own accord ; if he be
unthrifty it would be better for him, so far as opulence is concerned, if he were constrained to do so. But this is to invade
his liberty. True ; and upon other grounds than that of
procuring abundance, it may be better not to constrain him ;
but that is another question. The question we have before
us is, " How shall he obtain the greatest abundance ? " There
can be no sound reasoning if we fly off from the point under
discussion.

Now let us consider a nation, say, the United States. It
possesses a decided advantage in growing cotton. Are we to
confine ourselves, fifty millions of us, to growing cotton ? It
is only necessary to ask the question to make the absurdity
apparent. We have also an abundance of cheap land, capable
of yielding agricultural products for seven hundred millions
of people, and at our present rate of increase we shall grow to
be a hundred millions in twenty-five years ; and to two hundred millions in half a century. Some twenty-five millions of
people three thousand miles away are willing to take a few
agricultural products of us, and they say they will give us in
return manufactured products cheaper than we can make
them ourselves, while land is open to all at a nominal price.

Twenty-five millions of people (a minute portion of the
human race) propose to do the mechanical and manufacturing
work for a thousand millions. But a thousand millions of
people can raise raw agricultural products for three thousand
millions ; where are the other two thousand millions ? Or, to
put it in another shape, three hundred and fifty millions can
raise raw agricultural products for the world ; what are the
other six hundred and fifty millions to do while the English
Islands do all the mechanical and manufacturing labors ?
England teaches free-trade doctrines, and these *promise* a
greater abundance than is practicable with protection. We
have a right, then, to assume that she promises the world at

least as great an abundance of mechanical and manufactured products as are enjoyed by the people of the United States who are so silly and unscientific as to help themselves. They consume per head a value of $100 in such products. A hundred dollars each for one thousand millions of people is one hundred thousand millions. The remuneration of capital and labor for converting the raw material, even at a low rate, would be thirty thousand millions of dollars, or about six times the total annual production and consumption of the whole British Islands! Here we come to an absurdity. The dream of being the workshop to the world enjoying abundance is seen to be only a dream. If those Islands were called upon to supply the United States alone, profits and wages would speedily be doubled or trebled there, and the cheapness which exists during lack of demand would vanish. But what she could give us of finished products would be limited by the amount she could consume of our raw products ; and a very short calculation will show that the quantity would be only a small fraction of what we get by helping ourselves even now, and twice as inadequate twenty-five years hence.

Any one who has been taught simple arithmetic can see that Great Britain cannot give us abundance at any price. She can give us cheapness *and* scarcity if we will first allow her to destroy our own industries and drive an undue proportion of us on to farms; but we can have an abundance of finished products *only* by manufacturing ourselves. In this way we can have all we need without paying more in labor and abstinence than we pay for raw products.

Chapter XIX., — "National Independence."

A chapter so full of inveracity, audacious misrepresentation, and declamation as to be positively wonderful. It says in substance that : —

"With free trade and mutual independence would come eternal peace! 'Interest' — that is, the immediate selfish interest of the unbridled individual — is the necessary, eternal, and indestructible mover to the guidance of which *Providence* has confided human perfectibility. The 'spoliators' declaim against the beautiful harmony which God has been pleased to establish in the moral world," etc., usque ad nauseam.

The fact is that the most wicked wars of modern times have been waged to promote free trade, and more would be waged were it not that the great protectionist powers are too strong to be attacked.

Chapter XX., — " Human Labor — National Labor."

M. Bastiat maintains that the destruction of machinery and the prohibition of foreign goods are two acts proceeding from the same doctrine.

This only proves that M. Bastiat was entirely ignorant of political economy. He takes the case of machinery and shows easily enough that its introduction is advantageous. The gross annual product is not diminished, the immediate loss which falls upon the displaced laborers is made good to labor in general by the expenditure of the sum saved. Thus far, all right ; but his next step is a blunder.

Ten millions of hats produced in France at fifteen francs makes one hundred and fifty millions of francs. Import from abroad at ten francs, and they will cost one hundred millions ; and the fifty millions saved being spent for other articles or services, M. Bastiat imagines that all will be serene the same as in the case of machinery. But he overlooks the fact that the one hundred and fifty millions' value of hats provoked and remunerated other French labor, producing values of one hundred and fifty millions ; the sum of products, then (the whole price of which was net individual income to Frenchmen ; see J. B. Say), was three hundred millions. Bring in the English hats, and the French products to pay for the hats (supposing complete reciprocity) will be one hundred millions. If the fifty millions saved on the hats be spent for other products, or say for more hats, then the gross French product will be one hundred and fifty millions. France altogether will have lost one hundred and fifty millions. The case is totally unlike that of machinery. If M. Bastiat had been competent to instruct the American people, he would not have made such a blunder.

Chapter XXI. is entitled " Raw Material."

Here the blunder just noticed comes on the stage again. M. Bastiat quotes M. de St. Cricq as saying : —

" ' Labor constitutes the riches of a nation, because it creates supplies for the gratification of our necessities ; and universal comfort consists in the abundance of those supplies.'

" Here," says M. Bastiat, " we have the principle.

" ' But this abundance ought to be the result of *national* labor. If it were the result of foreign labor, national labor must receive an inevitable check.'

" Here," says M. Bastiat, " lies the error. (See the preceding fallacy.)"

There are inaccuracies of expression in what is represented to have been said by M. de St. Cricq, but it is plain enough what he means, if one wishes to understand. Labor does not constitute the riches of a nation ; but labor produces or causes the riches of a nation, because it creates supplies for the gratification of our necessities, and universal comfort consists in the abundance of those supplies ; and the labor *must* be national labor. It cannot by any possibility be foreign labor, for that will not give an atom of its products except in exchange for an atom of ours, or for bonds which are mortgages, or for treasure. If nation A produces articles with less labor than nation B, and nation B produces other articles with less labor than nation A, it will be well for them to exchange, provided the gross annual product of each nation remains undiminished. If it be diminished in either nation, then clearly that nation is the loser. How can this be when both are getting things cheaper ? Because the articles and services in demand in each country are not infinite in number, but limited ; nor are they in infinite demand as to quantity, but also in limited demand. Nation A produced both articles, x and y, enough for its demand at the cost price. Nation B also produced both articles, x and y, enough for its demand at the cost price. Nation A now transfers to nation B the industry producing x, and nation B transfers to nation A the industry producing y. The aggregate demand for products and services in general is diminished in one or the other nation unless x and y balance.

If the demand in nation A for B's cheaper product y be 1 and the demand in nation B for A's cheaper product x be 5, the extra 4 can only be had by nation B so long as its treasure and securities hold out.[1] Thereafter it must be content with one fifth of the article x that it had before, and this deplorable result will be arrived at by an appreciation of the value of gold, making all debts, public and private, more onerous, and reducing the exchangeable value of its whole accumulated capital in the market of the world. The accepted theory of international exchange leaves out of sight three not altogether insignificant facts, — the first, the fact that there is such a thing as money in the world ; the second, that nations can and do run in debt to other nations ; the third, that the debtor nation must sell its products for what the creditors are willing to give. Bastiat assumes falsely that, if France gives up making hats and takes them from England, then England will increase its consumption of French articles to the same extent. The increase in the English field of employment consequent upon the new demand for hats will give England a greater power of consumption ; but this power will be exerted in buying more of everything (commodities and services) which England habitually desires and buys. Only a small portion of the increased consumption will fall upon French products ; the balance must be paid in treasure. *If* this be recovered from other nations it will only be by offering them French products cheaper than before.

Abundance then cannot be the result of foreign labor ; the foreign products can only be obtained in exchange for national products, or for money or for bonds, that is, by running in debt ; and the introduction of the foreign product, even at a two-thirds price, may lead to a marked impoverishment of one or the other of the exchanging nations. One or the other may have a greater power of purchase at the high price, than it has at the lower price.

The rest of the chapter is a conversation between manufacturers who wish to have materials introduced duty free, and M. de St. Cricq.

Manufacturers often wish their own individual interests, or *supposed* interests, to be made the concern of the State ; but

[1] See note 3, page 79.

no protectionist, properly so called, considers any but the
problem of how the nation may become wealthier, wiser,
and better. It is unnecessary to examine what M. Bastiat
puts into the mouths of the manufacturers any more than his
declamations about spoliation. These last are the arts of the
sophist, essentially dishonest and disreputable, and discredit-
able alike to the author and to those who have made themselves his sponsors to the American public. Nobody supposes
or affirms that labor itself, aside from its products, is the
desirable object, so far as direct effects upon opulence are
concerned; and in combating such a proposition, M. Bastiat
simply makes a false issue.

Chapter XXII. is entitled "Metaphors."

In this chapter, M. Bastiat inveighs against the use of the
expressions : invasion of foreign products; an inundation
of foreign goods; paying tribute to a foreign nation. He is
quite right to inveigh against their use as arguments. They
are not arguments. Neither is the denunciation of their use
an argument. If the free-trade doctrine be right, they are
improperly used, not being descriptive of facts; if the protectionist doctrine be right, they are oftentimes very descriptive
of most calamitous facts. Which is right and which is wrong
can never be ascertained by declamation and much calling of
names.

CONCLUSION.

M. Bastiat says of his book : —

"Among the sophisms which it has discussed, each has undoubtedly
its own formula and tendency, but all have a common root; and this
is *the forgetfulness of the interests of men, considered as consumers.*"

M. Bastiat imagines that the interest of the consumer is
promoted by offering him commodities at a low price, regard-
less of whether he has or has not anything to buy with.
The protectionist maintains that the interest of the consumer
is best promoted by not only offering him commodities, but
seeing to it that he has the means of purchasing. If he cannot buy, it is mere trifling to offer him an article for little

money. Give him the means of purchase, and the price is comparatively unimportant. *Scarcity* to the consumer is often accompanied by lowness of price; while abundance goes often hand in hand with a high price. M. Bastiat concludes that he will be satisfied if he has brought the reader to doubt —

"1. The blessings of scarcity.

"2. The beneficial effects of obstacles.

"3. The desirableness of effort without result.

"4. The inequality of two equal values when one comes from the plough and the other from the workshop.

"5. The incompatibility of prosperity with justice, and of peace with liberty, and of the extension of labor with the advance of intelligence!"

The protectionist believes that in the existing state of the world *abundance* cannot flow from free trade; that to acquire abundance a nation must erect an obstacle to the maliciously destructive competition of a community, which, having reduced its own labor to misery, can and will, if permitted, bring others down to its level. Protection does not maintain that effort without result is desirable, but only that it is desirable to enlarge the field in which effort is possible, so far at least as to obtain the greatest possible gross annual product for the nation. Protection has nothing to do with the proposition that any two equal values are unequal, nor with any other absurdity; and, finally, protection maintains that under its system, and only under its system, will prosperity and justice, peace and liberty, labor and intelligence, be found in accord.

To be sure, there is a difference in the meaning assigned to justice and liberty by M. Bastiat and by the protectionist. The latter considers it just that the individual, who prospers with and through the prosperity of the society, should be allowed to follow that private selfishness, which, if followed by all, would destroy the prosperity of all, and which would cease to be advantageous to the individual himself the moment others followed his example; but the protectionist understands by liberty, the liberty of the whole community to pursue the course most advantageous to the whole community, the individual included; it does not understand by liberty the right of one man to veto and prevent the efforts of the whole for the good of the whole, the individual himself included. We have conquered state rights when construed to include nullification; we are not likely then to allow individual rights to be pressed to the same extreme.

M. Bastiat concludes by charging upon protectionists spoliation and robbery, which is rather cool in face of the facts. Great Britain, at the instance of her manufacturing classes, has found them markets by force wherever she could, — notably, in China, India, Japan, and Ireland. She now is attempting the same thing by sophism in France, the United States, and her colonies. She cannot use force in the latter cases; but she can scatter the specious fallacies of such writers as Bastiat, and this she is doing with a free hand.

PART II.   Chapter I. is entitled "Natural History of Spoliation."

In this chapter the evils of war, robbery, slavery, and monopoly are enlarged upon, and the protectionist policy is then quietly classed with the rest as being monopoly. This, too, addressed to thirty millions of Frenchmen; and, now, addressed to fifty millions of Americans, every one of whom is free to go into any of the trades or manufactures enjoying the *monopoly*. Good rhetoric, only untruthful and deceitful.

Chapter II., — "Two Systems of Morals."

This chapter explains that economical morality (that is, free trade) does not exclude religious morality, which may still find something to do in the world! This is fortunate for religious morality!

Chapter III., — "The Two Hatchets."

This is the same wearisome untruth once more: a carpenter is represented as holding forth that by means of the protective laws he is robbed of half his earnings, and so he asks for a law that only dull hatchets be used so that the amount of carpenters' work should be doubled. In such mixed fabrics of exaggeration and absurdity, M. Bastiat stands easily first. Nobody proposes any sort of protection which will diminish the efficiency of labor, or which will other than augment the national gross annual product. Nobody believes that half of a French carpenter's wages are taken away by protection; although it is very possible and probable that free trade would diminish them one half.

Chapter IV., — " Inferior Council of Labor."

Here laborers, blacksmiths, and carpenters are represented as declaring that they pay more for bread, meat, sugar, thread, etc., on account of the tariff.

They would like to get their bread and meat, their sugar and thread, everything they eat, drink, clothe, or warm themselves with, from foreign countries; and suppose that, under such circumstances, there would be abundant French customers for tailors and blacksmiths.

The unmeasured and incredible audacity of M. Bastiat makes any sober answer difficult.

He pretends to believe that all laborers having carefully considered their position might rationally come to the conclusion that they found relevancy in the proposition that " It is better to support one's self, surrounded by well-to-do neighbors, than to be protected in the midst of poverty." He feigns to believe that well-to-do neighbors will be generated by a system which proposes to an idle population to buy everything where it is cheapest. Buy! What is a man to buy with who has nothing to do? He fancied that the amount of labor employed depended upon capital. He did not know that quite another cause mastered or limited first the accumulation of capital and then the employment of laborers. What other cause? The extent of the field of mutually satisfying desires. The community as a whole offers to the community as a whole — wheat. There are individuals who desire more wheat than they use; but they have not the means of buying it. Why? Because they produce nothing the community desires in exchange for wheat. Let these wishers for wheat discover a new convenience, or a new service for which others have a desire, and the satisfaction of the new desire will give wheat to those who before were sighing in vain for it. More still; the sale of an additional quantity of wheat will enable the grower of wheat to satisfy perhaps some before unsatisfied desire. The newly discovered or invented want is seized upon by labor and by capital (both of which are normally in excess in a community where diversified employments exist), and the field of employment is permanently enlarged. The community as a whole produces more than before, and so there is more to divide. *Wages, profits, rents, all rise together.* Not so when the people, seduced by witless manipulators of words, adopt the free-trade panacea. " Let us buy in the cheapest market," say they. " Let us get our cotton and metal fabrics from England, our woollen goods from Germany, our coal from Nova Scotia, our sugar from the West Indies, our hemp and tallow from Russia, our lumber from Canada, our wool from Australia." Here are industries which respond to what now (1881) amount to, say, over twelve hundred millions of dollars of annual wants in the United States, the satisfaction of which supports a population whose demand for the productions of other industries creates a market to an equal amount.

Transferring these industries to foreign nations would reduce the purchasing power of the United States by twelve hundred millions of dollars, would diminish the gross annual product, the fund out of which all *wages*, all *profits*, all *rents* are paid by that amount, which means by one sixth part. But this is not the worst. The foreign markets, oppressed with an additional twelve hundred millions of our products, would refuse them, except at a greatly reduced price, and we should find that many of the remaining unscalped industries would gradually die out for want of a market. The over-anxious manufacturer, clutching after a foreign market, would find himself bereft of a market ten times greater at home ; the clergyman, lawyer, physician, who coveted cheap clothes *with* ample incomes, would find the people too poor to pay the ample incomes. The carpenter, blacksmith, mason, painter, paperer, etc., who had been told that " houses were never imported," would find out, to their cost, that houses were built in proportion· to the means of the community.   The owner of railroad stock, bank stock, manufacturing stock, of houses, of stores, of forges, of farms, would find out at last that they were in the same boat as the day laborer, and that they could not thrive while he starved.

Chapter V., — " Dearness — Cheapness."
Here is only a repetition of the old fallacy which teaches an individual who has work for only four days out of six, that he will become rich faster by spending a portion of his four days' earnings to *buy* than he will by keeping all his earnings and doing for himself during the unemployed two days that which he requires to have done ; and which teaches a nation that it will become rich by buying at a cheap price what its unemployed labor and capital can make for nothing. Here also. is a repetition of inveracious assumption, as follows : —

" Therefore the question, the eternal question. is not whether protection favors this or that special branch of industry, but whether, all things considered, restriction is, in its nature, more profitable than freedom.

"*Now no person can maintain that proposition.* And just this explains the admission which our opponents continually make to us : ' *You are right, on principle.*' "

As before observed, some protectionists, feeling themselves unable to unravel all the innumerable Protean, " Achilles and Tortoise " puzzles which men like Bastiat propound, may have found refuge in the absurdity of saying, " So and so may be good in theory, but is not good in practice ; " but it is not the refuge of any protectionist who has the time and patience to follow up and refute a hundred times over the parroted fallacies of free trade.

. There is nothing new in Chapter V.   It is only a repetition of positions and assumptions already over and over again refuted.

Chapter VI., — " To Artisans and Laborers."
Here is more repetition.   Tariff duties are a tax, therefore

they are of the same nature as all other taxes.   This is like the syllogism *with four terms* which runs thus: —

Files are instruments made of steel.

A regiment marching in regular order is composed of files.

Therefore a regiment marching in regular order is composed of instruments made of steel.

Some taxes take money from the people and give nothing in return.

Tariff duties are taxes.

Therefore tariff duties take money from the people and give nothing in return.

Such is free-trade *logic!*   Professors who write books upon political economy would do well to have their manuscripts examined by their fellow-professors who teach the science of logic, before they stereotype their productions.

Again M. Bastiat says: —

"I believe that we can call that the *natural* rate of wages which would establish itself *naturally*, if there were freedom of trade.   Then, when they tell you that restriction is for your benefit, it is as if they told you that it added a *surplus* to your *natural* wages.   Now, an *extra natural* surplus of wages must be taken from somewhere : it does not fall from the moon ; it must be taken from those who pay it.

"You are then brought to this conclusion, that, according to your pretended friends, the protective system has been created and brought into the world in order that capitalists might be sacrificed to laborers.

"Tell me, is that probable?"

That is to say, M. Bastiat, whose work has been translated from the French by the Free Trade League in order "to educate public opinion ; to convince the people of the United States of the folly and wrongfulness of the protective system," — this M. Bastiat did not know that a fully occupied people and capital would produce a greater mass of commodities than they would produce if a third or a half of them were unemployed.   He did not know that a large annual product gave much to be divided between wages, profits, and rent; and he did not know that the portions falling to profits and rent were nearly all distributed again to labor. He did not know that not only the recipients of profits and rent, but still more the recipients of wages, were supremely interested that the gross annual product should be the greatest possible, and that this desirable result was not to be obtained by sitting idle and buying cheap goods of other nations.

But in spite of this ignorance, M. Bastiat was selected as the best teacher of political economy which the League could find for the people of the United States.

One can imagine the grim humor with which the clear-headed workmen of the United States no doubt contemplate the condescension of the League.

Chapter VII., — " A Chinese Story."

This is the obstacle fallacy over again.

The free-traders discovered that obstacles, many of them, were the cause of expense, or that their existence increased the cost of commodities, without in any way increasing the gross product, or means of payment. They then discovered that a duty upon imported articles increased — sometimes — the price of similar articles produced in the country. We say *sometimes*, for Bastiat himself admits that they do not always do so ; and the fact is notorious that they do not do so for any considerable length of time, to nearly the amount of the duty, and that they often, by stimulating home skill and competition, cause a lower price than existed before. Never mind ! they are an obstacle to importation, so they are obstacles ; and by simply calling them obstacles, pure and simple, it is made to appear that they are not only obstacles to importation, but also obstacles to opulence. They are obstacles ; so also are fens, mountains, stormy seas, distance, obstructed canals, bad tools, etc., etc. The last being seen to be really obstacles to opulence, the free-traders jump you to the conclusion that everything called an obstacle is an obstacle to opulence. Several phenomena called obstacles being seen to be really obstacles to opulence, inasmuch as they raise the price without augmenting the national product, everything called by the same name is inferred to be of the same effect. *Those* obstacles increase the cost in labor, say, 25 per cent; this obstacle — the duty — also (we will suppose for the sake of argument), raises the cost in labor 25 per cent. They are, then, exactly alike! and so they are, thus far, or rather in these particulars; but in *the important* particular they are exactly opposite. Those obstacles increase the cost in labor of everything, — of that which it is desirable to import as well as of that which it is not desirable to import. This obstacle does not lay a finger upon the importation of tropical products which our climate cannot produce, does not prevent or render more difficult immigration, travel, the personal inspection of foreign arts and sciences and social organization; but it does prevent *that* industrial competition which makes it impossible for us to acquire such arts as we are perfectly able to acquire, and which both during the process of acquisition and thenceforth, forever, will add to the gross annual product of the nation, which is the same thing precisely as the aggregate net individual income.

This obstacle also discriminates and shuts out those products in which foreign nations excel only by reason of the lower rate of wages and by the introduction of which our own existing system of civilization (based as it is, upon a high scale of remuneration to labor *of every sort*) would be impaired if not entirely overthrown. The duty is a *discriminating* obstacle in which all that is good in the natural obstacles is retained, and all that is bad is discarded; this opposes baneful intercourse; those oppose alike every kind of intercourse, the benignant as well and as much as the baneful; this is an obstacle reared by human intelligence for a definite purpose; those are obstacles arising out of the constitution of the world. A mind may be presumed to have been given to man to enable him to discriminate between different things, even when called by the same name. Even a free-trader can perceive that there is a difference between a file of soldiers and a file of a carpenter; by and by perhaps they may develop sufficiently to see that there is a difference between a tax which simply takes a dollar, and a tax which, where it takes a dollar, gives five; and they may grow to see that there is a difference between an obstacle which simply obstructs and an obstacle which overcomes and annihilates a far greater obstruction.

Chapter VIII., — "*Post hoc, ergo propter hoc.*"

The free-traders say, " See how prosperous England has been since she adopted free trade ! " They exaggerate every picture of her wealth, wink out of sight the panics of 1866 and 1873, with their attendant horrors, point to the industrial troubles in the United States in 1873–1879, but say nothing about the sufficient cause of a contraction in the currency, the like of which worked far greater mischief in 1819 in England ; say nothing, either, of the wonderful recovery of the United States *under a higher tariff* in 1879–80 ; say nothing about the prosperity of France since 1845, — far more astonishing than that of England. They say nothing about the advantages that England has derived from investments in protectionist countries. No !

England adopted free trade.

Post hoc, England showed some very decided evidences of prosperity. *Ergo*, the prosperity, such as it was, came from free trade.

Chapter IX., — " Robbery by Bounties."

Here we have the public duped ; the public robbed, — robbed by tariff, robbed by bounties, robbed by fraud, robbed by force, etc. In fact, the chapter may be called a war-dance to the tunes of robbing, cheating, pillaging, stealing, swindling, monopoly, etc. Those who mistake abuse for syllogism can read it, no doubt, with amusement. There are, moreover, two really funny things in it. One where M. Bastiat says: " They find my little book of Sophisms too theoretical, scientific, and metaphysical ! " The other is where he says : " More than sixty years ago Adam Smith said, ' When manufacturers meet it may be expected that a conspiracy will be planned against the pockets of the public.' "

Did M. Bastiat suppose the world was ignorant of the fact that the free-trade measures adopted in Great Britain were adopted at the suggestion of a cabal of manufacturers ; that they were designed to forward the interests of that class at the expense of the landed aristocracy and the people alike, and that they were forced through by the most lavish use of money to promote publications, meetings, addresses, distribution of pamphlets, etc., etc., and that they prolonged the sacrifice of India, Ireland, and, for a time, the colonies, to Manchester?

The same system is now being applied to the United States. Pamphlets and books are being distributed by the myriad, and these wily manufacturers of Manchester, etc., would persuade us that they are taking all this trouble and going to all this expense to free *us* from *American* monopolists ! If there be an irrepressible contest between American monopolists and English monopolists, and if (as Adam Smith and Bastiat would have us believe) they are all rascals, then the American people are very likely to rally to the support of their own rascals. These at least can be reached by the law and by competition ; and whatever they do make must at all events be either spent or invested in the United States, and, in either case, gets at last into the hands of those who work.

Chapter X.,— "The Tax Collector."

The tax collector takes six out of twenty hogsheads of wine, which Jacques Bonhomme, wine grower, has produced with much care and sweat.

The first goes to the creditors of the state, the second goes to the civil service, two go to the army and navy, the fifth goes to Algeria, the sixth goes in bounty to encourage manufactures. There are fourteen hogsheads left, and Jacques Bonhomme is assured that these will buy only half as much as they would if he, good man, could be allowed to buy everything from the foreigner. There is the same confusion about taxes which do, and those which do not, lead to an increase of the nation's annual product, which we have before noticed, and the same exaggeration which runs through the whole book. English iron is cheap when it is not in demand.

M. Bastiat assumes that it will be just as cheap when France and the United States and all the rest of the world are clamoring for it. The wine grower is advised to buy everything abroad which can be made cheaper there, but he is not told that there would soon under such a *régime* be few able to buy his wine.

Chapter XI., — " Utopian Ideas."

This chapter is based upon the assumption that the just and the useful must agree. Very likely they must; but nevertheless it may be that the author has a mistaken idea of what is *just* and an equally mistaken idea of what is *useful*. He assumes that an individual has an undoubted right to do whatever he pleases with that which he acquires in the community. It is *just*, according to M. Bastiat, for him to benefit by the advantages growing out of the association, but at the same time to refuse to act in that manner which the association finds to be essential to the interests of all, himself included. It is *just* not only because a man has a right to do what he pleases with his own, but also because by the providence of God this world has been so arranged that the blind instincts of every uninstructed individual, seeking only his own advantage, necessarily lead him to the very acts which best promote the interests of the whole community. The individual instinct of every man, however ignorant, selfish, and gross, is surer than the judgment and reason of all men, including all statesmen and philosophers.

This is an extraordinary proposition indeed. It is not self-evident. It must then have been arrived at by induction, or deduction, or both ; and in point of fact we find that it was first put forth by Adam Smith in the second chapter of the fourth book of the " Enquiry into the Nature and Causes of the Wealth of Nations." He thought that men, in some cases, when pursuing their own interests, did at the same time promote the interest of the nation. The cases he adduced were very uncertain, it being by no means sure that men would act as he imagined ; by no means certain that among the manifold motives of man, Adam Smith did really select those which

would prevail in the cases imagined. But never mind; they
suited his purpose, and he jumped his readers to the conclusion that in "these as in many cases the individuals were
led by an invisible hand to promote an end which was no part
of their intention." It will be observed that with Adam Smith
this was little more than a pretty piece of rhetoric; and in
other parts of his work he affirms most vehemently that the
private interests of large classes are adverse to the interests
of the community as a whole; but a pretty piece of rhetoric
is as good as the strongest syllogism to the man who was not
born with the ability to reason, and has never acquired the
ability through education. Everybody who knows the canons of inductive logic is aware that a single negative instance
absolutely forbids the forming of such a "general proposition;"
and everybody who has read enough of political economy to
warrant writing upon the subject, knows that the negative
instances with respect to this proposition are innumerable.
The proposition belongs to the domain of noodledom, —

> " A limbo large and broad, since called
>   The Paradise of Fools."   *Milton.*

And yet such is the looseness with which political economy
is treated that writers of some authority refer to it as if it
actually carried weight into the discussions upon free trade
and protection. If, then, M. Bastiat is in error as to what is
useful, he may be equally in error as to what is just; and it
may turn out that justice and utility do agree and go hand
in hand; only they are not what he calls justice and utility,
but something very different.

Chapter XIII., — " The Three Aldermen."

This is a delightful piece of persiflage. The introduction
into Paris of three industries totally unsuited to the place is
described, and to this absurd imagining are applied the arguments which are justly and properly used in favor of the
introduction into a nation of industries for which it has
every natural advantage, and in favor of maintaining them so
long as their products will in the end cost less (in labor and
abstinence) than similar products brought from abroad. This

is the case of the United States *v.* Great Britain, and it is as an argument applicable to this case that the "Sophisms" of Bastiat are presented to the people of the United States.

An individual becomes wealthy by acquiring from others a portion of the already existing instruments of production. He may acquire enough to support him a thousand years. A nation can do nothing of the kind. *It* becomes wealthy in proportion to the increase of its annual product of commodities. But its annual product must be annually consumed, even that portion of it which is *saved;* that is to say, the portion which is converted by labor into instruments to facilitate and enlarge future production and comfort. It must be consumed, or else it lies in immoderate stocks, paralyzing industry. Taking the average of years, it is consumed. The richest nation then is the one which first produces and then consumes the largest annual product of commodities; and here we stumble headlong upon a most vital proposition, which is, that the richest nation is that in which the great bulk of the people, the workers with hands and the workers with brains, enjoy the highest real wages.[1]

What, then, can come of the plans which are built upon a reduction of the real wages of a people? Inevitable national impoverishment. *The gross annual product* pays all wages, all profits, all rents. Increase it, — they all increase. Diminish it, and they all dwindle away together.

Chapter XIV., — "Something Else."

Here are twelve pages of puerilities which are, nevertheless, specious, and must be dealt with, even at the risk of wearying the reader.

"Restriction and prohibition," says M. Bastiat, "bear the same relation to one another that an arc bears to a circle. One cannot be bad and the other good, any more than an arc can be straight if the circle be curved."

Straight and curved, mathematical terms signifying the same things under all possible circumstances, cannot, according to M. Bastiat, be predicated with any more certainty of a line, than the words good and bad can be predicated of restriction and prohibition in political economy.

[1] See note 4, page 79.

It is only necessary to show a single class of cases in which prohibition would be bad and restriction good, and the thinness of M. Bastiat's supposed logic will be apparent; and it is not necessary that the case adduced should absolutely exist. It is sufficient that it might exist.

Well, then, there might be two countries which produced silk piece goods. Call the countries A and B. In A the rate of wages is only one half what it is in B, but for reasons which seem satisfactory to the people generally it is considered to be both desirable to maintain the rate of wages in B and also to maintain the manufacture of silk goods. Evidently the manufacturers must be protected sufficiently to offset the difference of wages. This is one case; and, to prevent the free-trader from making a specious although unsound cavil, let us look at another possible case. Nation B, by reason of improvements in the application of its labor and the efficiency of it, can weave silk even a little cheaper than nation A; but the manufacturers in nation A, being vastly richer than those in nation B, can (and do, whenever they have a chance) sell at a loss, in order to destroy the manufacturers in nation B, and thereafter be free to charge their own prices. In this case, also, it would be necessary to give such protection as would overcome the existing obstacle to the maintenance of the silk industry in nation A. Here, then, restriction would be good, while prohibition might be good, bad, or indifferent, according to circumstances. IF (as alleged by free-traders to be sometimes the case) the silk manufacturers in nation B were lazy and unenterprising, using inferior machinery, and consequently turning out silk piece goods at an unnecessarily high price, — IF, we say, this were the case, then prohibition would be bad, and too high a duty would be bad; while some duty would be good, as preventing the demolition by foreigners of an industry desired by the people.

Let, now, the Free Trade League show a case where an arc of a circle is a straight line, or else confess that M. Bastiat's reasoning is flippant and unworthy to be offered to the American people.

Again, M. Bastiat declares that the definite effect of protection is to require from men *harder labor for the same result.* Let us see how this is made out, in respect to the United States, for the education (!) of whose people this and other books of a similar character are distributed. Mr. Mongredien, writing for the Cobden Club, shows us the method. The cost of American manufactured products, he says, is 40 per cent above the cost at which similar products can be imported. Why? Because the duty is 40 per cent and over, and in spite of the duty *some* goods are imported. That is, if some kinds of goods can be imported in spite of a duty of 40 per cent, then the native goods (if there be any of the same kind) must cost 40 per cent more than they could be imported for. Then *some* goods (those of which the like are imported) cost 40 per cent more by reason of the duty. Therefore *all* goods on which there is a duty (those kinds which are not imported as well as those which are) must cost 40 per cent more than they could be imported for !

From deductive reasoning one would have supposed that the internal competition of fifty millions of people might, perhaps, reduce prices considerably below the maximum possible price ; and a little inquiry as to facts would have shown that a large part of American products are actually as cheap, or very nearly as cheap as they could be imported for, even if there were no duty.

But Mr. Mongredien preferred to ascertain the cost by logic ; and he told the American farmers they could have for one thousand millions of dollars from England what they paid fourteen hundred millions for to the native mechanics and manufacturers. The farmers being about half the population, the whole country would save eight hundred millions, getting from England for two thousand millions what they now pay twenty-eight hundred millions for ; and all this built upon a syllogism in which a distributed conclusion is drawn from undistributed premises. Would it not be well for the Cobden Club to send Mr. Mongredien to school for a year or two before allowing him to write another book for the instruction of the American people? But to return to M. Bastiat. The Free Trade League, through him, tell the American people that the definite result of protection is to require from men *harder labor* for the same result. This inference is founded upon the well-known " Fallacy of Division," of which Archbishop Whately observes : —

" This is a fallacy with which men are extremely apt to deceive *themselves;* for, when a multitude of particulars are presented to the mind, many are too weak, or too indolent, to take a comprehensive view of them ; but confine their attention to a single point in turn, and then decide, infer, and act, accordingly ; *e. g.* the imprudent spendthrift, finding that he is able to afford this, or that, or the other expense, forgets that *all of them together* will ruin him."

M. Bastiat, referring to France, maintains that iron, being produced in England for less labor and abstinence than in France, had better be bought by France by means of some product in which she has an advantage ; then clothing had better be bought in a similar way of Belgium ; then food of Hungary or the United States ; and so on, forgetting that all the needs of France together which could be supplied more cheaply from abroad would come to many times more than would the aggregate requirements of foreign nations for the products of the remaining industries in which France has a decided advantage.

With regard to the United States, the chapter has no relevancy ; for almost everything we produce is produced with as little *labor* and *abstinence* as anywhere in the world. Many things can be brought here and sold for less *money;* but this is because our wages are high, and our labor altogether so much more productive that gold and silver are cheap with us. Were we to open our ports and give up to the foreigner a large portion of our " field of employment," — wages and money-prices would doubtless decline; but nothing would be produced with less labor and abstinence than it is now. Our foreign market might be increased a little ; but our home market would be reduced many times as much ; and profits, rents, fees, salaries, and incomes of every description would be diminished in proportion. Why so? Because the gross annual product would be diminished enormously, and it is this which pays all wages, profits, and rents. But why would our gross annual product be diminished enormously? Because nowhere in this planet could be found markets for four thousand — soon to be ten thousand — millions of the products in which we have an advantage, in addition to what we now export, nor could markets be found for even a third part of those vast amounts. We should not only rob ourselves of a large part of what we now get from the mechanical and manufacturing arts, but we should transfer to the foreigner all the advantages we now derive from agriculture.

The chapter consists chiefly of a conversation between Robinson Crusoe and Friday, whose situation was not at all analogous to that of an industrial community; and afterwards of the doctrine that, when one of the industries of a society is given over to a foreign country the displaced labor will occupy itself about

SOMETHING ELSE.

This conclusion is drawn from Adam Smith's doctrine " that each industry is prevented from increasing by the want of capital ; " it has no place in a world where each industry has unemployed capital, and is prevented from increasing for want of a " field of employment." In such a world the displaced labor and capital can only — in the words of Mr. J. S. Mill — squeeze out a living by competition with other labor and capital. Both the wages and profits appertaining to the remaining industries must be diminished whenever one is given up to the foreigner, for the reason that the extruded industry furnished a market to nearly its full value for other products, while the substituted foreign industry increases the foreign demand by only a small percentage of its amount.

Let us represent the various industries (both productive and unproductive) by the letters of the alphabet, A, B, C, etc. Then $VA + VB + VC$, etc., may represent the annual

exchangeable value contributed by each description of industry and each description of service to the gross annual
exchangeable value, and $VA + VB + VC$, etc. $= TAP$; or,
the total annual product. A purchases of B, C, etc., portions
of their annual products equalling in the aggregate VA,
and so do B, C, and each of the others. Now transfer
industry A to another nation, and immediately TAP becomes $TAP - VA$; that is, the capital and labor before
employed by industry A are in excess, and cannot find employment by spreading themselves through the other industries or classes of service already fully supplied. A portion
of the products of B, C, D, etc., must go abroad to pay for
the foreign products which have displaced industry A. If
these cost 25 per cent less than the native, then a value equal
to $\frac{3}{4} VA$ will go abroad, and a value equal to $\frac{1}{4} VA$ will
remain distributed among B, C, D, etc., as stock *in addition*
to their previously existing surplus stocks. There will be a
greater or less glut of commodities and services throughout
the society; and the exchangeable value of B, of C, of D,
etc., etc., will each be found to be diminished, probably to a
greater amount, perhaps to a much greater amount, in the
aggregate, than the $\frac{1}{4} VA$ expected to be saved by importing
from abroad. The effective demand, then, of the whole community, less industry A, for the imported article at, say, three
dollars, will be less than was the effective demand of the same
persons for the native article at four dollars, and there will be
also a necessity for supporting the labor of industry A in idleness. This labor cannot do "something else," for everything
else desired by the community was done before to the full
extent of the *then* effective demand which is *now* diminished;
and not only this, but production must be also lessened in each
of the remaining industries. So far from industry B having
more to spend for the products of C, D, E, etc., industry B
will find its own annual products selling for less money than
they did when A got four dollars for what the foreigner now
brings for three dollars.

France " has the advantage " of other nations in the production of many articles of taste, and also in some kinds of

wine. She exports these to the extent of about six hundred millions of dollars. It is highly improbable that the opening of her ports to other nations could cause any great increase of consumption of her products upon their part; while the products which she produces for herself at no advantage or at a disadvantage come probably to three thousand millions. Evidently she could not obtain any considerable increase of the articles she produces at a disadvantage, except by paying out of her accumulations of treasure. M. Bastiat thought she would get the needed treasure from Peru; but this only shows that his education had been neglected in the branch of arithmetic. The whole of the annual production of precious metals added to the whole of the large amount accumulated by France during the whole period of her existence would not suffice to purchase abroad for a single year the commodities which France makes for herself at more or less disadvantage, compared with this, that, or the other foreign country. As he suggests, she might import treasure from Peru, and this would suffice to buy this article, or it would suffice to buy that article, or it would suffice to buy the other article; but when it comes to adding all the articles together, the insufficiency of the proposed resource becomes so manifest as to be ridiculous. It is the fallacy of division fooling with the lives and fortunes of thirty-four millions of people.

Chapter XV. is the " Little Arsenal of the Free-Trader." These are short sentences embodying the fallacies already sufficiently answered.

Chapter XVI. proposes a number of funny absurdities, which M. Bastiat imagines to be of the same nature as protectionist arguments; but which only show that he either did not understand or did not choose to understand the protectionist arguments.

To work with the left hand rather than the right, to prevent the use of machinery, to dull the axes, to fill up canals, etc., etc., would not increase the gross annual product. To employ a portion of the population upon industries in which the nation stands at no advantage, or even at disadvantage, when the whole population cannot be employed upon the industries in which it has an advantage, or cannot be so employed without throwing away the natural advantage, would increase the gross annual product. That is just what M. Bastiat did not know; and that is why his teachings should not have been offered to the American people.

Chapter XVII., — "Supremacy by Labor."
It is impossible to do justice to the sophistry of this chapter without quoting. It says: —

" As, in time of war, supremacy is obtained by superiority in arms, can, in time of peace, supremacy be secured by superiority in labor ?

" This question is of the greatest interest, at a time when no one seems to doubt that, in the field of industry, as on that of battle, *the stronger crushes the weaker.*

" This must result from the discovery of some sad and discouraging analogy between labor, which exercises itself on things, and violence, which exercises itself on men; for how could two things be identical in their effects, if they were opposed in their nature ?

" And if it be true that, in manufacturing, as in war, supremacy is the necessary result of superiority, why need we occupy ourselves with progress, or social economy, since we are in a world where all has been so arranged by Providence that one and the same result, oppression, necessarily flows from the most antagonistic principles ?

" Referring to the new policy towards which commercial freedom is drawing in England, many persons make this objection, which I admit occupies the sincerest minds : ' Is England doing anything more than pursuing the same end by different means ? Does she not constantly aspire to universal supremacy ? Sure of the superiority of her capital and labor, does she not call in free competition to stifle the industry of the Continent, reign as sovereign, and conquer the privilege of feeding and clothing the ruined peoples ? '

" It would be easy for me to demonstrate that these alarms are chimerical ; that our pretended inferiority is greatly exaggerated ; that all our great branches of industry not only resist foreign competition, but develop themselves under its influence ; and that its infallible effect is to bring about an increase in general consumption, capable of absorbing both foreign and domestic products."

This is the language of the Anti-Corn-Law League, of the Cobden Club, of the Manchester manufacturers, — of the spider to the fly.

Labor in its nature is opposed to war. Labor produces; war destroys. Labor employs itself on things ; war employs itself upon persons. Opposite causes cannot produce identical effects. Does this, O reader, persuade you that there is no valid analogy between the struggles of opposing armies for the possession of a province, and the struggles of competing industries for the possession of a market? To seriously ask the question would be to insult you; and yet the trash is persuasive to the hasty reader. When he pauses for a moment and reads again he sees that he is trifled with.

That which moves to war is the desire to overcome an opponent. That which moves to industrial competition is the desire to overcome an opponent, — to overcome one who prevents your selling as much or as dearly as you would. The causes are similar. It is only the methods of procedure which differ. The paragraph about manufacturing, supremacy, Providence, oppression, and antagonistic principles is a similar logical puzzle, which any intelligent reader can solve for himself. It assumes that there are antagonistic principles wherever the methods of procedure, the instruments used to obtain the end, are dissimilar. The paragraph commencing, " It would be easy for me to demonstrate," is a bundle of assertions, pure and simple. There is not a particle of argument in it. The " proof" comes afterwards and consists in this : —

" If we see in any product but a cause of labor. it is certain that the alarm of the protectionists is well founded. If we consider iron, for instance, only in connection with the masters of forges, it might be feared that the competition of a country where iron was a gratuitous gift of nature would extinguish the furnaces of another country, where ore and fuel were scarce.

" But is this a complete view of the subject? Are these relations only between iron and those who make it ? Has it none with those who use it ? Is its definite and only destination to be produced ? And if it is useful, not only on account of the labor which it causes, but on account of the qualities which it possesses, and the numerous services

for which its hardness and malleability fit it, does it not follow that
foreigners cannot reduce its price, even so far as to prevent its production among us, without doing us more good, under the last statement
of the case, than it injures us under the first?

  " Foreign superiority prevents national labor only under some certain form, and makes it superfluous under this form, but by putting
at our disposal the very result of the labor thus annihilated."

  This is wonderful! What earthly relevancy has the second
paragraph? Is not French iron hard and malleable? The
French have iron in either case. The only question is whether
they shall have it at one price made at home or at another price
made abroad; and in a former chapter M. Bastiat put the
price at twelve francs for French and eight francs for English
iron. But he argues that to procure the English iron, France
will have only to "detach" from her general labor a smaller
portion than she would require to produce it herself. France
would save one third of the labor before used in making iron.
The careful reader will see that he assumes that the whole
labor power of the country is employed in either case; while
the fact is, and must be, that the whole is *not* employed in
either case. Even when France makes her own iron, every
industry within her borders is limited by the limits of the
field of employment. There are so many desires known to
her people which they have found out means of gratifying
with such expenditure of effort as they are willing to pay, —
so many and no more. Their desires even are not infinite; but
even if they were, the desires they know how to gratify without more exertion than they are willing to make, are very far
from infinite; they are quite limited. Their aggregate of
these constitutes the field of employment, outside of which
there are always (except during periods of abnormal excitement and perhaps even then) many unemployed persons,
many half employed persons, many persons helping others to
do what they can well enough do alone. This unemployed
labor is constantly striving to find something to do, and the
unemployed capital of the country is constantly striving to
find something to do, — some means of gratifying a desire at
such price as the community will be willing and able to pay.

The community, then, does not "detach" a portion of its previously employed labor to make iron, but a portion and only a portion of its previously *unemployed* or half employed labor, and the then more fully employed labor has the means of buying from all the other industries; their field of employment is increased. According to M. Bastiat's philosophy, if iron and its products should suddenly be rained down out of the sky already shaped for use, the United States would immediately have set free an amount of labor that would produce "something else" to the value of, say, three hundred millions of dollars. But "everything else" for which the people have a desire is already produced to a somewhat greater extent than can be sold, as is evidenced by the existing surplus stocks of commodities. The total industry of the community is kept up by motives, and one of these motives is the desire for iron. The immediate effect, then, of iron dropping down ready fashioned from the skies would be to diminish the field of employment to the extent of, say, three hundred millions; but as iron is only a means towards procuring other things, notably, food, clothing, shelter, and transportation, the getting iron for nothing might make it possible to procure a greater supply of food, clothing, shelter, and transportation, with the same effort, and the *ultimate* result *might* be that as great or even a greater field of employment would be found in producing a greater supply. But meanwhile, during the growth of a larger demand for food, clothing, shelter, and transportation, between two and three millions of people would have to go without food, clothing, shelter, and transportation, or squeeze them by competition out of the balance of the community. The immediate effect would certainly be a great diminution of the effective demand of the community for food, clothing, shelter, and transportation, — a glut. There would be much more of all these than the community as a whole had means of buying. There would be a period of distress and depression, and political economy does not perhaps, at present, possess the means of saying how long such depression would continue, nor even of saying decisively that it would not end in a permanent deterioration of the condition of the community; in which case the seeming gift would prove to be a gigantic evil, somewhat analogous to the fortune with which a fond father paralyzes the powers and prevents the development of his children. It is to be hoped that political economy will not always be incompetent to solve such problems; but it certainly will be as long as it remains innocent of all knowledge of their existence; so long as, with M. Bastiat and Mr. J. S. Mill, it supposes that displaced labor and capital always find "something else" to do.

The writer feels guilty for having mentioned so upright and serious a writer as Mr. J. S. Mill in the same sentence as M. Bastiat; but they agreed in supporting the same doctrine as to capital and its effects upon industry, and in the deductions from that doctrine; in all else they are very wide apart. In reviewing Mr. Mill, one would be spared the disagreeable task of combating the arts of the rhetorical sophist, the appeals to prejudice, to anger, to pity, to greed, to superstition, to misguided or affected philanthropy. He would meet with some very important errors in reasoning, strange as this is in an unquestionably pre-eminent logician; but everything is honest, straightforward, and such as the spirit of the great reasoner, looking back upon life, need not blush to have written. M. Bastiat closes his "Sophisms of Protection" as follows: —

" Let us decide that supremacy by labor is impossible and contradictory, since all superiority which manifests itself among a people is converted into cheapness, and results only in giving force to all others. Let us, then, banish from political economy all those expressions borrowed from the vocabulary of battles: *to struggle with equal arms, to conquer, to crush out, to stifle, to be beaten, invasion, tribute.* What do these words mean? Squeeze them, and nothing comes out of them. We are mistaken; there come from them absurd errors and fatal prejudices. These are the words which stop the blending of peoples, their peaceful, universal, indissoluble alliance, and the progress of humanity."

So writes M. Bastiat. Now compare with his words those of Horace Greeley. Speaking of some strictures upon the effects of reckless competition, he says: —

" The justice of these strictures I have at least twice seen realized on a gigantic scale, in the general prostration of the manufacturing industry of my countrymen under the pressure of European, mainly of English, competition. That industry was thus crushed out after the peace of 1815, when the eminent Henry Brougham (afterwards Lord Brougham) remarked (when Great Britain was pouring out the goods that crushed our then infant manufactures) that ' England can afford to incur some loss *for the purpose of destroying foreign manufactures in their cradle ;* ' and the noted economist and free-trader, Joseph Hume, made a similar remark in 1828. Our tariff enacted in that year rendered all efforts to cripple and prostrate our manufacturing industry temporarily fruitless ; but it was otherwise after the compromise tariff of 1833 began to take full effect. in the reduction of the duties to a (presumptively) revenue standard which culminated in the collapse alike of industry and revenue in 1840-42.

" A report on strikes made to the British Parliament in 1854 significantly said : —

" 'Authentic instances are well known of (British) employers having in such times (of depressed prices), carried on their works at a loss amounting to three or four hundred thousand pounds in the course of three or four years. If the efforts of those who encourage the combination to restrict the amount of labor, and to produce strikes. were to be successful for any length of time, the great accumulations of capital could no longer be made which enable a few of the most wealthy capitalists to *overwhelm all foreign competition* in times *of great depression*, and thus to clear the way for the whole trade to step in when prices revive, and to carry on a great business before foreign capital can again accumulate to establish a competition in prices, with any chance of success. The great capitals of this country are the great instruments of warfare against the competing capitals of other countries, and are the most essential instruments now remaining, by which our manufacturing supremacy can be maintained ; the other elements, cheap labor, abundance of raw materials, means of communication, and skilled labor being rapidly in progress of being equalized.' "

It will be seen that Mr. Greeley bears witness to our industries having been twice prostrated by their English competitors in his time, and it is matter of general knowledge also that the same thing happened to the Portuguese industries after the treaty of Methuen, and to the Irish industries after the union, and so with Turkey and India.

The reader can then form his own opinion about the hardihood of M. Bastiat when he attempted to prove that such things cannot happen, by a process of false logic which has been the somewhat disagreeable task of the writer to expose. The rest of his book is made up chiefly of rhetorical sophisms, in which taxes and obstacles which *do* increase the productive power of the community are classed with the taxes and obstacles which do *not* increase it ; of appeals to our pity that the "*poor workman*," after getting his wages from his fellow-citizens, should not be allowed to spend them among foreigners, and in appeals to class prejudices by abuse of every description poured out upon everybody who is protected from the English manufacturer. They are cheats, swindlers, robbers, monopolists, oppressors, thieves!

Now it has been held by every respectable economist, from Adam Smith down, that it is impossible for any industry to long obtain a profit above that usual in the community ; and it would seem, therefore, that all this abuse is as unjust as it is unseemly ; *but* if there be in any case reason to fear that manufacturers may combine to exact a higher profit, our own are within reach of control. Let the fact be proved, and nothing is easier than to bring them to reason, by simply reducing the duty to what will give them an adequate and not an excessive protection. We should have no such power over the foreigners. When they have once ruined our own industries they can, if they combine, charge us whatever they please.

If, then, there be any foundation for the cry of monopoly, the possibility of such a combination is the best of all reasons for standing by our own and not the alien manufacturers. These can be ruled. The others cannot.

PART III., — "Spoliation and Law."

This supremely sophistical chapter endeavors to connect, in the mind of the reader, the totally different matters of protection and communism. At the time it was written, society in France was alarmed at the pretensions of communism, and the endeavor to make out some similarity between it and protection was as shrewd as anything can be which is absolutely dishonest. The same attempt has been made by the unscrupulous upon this side of the Atlantic.

Civilized men everywhere recognize, either consciously or unconsciously, the fact that, without the aid of tools, machines, improved farms, mills, forges, railroads, stores of food, materials, and shelter, etc., — without, in short, the aid of instruments of production, the gross annual product of labor would be incomparably less than it is; they recognize, also, that these instruments of production cannot come into existence nor be kept in repair, except through abstinence, which is, therefore, entitled to such portion of the increased product as demand and supply determine to be the just value of their use; they recognize, also, that to allow individuals to possess these instruments and enjoy said portion of their fruits is the most economical and efficient method for bringing them into existence and keeping them in repair, utility being here completely at one with justice; they recognize even that those proprietors who do nothing except to live within their income do, nevertheless, thereby render a most essential service to society, for living within their income is nothing less than keeping in repair the " instruments " which furnish them with incomes; and in recognizing, consciously or unconsciously, these facts, all men of common sense perceive the rights of property to be based upon the all-sufficient foundation of the greatest good to the whole society, — not the greatest good only for to-day, or this year, but for all time. But the common sense of mankind also recognizes that, while the greatest good of the whole is the foundation of the rights of property, it also puts limits to those rights. As they are founded and justified by the good of the whole, they must logically be restricted to that which in the long run is beneficial to all. No man is allowed to use his property to found a college for teaching what the community generally accounts to be vice, nor to run gambling-houses or lotteries, nor to erect unsafe houses, nor to sail ships which have become unseaworthy, nor to establish anything which is a nuisance or a source of disease, nor to run a bank except under conditions protecting public interests, etc., *ad infinitum.* Property is not weakened by these necessary and proper restraints, but only prevented from weakening its own just and legitimate claims, and becoming in some respects a nuisance, instead of a great blessing to the community. Indeed, he is no friend of property, but its dangerous enemy, who maintains that each single possessor has the indefeasible right to veto the decisions of the whole society, and that, too, in the cause of a pseudo-theory composed of a vast mass of bad logic and of totally irrelevant rhetoric. The argument that " the highest right of property is the right to exchange it for other property;" that, therefore, any restraint or regulation of this right, — in short, the forbidding of any exchange, however detrimental, — is an unwarrantable invasion of the rights of property, and therefore akin to communism, — this argument can only be used by one who has the incredible folly to suppose that the American people are a nation of unmitigated noodles.

In the first place, the right to exchange it is not the highest right of property. A higher right still is the right to an unmolested enjoyment either of the property itself or of the income thereof. Second, another higher right is the right to protection against foreign attacks, whether civil or military. Third, if even it were the highest right, this, like every other right of property, must give way before the vastly higher and more important rights of the whole community. Compensation is given where the case requires it ; compensation is not given where the interference produces no damage, but a great benefit, as when protective laws are passed.

" But," exclaim the free-traders, " protective laws are not a benefit, but an injury."

Ah, gentlemen, you undertook to bolster the doctrine of free trade by an argument from the rights of property ; but we now find that the argument about the rights of property breaks down unless we first assume the free-trade doctrine to be correct. You are attempting to make two doctrines hold each other up, when neither the one nor the other can stand alone.

If the free-trade doctrine were sound, the interference with foreign exchanges would be unwise, but by no means beyond the restrictive rights of the whole people ; if the protectionist doctrine be sound, the interference is eminently beneficial ; but, in either case, there is nothing resembling the proposed communistic abolition of property which would be ruinous alike to individual owners and to the public.

The attempt, then, to *smooch* protection by coupling it with communism is simply a dishonest rhetorical artifice, disgraceful to the author and insulting to the readers whom he addresses.   It is precisely equivalent to calling them fools.

And here we come to the end of a book which shows much wit, vivacity, ingenuity, and audacity, but which stands almost alone among transatlantic productions for the entire absence of that serious, earnest desire for truth which political economists usually display.   Others may involve themselves in logical puzzles ; but they appear to do so unintentionally.   Possibly this may have also been the case with M. Bastiat, and the semblance of flippancy and insincerity may be rather apparent than real ; but, at all events, one cannot rise from a diligent study of him without a profound conviction that no member of the Free Trade League can have carefully perused the book which they translated and printed in order " to educate public opinion in the United States, and convince the people of the folly and wrongfulness of the protective system."

Any other conviction would involve the gross insult of supposing them to be either exceedingly flat or exceedingly dishonest, or both.

Bastiat's sophistries are based chiefly upon the following erroneous propositions : —

" 1.   That industry is limited by capital, whereas both are limited by the field of employment.

" 2.   That human labor is never without employment.

" 3.   That the wages fund is a fixed amount, equal to the existing capital, and the whole of it always employed.

" 4.   That protective laws, which cause more people to be employed *with increased* production, are the same in effect as dull axes, obstructed canals, working with the left hand, amputating one hand, etc., which would cause more people to be employed *without* increased production.

" 5.   That inasmuch as many obstacles to exchanges are also obstacles
to opulence, therefore all obstacles to exchanges are obstacles to
opulence."

In short, the argumentative portion of the book displays
a neglect of every canon of logic, both inductive and deductive.   The rest is rhetoric, and is good of its kind, — witty,
vivacious, impressive, and well suited to impose upon those
who are not clever enough to see that it proves nothing, and
is totally inapplicable to any existing society or to any society
which could exist while man is constituted as he is.

Common sense is unconscious logic; logic not yet introspective; logic which has not yet named its processes, but
which sees and casts aside a blunder intuitively; and there
is too much of this sort of logic in the brains of the working
people of America to allow much harm to come from such a
book as Bastiat's "Sophisms of Protection."

[1] My friend, Mr. David H. Mason, observes here : "That, in point of fact, individuals do not possess the claimed right, and have least of it where civilization is greatest. The disposition of one's own property is not a natural right, but a conventional right, — a right limited by law or by custom, based on the views taken of the individual's obligations to the society of which he is a unit. Whatever may be said theoretically about the right of each individual to the free disposition of his own property, he does not in any civilized community possess such claimed right. Restraint, in a multitude of forms, confronts every member of the community in the disposition of his property. No person can legally dispose of his property in such a way as to interfere with the rights of his fellow-citizens. He cannot use his capital to erect a frame-building within the limits of a municipal fire-district. He cannot spend his money so as to commit a public nuisance ; as, for example, by locating a bone or soap factory, with its noisome stench, amid the residence quarter of a town. He cannot, without incurring heavy penalties, invest his means in publishing clearly immoral newspapers or books, which operate to debauch public sentiment. If he is an apothecary, he cannot sell poisons indiscriminately, but is therein subjected to various restrictions. If he is a manufacturer, he cannot purchase for use in his business any machinery which infringes a patent, without making himself liable for exemplary damages. If he is a publisher, he cannot, without violating the law and incurring its punishment, print a book for sale which has been copyrighted in his country, and for which printing he does not possess the *imprimatur* of the author or the permission of the owner. If he is a shipmaster, he cannot sail his vessel into the harbor of destination according to his own separate will, but according to the will of the health-officer of the port, who may force him into detention at quarantine quarters. Formerly in the Southern States it was legal to dispose of negroes as property. That was then a conventional right ; now it is a conventional wrong. A protective tariff rests upon the same general principle, that society is injured by permitting to individuals the *free* disposition of their property in purchase of or exchange for imported property."

[2] Much protection was taken from pig-iron, the base of our iron and steel industries in 1870, and there was a heavy reduction of duties on a wide range of manufactures in 1872. But for these changes the country might perhaps have escaped the panic of 1873 in spite of the contraction of the currency, &c.

[3] After all the treasure it can possibly spare is gone, government bonds, rail road bonds and stock, mortgages, &c., will go, and during all this process B will be unable to compete with A by manufacturing for herself. The industries in which she is inferior will be destroyed, and she will be kept continually in the condition of treasure-famine. She will never have enough of the precious metals to suffice as a basis for a safe and stable currency.

[4] There is an exception when the individuals of a community invest largely in other lands ; but this kind of wealth, as Adam Smith has observed, is of a very unstable and fugitive character.

REVIEW

Of Professor Sumner's article in the March number of the Princeton Review, entitled, —

"The Argument against Protective Taxes."

A PROTECTIONIST cannot even pass by the title without objection. A tax is not necessarily a burden. If the money be well and economically expended, and gives us good roads, good water-works, good police, and good government at what they ought to cost, then a tax is a great blessing and saving; but, unfortunately, the money is often expended recklessly and foolishly, and so, *through abuses*, the very name of tax becomes offensive. The free-trader who writes about "Protective Taxes" avails himself of this existing prejudice, with the effect of disgusting the reader with protection at the outset, in advance of all argument in respect to it. The word tax also gives two false impressions: first, that all protected articles cost the consumer more than they would if not protected; and, second, that when they cost more, the consumer gets no counterbalancing or greatly overbalancing advantage. In this sense Professor Sumner writes that, —

> "Every cent paid in protective taxes lessens the power of the citizen to pay revenue taxes for the discharge of the public burdens. Hence the fact that we have heavy public burdens is just the reason why we cannot afford to squander our means in paying taxes to our neighbors for carrying on (as they themselves allege) unproductive industries."

This argument was used by Adam Smith one hundred and thirty years ago in the lectures which afterwards were thrown into the form of the famous "Enquiry into the Nature and Causes of the Wealth of Nations;" but the human race ought to have learned something in one hundred and thirty years, and it has been many times shown, or at all events is easily shown, that where a protective law causes labor and capital, otherwise not occupied, to produce an article for $1.25 which could be imported for $1.00, the nation does not lose twenty-five cents but gains the dollar. The tax gives to the totality of consumers five times what it takes from them. To this it may be replied that labor never need be unoccupied where there is much land to be had for the asking, that it can always go to farming; but here comes in the fallacy of supposing that when we all went to farming there would be the same favorable market for our products that exists now. Agriculture, it is true, is the field in which we have the greatest advantage over Europe; but we might easily have so pressed the cultivation of this field as to have transferred the whole advantage to Europe and have kept no part of it for ourselves, — to have been compelled to eat Indian corn and rye, while we exported our wheat to buy a very small modicum of conveniences. We have had wisdom enough to stop short of this supreme folly, by turning a portion of our population upon other fields in which we are at some disadvantage as compared to Europe; and, by doing so, we have made the whole body of our labor vastly more productive,— more productive per man than that of any other country in this planet. Here a free-trader would point out some particular article which — perhaps only for the moment, but perhaps even permanently — costs in wheat, at the present price of wheat, more than it could be imported for; and he says to the individual farmer: " See how much more cheaply you could get this from abroad ! " and he persuades the farmer (and himself too) that the fact is the same with regard to every article; and, even then, he does not see that he is misleading himself and the farmer by means of the " fallacy of division." Farmer A, things being as they are, could get what he wants through wheat somewhat more cheaply than he now does; so could Farmer B; so could each one of the others; but they all of them together cannot, for wheat would fall to perhaps half its present price and, with twice as many farmers, only a very small portion of the surplus of wheat would be salable at any price. Such questions are practical questions, depending upon the possible foreign demand and the population of the country in question ; and no man who carefully considers the subject, will come to the conclusion that the people of the United States, if confined to those industries in which we have an advantage, could produce anything like the gross annual exchangeable value they are now producing. Here it may be urged that when farming ceased to be profitable, the other industries would establish themselves naturally and healthfully by the action of individual interests ; but this assumption was disposed of fifty years ago by John Rae.*

In his opening paragraph Professor Sumner shows very correctly that it is absurd to say that free trade may be good in theory but not in practice. Theory must be competent to explain observed facts, or it is no true theory ; or at all events lies under grievous suspicion of being faulty in some undiscovered point. Professor Sumner reads it the other way, namely, that no one can be sure of facts unless he be able to disentangle every train of argumentation, claiming to be theory, which seems to contradict the facts or show them to be impossible. Adam Smith, more than a hundred years ago, argued thus : —

"The general industry of the society never can exceed what the capital of the society can employ. As the number of workmen that can be kept in employment by every particular person must bear a certain proportion to his capital, so the number of those that can be continually employed by all the members of a great society must bear a certain proportion to the whole capital of that society, and never can exceed that proportion. No regulation of commerce can

---

* Rae shows very conclusively that an individual acting wisely for his own interests could never undertake the introduction of foreign arts except in the very rare cases where, with assistance, such arts might have been domesticated with advantage at a much earlier date.

Besides, it seems certainly wiser to gain the foreign arts by a system which keeps agriculture profitable, than to wait until stern necessity *forces* the ruined farmer to betake himself to other employments.

increase the quantity of industry in any society beyond what its capital can maintain. It can only divert a part of it into a direction into which it might not otherwise have gone; and it is by no means certain that this artificial direction is likely to be more advantageous to the society than that into which it would have gone of its own accord."

Thirty years ago Mr. John Stuart Mill repeated this argument, with variations, thus: —

"There can be no more industry than is supplied with materials to work up and food to eat. Self-evident as the thing is, it is often forgotten that the people of a country are maintained and have their wants supplied, not by the produce of present labor but of past. They consume what has been produced, not what is about to be produced. Now of what has been produced, a part only has been allotted to the support of productive labor; and there will not and cannot be more of that labor than the portions so allotted (which is the capital of the country) can feed and provide with the materials of production."

"Yet, in disregard of a fact so evident, it long continued to be believed that laws and governments, without *creating* capital, could create labor."

In the article under review, Professor Sumner repeats and varies the argument thus: —

"Any favor or encouragement which the protective system exerts on one group of its population must be won by an equivalent oppression exerted on some other group. To suppose the contrary is to deny the most obvious application of the conservation of energy to economic forces. If the legislation did not simply transfer capital it would have to *create capital out of nothing*. Now the transfer is not simply an equal redistribution; there is loss and waste in the case of any tax whatsoever. There is especial loss and waste in the case of a protective tax. We cannot collect taxes and redistribute them without loss; much less can we produce forced monopolies and distorted industrial relations without loss."

This is the theory which has, for one hundred and thirty years, deterred men from trusting either their eyes and ears, or that intuitive reason which conducts nine tenths of human affairs. Let us examine the reasoning. First, capital is defined to be those funds allotted to the support of productive labor; then it is said that there cannot be more industry than this capital *can* support. These two propositions together affirm, then, that industry never can be greater than it can be, — an identical proposition, which nobody can deny to the end of time, but which does not and cannot convey any information whatsoever. It leaves the whole question still unsolved before us. It is very true that the industry of the society cannot be greater than its capital, real and potential, *can* support; but what we are concerned to know is whether the industry of the society cannot be greater than its capital *does* support. If the normal condition of an industrial community be one in which a considerable portion of its capital is locked up in unsold goods, in which there are large amounts also capable of being turned on the instant from unproductive to productive purposes, then a protective law will find ample means for the inauguration of its new industry.

To Adam Smith's argument above quoted it has been replied that —

The number of workmen that can be kept in employment by any particular individual does not bear a certain proportion to his capital. When the market for his products is dull, a large part of his capital is locked up in unsold goods; he must then lessen his production and dismiss some of his workmen; and the same is true of society taken all together. In a normal condition of things there may be, for instance, a stock of goods equal to two months' consumption of the whole community, — a value in the United States at the present time (1881) considerably exceeding one thousand millions of dollars; and observe that these stocks of commodities are the very things — the food, the raiment, the tools, &c.— which are requisite, and in fact used, in carrying out new undertakings; and, besides these, there are also immense sums lying in the banks awaiting investment. The proposition, then, that industry never can exceed what the capital of the society *can* support, is totally irrelevant. It never can, for any considerable time, be nearly as great as the capital *can* support; for, if it were, there would be no stock of commodities, and this would cause such high prices and such high rates of interest as must check consumption on the one hand, and quicken production on the other.

One half of the capital normally unemployed is ample for the inauguration of gigantic enterprises; and these, if within the strength of the community, will not prevent anything being done which would otherwise have been done. On the contrary, the previously existing industries will be stimulated to larger production.

Let us suppose that the United States at the end of 1879 was producing and consuming commodities equal to a value of six thousand millions for the year, with a surplus stock equal to the value of one thousand millions. The bank deposits of money are known to exceed one thousand millions. If, at that time, they commenced forming new instruments (mills, forges, farms, houses, railroads, &c.) to the annual value of three hundred millions over and beyond the regular and normal movement, there would be, as we see, one thousand millions of unemployed floating capital, and immense moneyed reserves, to answer to the subscribed funds; but these subscriptions would go to recompense the producers of the new instruments, and would be by them expended, for the most part, for commodities, — thus relieving the capitalists of a portion of their stocks, and placing them in a position to employ more labor for the sake of enlarging their production of commodities. But whatever they thus expended in labor would lead to the production of more than twice the value expended in labor, as is shown by the returns of the census of 1870. This gives the total value added to materials by the manufacturing and mechanical industries of the United States as 1,744 millions, of which 776 millions went *directly* to labor. It might well, then, have happened that at the end of 1880 the gap made in the stock of unemployed floating capital was quite repaired, and the country as ready to continue a similar movement in 1881 as it was to commence it a year before. Meanwhile the extra recompense to labor during the year might have been not less than six hundred millions.

Vary the amounts as you please, but you will find that any new enterprise, not out of proportion to the existing surplus stock of commodities, will result, first, in an enlarged employment of laborers; and second, in the creation of new subsidiary capital,— or, say rather, of new instruments of production, which would not otherwise have come into existence. But a free-trader may ask: How do you know that there is any surplus stock of commodities? And we should reply that, in the first place, we know it as a matter of fact, which can be verified in State Street any day when production and consumption are in their normal condition. But, as our free-trade brethren do not like facts, nor believe in them unless they agree with conclusions deduced from postulates admitted by their own authors, we will try to show that in an industrial community there must be normally a stock of commodities or of unemployed capital.

First, then, take Industry A. Those who commenced it did so for the sake of profit. But so long as they obtained a satisfactory profit, the same motive would lead them to enlarge their production. If one man did not, another would; and so the increase of the industry would go on until it overran the demand. A stock would then accumulate, bringing down profits and locking up a portion of the producers' capital at the same moment. But what is true of Industry A, is true of B, C, D, &c.; and we thus arrive at the conclusion that each carries along a surplus stock. When this stock is diminished by a novel or increased demand, prices rise; when the stock is increased, prices fall, and the industry is checked.

No economist, as far as we know, has noticed the vast aggregate of these stocks, nor the manner in which they regulate the play of the industrial forces; and yet, without knowing about them, it is impossible to understand what happens upon the commencement of a great war or of a great industrial movement. When we have ascertained what the ordinary average stock is, whether equal to two, three, or more months' consumption, it may become possible to form a rational opinion as to how far any industrial movement can be pushed without bringing on a scarcity of floating capital and a stringency in the money market; but, meanwhile, it is something to have satisfied ourselves that such stocks must and do exist, and that systems framed in ignorance or disregard of them are necessarily erroneous.

Such a system is that of Adam Smith in his third paragraph above quoted. He starts with the self-evident axiom that "the general industry of the society never can *exceed* what the capital of the society *can* employ." He then repeats the idea, in different words, three several times; and then, mistaking apparently this rhetorical artifice for logic, he draws his conclusion that "a regulation of commerce can only divert a portion of the capital of the society into directions into which it might not otherwise have gone." This conclusion will follow from his axiom whenever an industrial community shall be found in which there exists no unemployed capital, and no funds, which, though originally intended for private expenditure, are capable of being diverted to the support of productive labor, the moment a protective law affords a sufficient motive for doing so.

Professor Sumner's argument appears to be only a variation of that of Adam Smith and Mr. J. S. Mill. He urges that if a law can do anything more than transfer, to the protected industry, capital that was or would have been applied to some of the old industries, then the law must *create capital out of nothing.*

This would be true if in civilized communities there were no capital seeking investment (a portion of the one thousand millions of bank deposits), and no capital locked up in commodities awaiting a demand. or materials delayed in conversion into commodities on account of the dulness of the demand; but it would seem to be untrue in the actual world we live in.

I respectfully invite Professor Sumner to examine this matter to the bottom. and see whether, in his theory, he does not overlook facts which, when taken into account, will necessitate another and very different theory. It is true that the argumentation on which his theory is built has stood more than a century without being picked to pieces; but the doctrine that the world was flat stood a great many centuries. The antiquity of an argumentation, the fact that it had been found satisfactory by three or four generations, was sufficient to warrant its acceptance by a teacher and its communication to pupils; but if it has been shown to be erroneous, both it and its corollaries ought surely to be abandoned forthwith.

The writer has no pecuniary bias in this matter, and no desire except to arrive at the truth; and he abhors, as much as Professor Sumner can, whatever is mystical, misty, indistinct, — everything in short which will not stand the test of the most minute and searching examination.

This leads me to object (without any disrespect to Professor Sumner) to such sentences as the following : —

" We cannot collect taxes and redistribute them without loss : much less can we produce forced monopolies and distorted industrial relations without loss."

Such words appear to me to mislead both writer and reader. They assume that under the régime of free competition in a nation of fifty millions there can be monopolies, and they assume that industrial relations, different from what would arise by themselves, are productive of national loss; and these assumptions appear to me to take for granted the doctrines of free trade, which are the very things under discussion.

Again, Professor Sumner remarks that —

" The notion that the Legislature has a wisdom greater than that of the people, and can point out the industries they ought to pursue, has been often refuted ; but the protective theory assumes more than that ; it assumes that the law can enlighten the desire for profit, and make it a more trustworthy guide than it would be under freedom."

But the question does not seem to be whether the Legislature has greater wisdom than the people, but whether the untrammelled action of each individual necessarily produces the best possible result, — such as cannot be improved by the collective wisdom; whether, in short, in this one field of human affairs, judgment and observation and study are utterly impotent to improve the accidental or, if you please, the natural course of events. I am not aware that the opinion that the collective action of the whole nation may produce advantageous results has been often or ever refuted. The most persuasive argument in favor of a negative decision, that I have seen, is contained in the Enquiry into the Nature and Causes of the Wealth of Nations, Book IV. chap. 11, § 4, *et seq.*, and it is very persuasive; but if Professor Sumner will examine it narrowly, and apply to it the logic which the article under review shows him to be master of, he will see the supposed demonstration crumble to pieces. To examine it in this article would exceed the limits of space and the patience of readers. Protection does not, I think, presume to enlighten the desire for profit, but only to place within the reach of unoccupied capital and labor an additional field of employment which they can take possession of with benefit to the *whole community.*

In the foregoing I have endeavored to show where and how protection exerts an effect on production, to increase it. I must now ask the indulgence of the reader, and of Professor Sumner, while I endeavor to show where and how free trade may exert an effect on production, to diminish it.

Let us take the three industries of cottons, woollens, and iron, and let us suppose, for the sake of illustration, that their aggregate product sells for one thousand millions; and let us farther suppose, for the sake of illustration, that the same products could be purchased abroad for seven hundred millions. The gross annual product of the United States I find set down in a Free-Trade Book, "The Balance Sheet of Nations," at £1,400,000,000 sterling, or say seven thousand millions of dollars, which appears to be not an unreasonable estimate.

It would seem that this seven thousand millions must pay all rents, all profits, all wages; must pay all productive laborers,

so-called, and all recipients of salaries, fees, or wages for services which do not issue either in commodities or in instruments of production. It would seem that the *proportion* of
the gross product which would fall to any capitalist for the use
of his particular instrument of production, or which would fall
to any salaried man for the services he renders, must depend
upon supply and demand; *e. g.* upon the number of persons offering to give instruction, compared with the demand
of the community for that much-honored service. Let us call
the share of the gross product falling to any one, X. Now in
the cases of the instructor, the clergyman, the lawyer, the
physician, or any other recipient of fees or salaries, it would
seem that they must be benefited by the drawing off, into the
cotton, woollen, and iron industries, of a multitude of men who
would otherwise be pressing into the professions. It would
seem that for each person in those professions the share represented by X must be greater by reason of the existence of
those industries, unless, upon their suppression, an equal field
would be found for that class of persons.

But the three industries in question produce (by the supposition) one thousand millions, or one seventh part of the
total annual product; that is, they support something over
seven millions of people. Every dollar gets into the hands of
either the producers of commodities and instruments of production (capital), or else into the hands of those who render
services — every dollar, save and except the comparatively
small sum expended for foreign products. Substantially, the
whole one thousand millions are expended for other American
products and services, and the amount expended for services
would be again expended for commodities or for capital; so
that in the end the thousand millions of those three industries would be paid for by one thousand millions of other
American products.

But, by the supposition, seven hundred millions of the other
American products would, *at present prices*, procure, if sent
abroad, the same amount of cottons and woollens and iron now
enjoyed and consumed. Suppress the cotton and woollen and
iron industries and — *if the exchangeable value of our own*

products remained undiminished when offered abroad in such greater quantities, and *if also the exchangeable value of foreign cottons, woollens, and iron* remained unenhanced when called for in such great quantities — we should thereafter get the cottons and woollens and iron as much as we now get them, but the seven millions of people, supported directly and indirectly by the three industries, would be without means of support; they would then have, as Mr. Mill expresses it, either to go without food and necessaries, or squeeze them by competition from the shares of other laborers.

But, to bring about even this result, we have had to suppose that the addition of seven hundred millions (to our present export of eight or nine hundred millions) would *not* depress the exchangeable value of the whole. If it did depress it, even fifteen per cent, then our cottons and woollens and iron would cost as much as now, and leave us our seven millions of unoccupied people besides; and, if the foreign iron and woollens and cottons advanced in exchangeable value, we should be worse off still. But it has been urged that the seven millions, or those who support the seven millions, would find occupation about "something else — " that they would build *houses* and *wagons*, &c.; but the effective demand of the community for houses and wagons, &c., will, by supposition, be diminished by the seven hundred millions sent abroad to buy cottons and woollens and iron before made at home; and, although houses and wagons " are never imported," their exchangeable value depends upon the effective demand.

Let us now try again to imagine how salaried men would be affected by the suppression of the three industries in question. Evidently the educated men, now employed in and about those industries, would become competitors over and above those now competing for pulpits, professorships, seats upon the bench, and other dignified occupations yielding salaries. The X representing any particular salary must then, after a while, come to be a smaller proportion of the total annual product available for home consumption, as already observed; and this last being, by the supposition, reduced by the one tenth part sent abroad, the particular salary would soon come to be not only a diminished proportion of the previous annual product, but a diminished proportion of nine tenths of the previous product. In short, less being produced in the country, there would be less to divide between rent, profits, and wages.

It is only a couple of weeks since I became aware that Professor Sumner had published in March the article now under review; and the present paper has been written in response to his request conveyed in the following sentence : —

" If this be not so, let some protectionist analyze the operation of his system, and show, by reference to undisputed economical principles, where and how it exerts any effect on production to increase it."

In return I have only to request that, if this paper has not duly met his requisition, he will point out with precision exactly where and how it is erroneous or defective. The subject is one of tremendous importance, and there are thousands of honest and intelligent men who desire to be shown exactly what is and what is not true with regard to it.

I have endeavored to avoid all side issues, and to go direct to the chief point in which the scholastic political economy appears to be erroneous. This is a small matter, indeed, when once pointed out; but it has been nevertheless sufficient to paralyze the keen intellects of its professors, sufficient to prevent their improving political economy into a real science, and sufficient to force them to conclusions the reverse of those drawn by the practical man from the industrial phenomena which he is obliged every day and hour to interpret, under the penalty of *ruin* if he fail to interpret correctly.

GEORGE BASIL DIXWELL.

REVIEW

Of an article by Prof. Arthur L. Perry, Williams College, Williamstown, Mass., in the Journal of the American Agricultural Association for July and October, 1881, *entitled,* —

"FARMERS AND THE TARIFF."

PROFESSOR PERRY states substantially as follows (his statements being merely condensed) that —

" the war of the American Revolution was waged mainly in the interests of a free trade; that one of the first acts of the thirteen colonies, April 6, 1776, was to establish free trade, which substantially continued until the present government was established in 1789 ; that no ill effects followed, and that the country was not flooded at that time with the cheap goods of foreigners, *because* the only way that can be brought about is for the natives to flood the foreigners with cheap native goods in exchange. In 1789 shrewd members of the first Congress, mostly from New England, at the instance and under the pressure of certain men who thought thereby to raise the price artificially of their own special home products, by means of lobbying and logrolling, caused to pass the first tariff bill, of which the preamble was : ' Whereas, it is necessary for the support of the Government, for the discharge of the debts of the United States, and the encouragement and protection of manufactures, that duties be laid,' and so on. The duties were low, but they introduced a false principle, — that a man's neighbors may be taxed indefinitely to hire him to carry on an alleged unprofitable business ; and this utterly false principle has brought on the protective system, which has grown so unjust, onerous, and abominable that no other free people would submit for a single year. It was well understood in 1789 that this system would be hostile to the interest of the farmers as such ; the fallacy that a home market in some mysterious way compensates the farmers was not then invented, and can now be exploded by a few words. These words are : ' Unless it can be shown that protection — that is to say, restriction — increases the number of births or diminishes the number of deaths, it is in vain to claim that there are any more mouths to be fed by the farmers than there would be under freedom.'

" Fisher Ames said in 1789 : ' From the different situation of manufacturers in Europe and America, encouragement is necessary. In Europe the artisan is driven to labor for his bread. Stern Necessity with her iron rod compels his exertion. In America, invitation and encouragement are needed. Without them the infant manufacture droops, and those who might be employed in it seek with success a competency from our cheap and fertile soil.'

" This lets the protectionist cat right out of her bag. Our people are not poor enough, and never were, to carry on unprofitable branches of industry to support which the whole community has to be taxed, and particularly the agricultural classes. What then is to be done? Why, drag down agriculture by abominable taxes to the level of the alleged unprofitable infant manufactures. ' Protection assumed at the outset, and has maintained to this day, an attitude of unceasing hostility to the tillers of the soil. Protectionist manufacturers, who are a mere fraction of the population, have cajoled the farmers, who are one half the population, to consent to pay for their supplies prices artificially enhanced by law, and to sell their produce at prices artificially depressed by law.' There never was a worse delusion than this on the part of the farmers, and there never was a worse swindle than this on the part of the party of the other part. But the manufacturers as a body are not benefited ; many of them lose two dollars by protection for every one dollar which they gain ; so that the free-traders of this country are fighting a battle in behalf of the manufacturers themselves (selfishness is always short-sighted) as well as in behalf of the farmers. That protective duties are a great burden is shown by the fact that the protectionist manufacturers never like to pay them themselves ; it seems that what is sauce for the agricultural goose is not good for the protectionist gander. Whether the farmers see their true interest or not the fact remains that they are the ass that bears most of the burden and eats least of the hay of protection."

Let us first examine the historical portion of this document.

It is undoubtedly true that one object of the War of the Revolution was to free the trade of the colonies from the restrictions which Great Britain had placed upon it for the benefit of her own commerce and manufactures. It was, therefore, in

one sense waged "in the interests of a free trade." But it was
not waged in the interests of any such free trade as Professor
Perry advocates, — a free trade which denies the right of a
nation to place any restrictions having in view the encouragement of industries deemed necessary or useful to the whole
community. On the contrary, the colonies strove for the right
to regulate their own commerce and industry as they pleased,
and, as soon as independent, they proceeded to exercise the
right. It was found, however, that the action of Virginia was
ineffectual without the co-operation of Maryland, and that
those two could not act effectually without Pennsylvania, nor
those three without New York, and so on. Mr. Madison,
writing to Joseph C. Cabell, Sept. 18, 1828, records these facts,
and adds in illustration the following: —

"There is a passage in Mr. Necker's work on the finances of France
which affords a signal illustration of the difficulty of collecting in con-
tiguous communities indirect taxes when not the same in all, by the
violent means resorted to against smuggling from one to another of
them. Previous to the late revolutionary war in that country, the
taxes were of very different rates in the different provinces. . . . The
consequence was that the standing army of patrols against smuggling
had swollen to the number of twenty-three thousand; the annual
arrests of men, women, and children engaged in smuggling, to five
thousand five hundred and fifty, . . . more than three hundred of
whom were consigned to the terrible punishment of the galleys."

The colonies, then, did not go to war to deprive themselves
of the right to regulate their own trade according to their own
notions of what is advantageous to the whole community; and
Professor Perry's labored introduction tends to produce an impression the reverse of what is true.

But this is a trifle to what follows, when he says that "no
ill effects followed this general liberty to buy and sell with
foreigners," &c.

The real facts are that upon the opening of the ports, after
the war, an immense quantity of foreign manufactures was introduced; and the people were tempted by the sudden cheapness of imported goods to purchase beyond their capacity for

payment. The bonds of men whose competency to pay their debts was unquestionable could not be negotiated but at a discount of thirty, forty, and fifty per cent; real property was scarcely vendible, and sales of any article for ready money could only be made at a ruinous loss. Property, when brought to sale under execution, sold at so low a price as frequently to ruin the debtor without paying the creditor. A disposition to resist the laws became common. Laws were passed by which property of every kind was made a legal tender in the payment of debts, though payable according to contract in gold and silver. Other laws delayed payments, so that of sums already due only a third, and afterwards only a fifth, was annually recoverable in the courts of law. Silver and gold departed to pay for the necessary and unnecessary commodities imported.

In this condition of financial matters, the public securities fell to fifteen, twelve, and even ten cents in the dollar, ruining a large portion of the warmest friends of the Revolution, who had risked their lives and embarked their entire property in its support.

In every part of the States the scarcity of money had become a common subject of complaint, and the difficulty of paying debts had become so common, that riots and combinations were formed in many places, and the operations of civil government were suspended.

The authorities for the above are, Dr. Hugh Williamson, Minot's "History of the Insurrection in Massachusetts," pp. 2, 13; Marshall's "Life of Washington," pp. 75, 88, 121; Ramsay's "South Carolina," vol. ii. p. 428; Belknap's "History of New Hampshire," vol. ii. pp. 352, 356, 429; Matthew Carey's works, and the "Questions of the Day," by Dr. Elder.

But Professor Perry says that "no ill effects followed this general liberty to buy and sell with foreigners," &c.

Let the reader pause a moment over this extraordinary misrepresentation. Had it been made by one who was impelled by avarice or revenge, there would be nothing marvellous about it; but here is a very different case. A professor in a respectable college, the author of a treatise on political economy said to be used in many universities, a gentleman whose official position makes him a trustee of the truth for the rising generation, should not be accused of wilful untruthfulness. No! it is more courteous, more agreeable, and doubtless more just, to trace the misstatement to an unfortunate habit of hastily concluding that events did actually happen in this or that manner, because, if his theories be correct, they must so have happened. He feels perfectly sure of his doctrine; and, such being the doctrine, the events must have been as stated; but, unfortunately for the deduced history, the doctrine itself cannot be maintained. Imports are not exchanged for exports. Imports are sold for money, and the money is thereafter either carried abroad or invested in exports, according to circumstances; or it may be invested in Government or other securities, and so run the country in debt. But paying in money or in securities has a limit which is speedily reached; and afterwards, imports must be limited by the foreign demand for exports, even if this pays for only a fifth or a tenth of what the country could produce and enjoy through its own labor. But before the free-trade disease reaches this chronic stage it must pass through the acute stage. There are the export of treasure; the contraction of all values as measured by treasure; the aggravation of all debts, public and private; forced liquidations; widespread bankruptcy, and a general diminution of employment to industry.

The theory which teaches that the only way in which a country can be flooded with the cheap goods of foreigners is for the natives to flood the foreigners with cheap goods in exchange is an incorrect theory; and the history deduced from it is consequently the opposite of the actual course of events, — all which proves only what common sense would have seen at once, namely, that history should not be inferred from theories, but ascertained by reference to the written and printed records of the times.

Another misstatement as to facts may be found in the allegation that in 1789 men had not yet invented the theory that protection would benefit farmers by enlarging the home market.

In Adam Smith's lectures, afterwards published (in 1776) under the title of " Inquiry into the Nature and Causes of the Wealth of Nations," the idea of the great advantage of the home market crops out frequently, and may be found more particularly in bk. iv. chap. ix., last paragraph but four, where he says : —

" Whatever, then, tends to diminish in any country the number of artificers and manufacturers tends to diminish the home market, — the most important of all markets for the rude produce of the land."

The same idea appears frequently in Alexander Hamilton's writings. He says : —

" There appear strong reasons to regard the foreign demand for that (agricultural) surplus as too uncertain a reliance, and to desire a substitute for it in an extensive domestic market.

" To secure such a market there is no other expedient than to promote manufacturing establishments.   Manufacturers, who constitute the most numerous class after the cultivators of the land, are for that reason the principal consumers of the surplus of their labor.

" The idea of an extensive domestic market for the surplus product of the soil is of the first consequence.   It is, of all things, that which most effectually conduces to a flourishing state of agriculture."

Benjamin Franklin, writing home from London in 1771, says : —

" Every manufacturer encouraged in a country makes part of a home market for provisions among ourselves, and saves so much money to the country as must otherwise be exported to pay for the manufactures he supplies.   Here in England it is well known that wherever a manufacture is established which employs a number of hands, it raises the value of land in the country all around it.   It seems, therefore, the interest of our farmers and owners of land to encourage our young manufactures in preference to foreign ones."

Professor Perry says that this doctrine, which he calls a fallacy, had not been invented in 1789!   The reader will see that he is here again in error as to matters of fact.   The doctrine was well established long before the date named, and has never been shaken. It was reaffirmed by General Jackson in his celebrated letter to Dr. Coleman in 1824, and by John Stuart Mill, in his Political Economy, thirty years later. Indeed, it is nearly self-evident; but Professor Perry denounces it as a fallacy which a few words will explode, and he gives us the few words, which are : —

"Unless it can be shown that protection — that is to say, restriction — increases the number of births or diminishes the number of deaths, it is in vain to claim that there are any more mouths to be fed by the farmers than there would be under freedom."

This is a question about which a farmer is as good a judge as any professor. In twenty-five years the population of the United States will be doubled, — it will be 100,000,000, — capable, if all employed in agriculture, of producing food and raw materials for 250,000,000 to 300,000,000 of people. Nowhere on this planet are to be found the requisite number of purchasers. In England and Scotland and Wales the people (less than 30,000,000) have been rash enough to make themselves largely dependent upon foreign food ; but even their demand is liable to very great variations. Other countries pursue the more sensible policy of raising in ordinary seasons enough for themselves.

To repeat: in twenty-five years the population of the whole country will be doubled ; that of the now less settled portions will be increased three, four, or five fold. Let the farmer in such portions consider whether he would prefer the increase of population to be mostly farmers or mostly people who buy and do not produce farm products. It will not take him long to make up his mind, and his judgment will be worth as much as that of all the political economists in Europe and America. His judgment will agree with the mature and deliberate opinion of such men as Franklin, Hamilton, Jefferson, Andrew Jackson, Henry Clay, Daniel Webster, and the majority of the great statesmen who have been the pride of our country.

The article now under review contains two argumentations which it may be well to examine, coming as they do from a noted political economist.

The first is in favor of free trade. It runs thus : —

" Free trade does not compel anybody to trade; it does not even recommend anybody to trade ; it merely allows those persons to trade who find it for their profit to do so. Unless it be profitable for them to trade they will not trade. They have no motive to trade."

The original free-trade argument (by Adam Smith) went farther, and maintained not only that each individual knew his own interest (both immediate and permanent) better than any statesman or law-giver could, but also that what the individual elected to do must necessarily be that which best promoted the national wealth. These extravagant propositions were repeatedly shown to be untenable, were abandoned by Mr. John Stuart Mill, and are abandoned by Professor Perry, inasmuch as in the very article now under review he maintains that the manufacturers do not understand their own interests, that the farmers do not understand theirs, and that a majority of the American people have for a hundred years been pursuing a pernicious and pauperizing policy.

But in place of these abandoned positions Professor Perry gives us the following : —

" If it *be* profitable for any two persons to trade, and a law steps in to prevent it, then that law destroys property, interferes with rights, and makes the persons subject to it so far forth slaves."

But as the identity of individual and national interests has been abundantly disproved, this proposition is exclusively one regarding the rights of property. It is a proposition in law or in social science. It cannot be maintained either in law or in social science ; but if it could, it would still be out of place in a discussion as to whether free trade or protection will best promote the wealth of a particular nation. Both law and social science demand that the individual interest shall give way to the national interest; with compensation, it is true, in some cases, but not in those cases where the betterment outweighs the damage. To suppose that property confers the right to nullify the social and economical *régime* under which

it was acquired would, I think, have astonished Socrates or
any subsequent moralist; and to expect that a discussion of
the rights of property will reveal the secrets of the nature and
causes of the wealth of nations would equally surprise all
political economists save Bastiat and his imitators.

The second and last argument which it will be necessary to
look at is the following: —

"Your protectionist thinks it is a very good thing for the farmers and
for the people generally to pay protective prices, *but he never likes* to
pay them himself. He has no scruple in evading them, if he can do
so by any possibility. He denies by his own actions, which speak
louder than words, what he is constantly affirming in words, namely,
that protection is a good thing."

Let us test this method of reasoning. A just, efficient, and
economical government gives us good roads, good water, safe
buildings, defence against public and private violence, and a
thousand other desirable things; but it costs money, and many
individuals, after enjoying its benefits, are unwilling to pay
their proportion of the expense. They thus deny by their
actions, which speak louder than words, what they are constantly affirming in words, namely, that a just, efficient, and
economical government is a good thing.

Again, laws against cheating and robbing are generally
thought to be good; but many men, while they themselves
enjoy protection against cheating and robbing on the part of
others, will not hesitate, whenever they can, to cheat and rob;
thus denying by actions, which speak louder than words, what
they are constantly affirming in words, that cheating and robbing ought to be suppressed.

Again, if the protectionist doctrine be correct, the American
system vastly increases the gross annual product of the country,
which pays all rents, profits, fees, salaries, and wages, which
has endowed our institutions of learning, and brought our prosperity and civilization to its present height. Nevertheless, the
wealthier classes generally keep themselves in a fever because
under this system their champagnes, gloves, ribbons, silks,
satins, and fine broadcloths, brought from abroad, cost much

higher than they would were there no duties. They do not like to pay the cost of the prosperity they enjoy. But this does not prove that prosperity is a bad thing. The farmer sees that without protection he would have to go without three fourths of the comforts he now possesses; the rich do not see that under free trade reduced incomes would compel them to forego a large portion of their present luxuries. They deny the allegation with emphasis; but neither the denial nor the emphasis proves anything. The proof must be sought from *combined* observation and reasoning. Patient and truthful search after facts, patient and truthful reasoning from them, patient and truthful examination and re-examination of *both* facts and reasoning, when they appear to disagree, may at some future time build up a solid and enduring *science* of political economy. Violence, denunciation, rhetoric, fierce onslaughts upon individuals or classes, vehement appeals to the short-sighted pocket, will in no way assist in its construction.

Having examined Professor Perry's historical and logical methods, we are in a position to form a correct judgment as to the rest of his article.

He asserts that the manufacturers are so foolish as to support measures which do not benefit them at all as a whole class. Some of the shrewdest and most unscrupulous are benefited; and these wicked, selfish, mendicant swindlers have cajoled the farmers into consenting to pay for their supplies prices artificially enhanced by law, and SELLING THEIR PRODUCE AT PRICES ARTIFICIALLY DEPRESSED BY LAW. This they have done by lobbying and log-rolling, — that is, by either deceiving or corrupting a majority of the Representatives and Senators in Congress. A majority of the American people for a hundred years have been either fools or knaves, or both; and the farmers especially are " the ass that bears most of the burden and eats least of the hay of protection." The only pure, patriotic, and intelligent people in the country are the free-traders. No evil has ever been experienced from free trade; no good has ever come from protection.

The actual history from beginning to end has been precisely opposite to that which Professor Perry has laid before us.

In 1789 it was well known to thinking men that the steady and permanent interests of farmers could be secured only by increasing the proportion of the community which consumed and did not produce farm products.

In the years immediately preceding 1789 free trade had brought intolerable evils upon the country ; and it was for this reason, as well as with the design of benefiting the farming in. terest by adding to the number of their customers, that duties were imposed upon imported manufactures. The Napoleonic wars followed with a great demand for our exports, and then came the period of the embargo and the war with England of 1812-15. During the period of non-intercourse and the war our manufactures increased greatly ; but after peace was declared there came a period of excessive importations similar to that which followed the War of the Revolution. Although free-traders assert that " the only way a country can be flooded with the cheap goods of foreigners is for the natives to flood the foreigners with cheap goods in exchange," the facts were the reverse of those deduced from their theories. In point of fact our country *was* flooded with cheap foreign goods ; in point of fact we *did* buy enormously beyond the amount which the foreigner would take pay for in goods ; in point of fact our treasure *was* exported, and this (contrary again to free-trade theories) *did* plunge the country into immeasurable distress, destroying a vast number of our manufacturing establishments, and affecting in a disastrous manner the farming interests as well.

It was then perceived that the protection which the existing tariff gave to manufactures was entirely insufficient in times when English speculation or distress threw immense masses of goods upon our shores ; and it was perceived that the ruin brought down upon every interest by a short period of great cheapness cost the country a hundred times what it gained by the momentary and illusive advantage of a low-moneyed price. It was in 1824 that General Jackson asked, " Where has the American farmer a market for his surplus products ? " and recommended as a remedy to draw from agriculture the superabundant labor, and employ it in machinery and manufactures.

It was to benefit the farmer that he proposed such higher duties as would make the other industries safe in times of foreign panics or periods of speculation. There would have been a diverting scene had any one assured the clear-headed old warrior and statesman that commodities are always paid for with commodities, and that no harm can come to a country from an inundation of foreign goods.

In 1833, in consequence of the threatening attitude of several of the Southern States which, under the slavery *régime*, were unable or unwilling to establish manufactures, the tariff was reduced ; and in the ensuing panic of 1837 the lessons of 1786 and 1820 were repeated, and it again became apparent that the farmer absolutely required the custom of the manufacturing and mechanical classes, and that these could only be rendered safe by duties sufficiently high to prevent foreign competition not merely in ordinary times, but also and chiefly during periods of financial disturbance in England. Any other policy would be as wise as it would be for Holland to build her dikes only high enough to exclude the ocean in ordinary weather, preferring occasional submergence to a somewhat more expensive security. Nay, it would not be as wise, for the higher duty does not entail higher prices. These, as regards such goods as concern the great mass of the people, are determined by internal competition. They will be as low as they can be under the circumstances of the country, whether the duty be forty per cent or sixty per cent; indeed, the higher duty would be more likely to lower the price by giving a greater sense of security, and thereby attracting more capital to the industry. I am not aware that any respectable economist, from Adam Smith's days to ours, has written anything which contradicts this proposition. The goods produced at home are in a few years much cheaper than the foreign goods with duty added, and they gradually grow cheaper and cheaper as skill and the increasing use of machinery more and more counterbalance, and in many cases overcome, the effect of a higher rate of wages and a higher rate of interest. The heavier cotton goods were long ago cheaper even in money than they could be imported, duty free; and free-trade writers

allege that heavy woollens have reached nearly an equality
in cost with foreign goods. To be sure, after making this
allegation they state that the duty is 135 per cent, and invite the "hod-carrier and the poor sewing-girl" to believe
that they pay, and the manufacturer pockets, the 135 per cent;
but everybody knows that any reasonable prospect of making
ten per cent a year would cause a hundred millions to be invested in new woollen mills; and the inference is unavoidable
that the poor get their clothing at what it costs, and a profit
averaging about the same as is made in other industries.

In every industry the demand occasionally outruns the
power of production, and then there are large profits; and
occasionally the power of production outruns the demand,
and then there are severe losses. The steel rails of Professor
Perry's article are in point. The productive capacity of England in 1880 was about one million tons, and that of the United
States the same, with the prospect of reaching a million and a
half in 1882. Before steel rails were made in this country the
price was not less than $150 a ton, and the demand has so
suddenly outrun the means of supply, that the same price
would very probably have been reached again had we depended
upon England. The present price in England is what answers
to a demand for one million of tons, and Professor Perry bases
his calculations upon the assumption that the price in Great
Britain would have been the same in the face of a demand for
two millions of tons, and in face of a knowledge that the Americans could not make a ton for themselves! As it is, the
manufacturers of steel rails are making money, — perhaps a
great deal of money, — and the country is made to ring with
denunciations of the wicked and deplorable fact. By and by
they will be losing money, and then the free-trader will try to
gain influence with them by urging that they are being ruined
by the duties upon iron. But the country can console itself by
the reflection that whatsoever they make, be it much or little,
finds its way, every dollar of it (save and except what is spent
upon foreign goods) into the hands of the American working-
man.

The observations of Fisher Ames, which Professor Perry

contrives to misunderstand, are simple enough. They assert merely that where every man can be a farmer if he pleases, and enjoy the competence and independence of that position, it is in vain to endeavor to form other classes unless the condition of those other classes be made sufficiently profitable to compensate them for leaving their farms or for abstaining from taking farms. On these conditions we can have all that the whole community can produce; on any other terms we can have only the food and raw products we ourselves need, and such amount of manufactured articles as will pay for what raw products foreigners desire to take from us. If we desire a far greater value of their products than they desire of ours, the advantage we possess in producing raw products will inure entirely to them; and, moreover, we shall obtain only a portion — in our case only a small portion — of what we desire, and shall either have large quantities of food to be given to animals or burned, or else be discouraged from producing more than a fraction of what we might produce under wiser arrangements. We should then enjoy in some sense a competency, for we should not starve; but we could not enjoy our present comparative opulence. If any one doubts this let him study Mr. J. S. Mill's chapter on international trade.

Professor Perry is an admirer of Bastiat, a writer who endeavored to bolster a weak cause by importing into economical questions the virulence of personal and class abuse, and the inexhaustible resources of rhetorical inveracity; a writer, however, of whose works one serves as a text-book at Harvard, while another — the worst of the whole — is recommended to youth by the authority of Yale. According to Bastiat, protectionists are cheats, thieves, robbers, swindlers, &c., and the denunciations of Professor Perry in the article under review are of a similar quality. If these were merited it would be high time that Harvard and Yale and our other universities looked into their records to see how large a proportion of their foundations had been derived from protectionists; to what extent, in short, they have been receivers of stolen goods; and they should lose no time in coming to a solemn resolution to accept nothing in future from so infamous and polluted a source! Meanwhile, it would gratify a natural curiosity if some one would tell us who were the wicked and selfish men who have for a hundred years cajoled the majority of the American people. The men who introduced the cotton manufacture certainly did not answer to the description; they were men with large heads and large hearts, many of them the sons of farmers, but quite able to comprehend and act upon the broadest views of statesmanship. They were not wicked, nor selfish, nor robbers, nor swindlers, nor men who would cajole anybody. They engaged in an enterprise in which immense capital was embarked, and so some of them became rich; but no one can truthfully allege that they used their wealth in a mean or selfish manner. As to this point Harvard College can be called as a witness. Certainly no more weighty witness could be summoned; but this grand old witness now testifies emphatically to the truth of the free-trade doctrines. How is this? Is it not almost conclusive? By no means! It is a transient humor. Her belief was very different in 1776 when men were in earnest; it was very different during the greater portion of the intervening years, and it will be different again as soon as it shall be generally seen that Great Britain, through her commercial, manufacturing, and educated classes, organized in the Cobden Club, is assailing our prosperity as perniciously as she could with shot and shell and ironclads and all the barbarity and devastation of war. The persistent pressure of transatlantic condescension will then cease to sway our literary classes; and we shall have not only free farmers and free working-men, but a whole population which will be free to reason for themselves, and which will bestow upon the faithful journalist, author, and teacher the all-sufficient reward of the sincere and enduring approbation of his own fellow-citizens.

To return to Professor Perry's article. We have seen —

1st, That with regard to the Revolutionary War, it so states the truth as to lead the reader inevitably to a false conclusion.

It does the same also with regard to the opinions of Mr. Madison, quoting words he used, but failing to quote the exceptions he insisted on.

2d, That with regard to the effects of free trade before 1789, and in regard to the time when the theory of the home market sprang up, it makes statements which are absolutely contradicted by historical records.

3d, That its only argumentative portions will not bear to be confronted with any known system of reasoning.

4th, That it speaks with indecorous and unwarrantable contempt of the majority of the people and statesmen of the United States, representing that the manufacturers are too stupid to know their own interests, and yet are clever enough to deceive or corrupt the statesmen and to cajole the farmers, whom it calls "the ass that bears most of the burden and eats least of the hay of protection."

5th, That its incautious author appears to have fallen into these incongruities in consequence of reasoning which involved a doctrine in political economy long since obsolete, — the doctrine, namely, that the immediate interests of the individual are always necessarily identical with the immediate and permanent interests of the community to which he belongs. This doctrine may linger in the seclusion of this or that university; but as each class emerges, annually, into the broad daylight of actual life, its members will quickly discover that those who would be leaders among men must possess themselves of some philosophy which does not flatly contradict all that their eyes and ears reveal to them in the world of firm, concrete, positive, indisputable fact.

GEORGE BASIL DIXWELL.

TARIFF COMMISSION.

TARIFF COMMISSION.

PHILADELPHIA, PA., OCT. 14, 1882.

PROF. W. G. SUMNER, of New Haven, Conn., addressed the Commission as follows : —

"I have noticed that in the discussions which have taken place before this Commission there has been a constant reiteration of some false doctrines of theoretical political economy about wages. If there is to be any theoretical political economy admitted, it is worth while to have it correct. I have therefore thought that it might be proper for me, as a professional student of political economy, to appear here and read a paper setting forth the true relations between protective taxes and wages."

Mr. Sumner assumes that, being a professor of political economy in a great institution of learning, he is competent to correct what he alleges to be a gross error in the public mind in regard to the relation between protection and wages. His reasons shall be carefully examined; but we must first ascertain how much deference we ought to pay to his opinions on the ground of his being a professor. What guarantee does that fact give of the accuracy of his doctrines? Let us see how it has been with others over whom Mr. Sumner could hardly claim superiority.

First let us take Prof. Adam Smith, the very distinguished author of the "Enquiry into the Nature and Causes of the Wealth of Nations." He was as certain as Mr. Sumner of the correctness of his opinions; indeed, he was not the least bashful about intimating that the "notions" of all statesmen and lawgivers were childish in comparison with his.

But Prof. J. R. McCulloch (equally positive) declared that Adam Smith was in error upon more than eighty points, many of them of great importance.

Mr. John Stuart Mill, also, who was so distinguished a thinker and reasoner as to be ranked perhaps almost upon an equality with the professors of political economy, declared that the work of Adam Smith was " in many parts obsolete and in all parts imperfect " ! and Mr. Mill could not agree with Malthus, Chalmers, or Carey.

But Professor Cairnes dissents in very important points from Mr. Mill, although declaring himself to be a humble follower; while Professor McLeod, in a work which has had an immense success upon the Continent of Europe, maintains that Mr. Mill and all his school are in error as to the very method of studying political economy, — they declaring that it should only be studied by the deductive, he that it can yield correct results only when investigated by the inductive, method.

Professor McLeod also, in his Dictionary, falls foul of other professors upon various points, especially upon their doctrine that absenteeism is no injury to a country; and he presses his own views with such vigor and warmth as might lead a hasty reader to infer that his opponents were little better than blockheads. But it would be a very precipitate reader who would draw such a conclusion. Each of these great thinkers made inestimable contributions to political economy, notwithstanding that each contradicts others and himself as well. To examine these contradictions and ascertain wherein and to what degree each was right, is a work to which plodding conscientious mediocrity is quite competent. The critic needs not the genius and inspiration of the author, but only the diligence which brings the author to the bar of his own methods of reasoning. Mr. Mill's great works upon Logic and Political Economy will furnish the tools by which to detect the few errors into which even Mr. Mill himself may have fallen ; but they will never be discovered by one who, like Professor Sumner, draws his inspiration from Bastiat, Mr. D. A. Wells, and the Cobden Club Essays, and who from inability to understand Mr. Mill's methods is quite incompetent to distinguish between the propositions which are and those which are not consistent with those methods. Professor McCulloch's paradox regarding absenteeism passed for science for thirty years without, however, making any impression upon the popular mind ; but at last the error in his reasoning was recognized, and his position abandoned by several even of the free-trade writers.

We see, then, that we cannot safely indulge our laziness in allowing a professor to think for us. He has no sources of information which are not equally open to statesmen and educated business men, all of whom have been pupils of the professors and afterwards pupils in the great school of practical life, where they often learn first to doubt and then to discard much which had been learned at college.

The professor, in fact, stands at some disadvantage. He is obliged to teach the same old propositions year after year, until they root themselves in his mind too deeply to be torn up; in short, he is very liable to fall into that condition which is described by Carlyle as being "possessed by Fixed Idea." In ordinary life he has nobody to challenge his opinions, and he must therefore be more likely than others to become dog-matic, and to be prone to wrath whenever he does encounter opposition.

Like Professor McCulloch in the matter of absenteeism, Mr. Sumner comes forward to sustain a paradox, and to prove by dialectics that wages are not higher by reason of protection; that is, he has set himself the task of proving that an opinion generally entertained upon both sides of the Atlantic during all past time is entirely erroneous. It was necessary in the interest of the free-trade party and of the Cobden Club that somebody should make the attempt, and it was perhaps judicious that he should be one who would carry before him the shield of a great institution of learning; but we have said enough to show that this, after all, amounts to very little, and that the reasons of a professor must be brought to the test as rigidly as those of any other individual. Let us now examine them.

"I learn, from the reports of the proceedings before this Commission, that some people believe that protective taxes make wages high, and at the same time that high wages make protective taxes necessary. If the Commission should act on these two doctrines, it would first raise taxes in order to raise wages in obedience to a delegation of workmen, and then raise taxes again in order to offset the previous increase, in the interest of a delegation of employers, and so on forever. These two notions, therefore, contradict each other and produce an absurdity. They are both false. Protective taxes lower wages, and high wages are a reason for free trade, not for protection. These two propositions confirm and sustain each other, and so ratify the truth of each."

The logical deception in this paragraph consists in the substitution of a universal for a limited proposition. Men who investigate cases in political economy, whether by the deductive or inductive methods, embody their conclusions in a set of words which, taken with the circumstances of the case known to all the world, are limited with sufficient exactness to prevent anybody of ordinary caution from falling into error.

Thus Adam Smith, Fisher Ames, Mr. John Stuart Mill, and many others have noticed that where cheap land is to be had men will flock to it, unless drawn to other pursuits by wages high enough to overcome the attraction of the land. Adam Smith, speaking of the Colonies, says: " From artificer a man becomes a planter, and neither large wages nor the easy subsistence which that country affords can bribe him rather to work for other people than for himself. He feels that an artificer is the servant of his customers, from whom he derives his subsistence; but that a planter, who cultivates his own land and derives his necessary subsistence from the labor of his own family, is really a master, and independent of all the world."

Here the inclinations of the individual are opposed to the interests of his class and to those of the whole community, which tends to become disproportionately agricultural, to depend more and more upon distant nations for everything except food, and to become poorer and poorer as it increases in numbers. The demand of the outer world for the food and raw materials of the United States cannot increase as fast as the home population ; for the outer world can take payment for the conversion of raw into finished products only in a few articles of comparatively easy transportation, while the home artificer and manufacturer take payment in every sort of product and every sort of service. Let the producers of food and raw materials allow to the other classes such emoluments as are sufficient to induce a portion of the community to abstain from becoming farmers, and the nation will grow symmetrically. The daily increasing numbers and skill of the other classes will give the market which will enable agriculture to avail itself of better tools, machines, drainage, and other improvements. The emoluments of the other classes, meanwhile, can never exceed the limit named, — to wit, that which balances the disposition of an individual to become an independent landowner. If it goes beyond this for a while, more persons will abstain from farming, and the balance will be restored. But before the introduction of manufactures there is not only the difficulty of high wages but also that of want of skill. Without a protective duty adequate to shut out the foreign article nothing can be done. The duty being laid on raises the price, but not to the extent of the duty, for the foreign price declines under the reduced demand. If, however, the duty be sufficient, the manufacture is introduced at a certain price which covers the higher wages and also the want of skill. This rise in price is for the moment a disadvantage to the portion of the community who before obtained a sufficiency of finished products; but the articles come at once within the reach of a wider circle, who before could not obtain them at all, or not in sufficient quantity, on account of the low price or unsalableness of their crops. The duty removes those who were causing an agricultural glut, and whose labor therefore produced less than nothing, and puts them upon the construction of finished products which are pure gain to the community. The gross annual product is increased by their whole value. There is more to divide, and demand and supply ultimately distribute the increase throughout the community. The farmer and planter are the first to feel it. Their occupation becomes more remunerative; and from this movement there *follows* a rise of wages in the non-agricultural portion of the community. The working of the economic forces is progressive, not simultaneous or instantaneous. The protective law first relieves the agricultural glut and apathy, and this in turn causes an increased demand for finished products. Wages in all departments will gradually advance, but they can augment no farther nor faster than the gross annual product. The protective *tax*, as Professor Sumner likes to call it, simply removes an obstacle which prevents the best and the natural distribution of the population. As skill increases, the price falls under home competition until it covers only the difference in the cost of labor;

and the skill may increase so as to cover this also, and give the community the article as cheaply as it could be imported without any duty. Such is the case with regard to tools, locomotives, agricultural machinery, and many other goods, including the greater part of the cottons consumed in the country. Such appears to be nearly the case with regard to the woollens used by the bulk of the people. The fine cottons and woollens which are objects of ostentation are still mostly imported. The duty on them gives a large revenue to the Government, and in reality comes out of nobody, as their higher price only fits them the better to enable A to appear as rich as B. It is these duties, however, — the duties upon objects of luxury and ostentation, — which irritate some of the salaried classes who do not understand political economy, and even some professors of the subject. They think themselves oppressed, they hate the manufacturers who live more showily than they can, and they make every effort to persuade the bulk of the people that they also are the victims of oppression.

If they understood the subject they profess, they would know that if its present objects were cheapened to ostentation, it would reject them and fly to others; and they would also know that whatever social *necessity* there may exist for such indulgences must surely in the long run be considered in the salaries paid them. But this necessity does not go a great way. The high respect which they and their families command on account of their much honored office relieves them from such necessity. The wise, temperate, truthful, benevolent, right-hearted professor is as welcome in homespun as is Crœsus in broadcloth; and if any individual fail to command respect, it can only be because he is an exception to the rule, and wanting in the high intellectual and moral qualities usually exhibited by professors. But to return to the price of manufactured goods. It must be sufficient to pay the wages of labor and the profit on capital usual in the community. Higher than this it cannot be for any long time, and it cannot be long lower. Monopoly has had no place in political economy since the discussion upon that point between Say and Ricardo.

It will be seen, then, that the propositions of the protectionists,— 1. That a duty raises wages gradually as the annual product increases; 2. That high wages (so far as wages affect the cost, and are not overmastered by greater efficiency) make protection necessary, — are limited. Within the limits naturally and necessarily attaching to them they are not contradictory, and they do not produce an absurdity.

But for these limited propositions Mr. Sumner substitutes two universal propositions, —

1. That a duty always raises wages, and raises them in proportion to its magnitude.

2. That high wages always make protection necessary, and necessary in proportion to their height.

These universal propositions he endeavors to impute to the protectionists, depicting the Commission first raising the duty in order to raise wages, and then raising it again to compensate the manufacturer for the higher wages, and so on. It is an ingenious sophism, well calculated to impose upon those whom a technical education has deprived of their natural intuitive judgment, while only half teaching them how to reason by propositions; but it would never impose upon any thoroughly educated person nor upon any practical man. The latter would put it aside at once as nonsense, and I fear would even think me a fool for spending time in showing it to be so.

What would the Commission have answered to a deputation of either workmen or employers asking for an advance of the duty for such purposes? Why, that if the industry already existed, and upon an average of years was paying the rate of profit usual in the community, then the duty had done all that it could do, — it had excluded the foreign product, and left the price and the wages to be arranged, as they must be, by the internal demand and supply. Higher duties, the Commissioners would have said, cannot raise your wages any more, nor raise your profits. An additional amount would positively have no effect.

To this the committees might say, Why not, then, raise the duties? And the only answer that could be given them would be, Because, if we raised the duties, it would be a handle for demagogues to use with those uninformed about such matters. It would be represented that the additional ten or twenty per cent was added to the price.

The "Boston Transcript," "Globe," "Herald," and even such high-toned papers as the "Advertiser," and the "New York Times" admit articles based upon this economic absurdity. The "Herald" even published an article which declared that the manufacturers of woollens could make the common goods suitable for the general consumption as cheaply as they could be made abroad, and yet took one hundred and thirty-five per cent profit to the detriment of the hod-carrier and poor sewing-girl! All business men who were in vain trying to find investments to pay six per cent were amused, but uninformed people were misled.

The next two paragraphs read as follows:—

"The interests of the man who pays wages and those of the man who receives wages are antagonistic. The one wants wages low and the other wants wages high. The protectionist legislator pretends to step in between them and satisfy both at once. He pretends to make both parties happy at once. 'I am going to make your wages high,' says he to the wage receiver. 'What, then, will become of me?' says the wage payer. 'I will make wages low for you,' he replies. 'How is that?' cry the laborers and all their friends; 'you are going to make wages low?' 'No,' replies the legislator, 'I mean that I will make the price of the products high, which will have the same effect for the employer.' 'But how is that?' cry the consumers; 'you mean to make prices high by law?' 'No,' replies the legislator, 'I do not really make prices high; it only looks so. My measures really make prices low.' We have here, then, the greatest miracle that has ever been accomplished. We have heard of making something out of nothing, but here we have creation and destruction in one and the same act. Certainly the problem of universal happiness is solved if we have found out how those who buy need pay little, and those who sell may at the same time receive much; how prices may be raised for the producer and lowered for the consumer both at the same time. As we are all producers and all consumers, we may all sell at the high prices and all buy at the low ones, and all get rich together. This is why it is that the protected manufacturers are found bulling what they are short of (that is, labor) and bearing what they are long of (that is, products). They have discovered this wonderful system by which all are to bull everything and bear everything at the same time, and win a big difference out of nothing. No wonder the protectionists are enraged at the economists who are still stupidly teaching that we can produce nothing except by applying labor and capital to land.

"Who is the beneficent genie, now, who works all the magic of the protectionist system? It is tax. If taxes are only rightly adjusted, says the protectionist, they make wages high and low and prices high and low both at the same time. When one hears this kind of nonsense, one is forced to believe that the sum of superstition in the world is a constant quantity. Superstition is a defective sense of causation. The savage who wears a bone tied to his arm as a fetich to ward off misfortune believes that there is a connection of cause and effect where there is none. The astrologer thought that the relations of the planets to each other affected the fate of persons born at a certain time. He saw a connection of cause and effect where there is none. The protectionist legislator lays a tax and goes home secure in the faith that wages will be high, prices low, and prosperity stable, as if there were a fixed, direct, and inevitable law of nature connecting taxes with social welfare and nothing else. This superstition is more wild than fetichism or astrology."

As Mr. Sumner says, " When one hears this kind of nonsense,[1] one is forced to believe that the sum of superstition in the world is a constant quantity ;" but if superstition be a defective sense of causation, then Mr. Sumner certainly is the most superstitious man on earth, for he shows an unparalleled inability to appreciate the action and reaction of economic causes.

General Jackson, writing in 1824, said : " The American farmer has neither a foreign nor a home market, except for cotton. Does not this clearly prove that there is too much labor employed in agriculture, and that the channels of labor should be multiplied? Common sense points out at once the remedy. Draw from agriculture the superabundant labor, and employ it in mechanism and manufactures, thereby creating a home market for your breadstuffs, and distributing labor to a most profitable account, and benefits to the country will result. Take from agriculture in the United States six hundred thousand men, women, and children, and you at once give a home market for more breadstuffs than all England now furnishes."

Benjamin Franklin, writing in 1771, said : " Every manufacturer encouraged in a country makes a part of a market for provisions within ourselves, and saves so much money to the country as must otherwise be exported to pay for the manufactures he supplies. Here in England it is well known and understood that, wherever a manufacture is established, it raises the value

---

[1] The nonsense is Sumnerian nonsense exclusively, and is founded on a misstatement. No protectionist ever pretended to " make wages high and low and prices high and low both at the same time."

of the land in the neighboring country all around it. It seems,
therefore, the interest of our farmers and owners of land to encourage our young manufactures rather than foreign ones."

The condition of affairs described by General Jackson was a
verification of the deductions made from Adam Smith's remarks
about the attractiveness of plentiful land. Reasoning led us to
the conclusion that the tendency was to become unduly and un-
profitably agricultural. Our country tried the experiment, and
found it was so. Mr. John Stuart Mill also recognized this tendency, and he recognized it as a difficulty out of which the efforts
of individuals to benefit themselves cannot extricate a community : that *laissez faire* is entirely impotent, and government
assistance — that is to say, the combined action of the whole
community — imperatively necessary.[1] Mr. Sumner lingers be-
hind Mr. Mill about a hundred years, and knows, or appears to
know, no more upon the subject than Adam Smith knew in
1755, when he gave his lectures, which were afterwards published under the title of an " Enquiry into the Nature and Causes
of the Wealth of Nations." How long will Harvard and Yale
insist upon being the Sleepy Hollows of Political Economy, from
which pupils emerge with ideas that have been obsolete for a
century ?

What Jackson recommended was done by the tariff of 1824.
The people, removed or retained from the land where they could
only add to a surplus already unsalable, produced finished products, and the whole value of their labor was just so much
added to the gross annual product of the country, which, being
distributed by demand and supply, could produce no other possible effect than to increase all incomes, — rent, profits, and wages.
The price at which the new products sold may have been at first
thirty, forty — if you please, even fifty — per cent higher than
they could be imported for; but we got the commodities, and
did not have to export money or commodities to pay for them.
The totality of consumers may have had to pay one hundred and
fifty millions for what before cost one hundred millions, and so
lost fifty millions; but they had the commodities, and in their
capacity of producers, or livers upon the rent or profits of pro-

---

[1] See Book V. Chap. XI. § 12 of his " Political Economy."

ductive instruments, or upon salaries drawn from the general prosperity of the country, they gained the one hundred millions which would otherwise be sent abroad; and as increasing skill produced the articles with less and less labor, the legislator's "little tax" became less and less.

Paragraphs 5 and 6 are as follows:—

"In discussing the effects of taxation, ambiguity is often introduced by not distinguishing carefully the alternatives which may be imagined. If we could imagine a state of society in which vice, passion, and other destructive forces no longer existed, government could be dispensed with, or it would sink into some low form of co-operation for common purposes. Taxes could then be dispensed with. If we compare our present condition with any such ideal state of things, all taxes are minus quantities, reducing by so much the available wealth and attainable comfort of the community. But such an ideal is a mere poetic dream. If we had no government we should have vice and passion running triumphantly through society, wasting and destroying on every side. Comparing our present condition with that state of things, the taxes which we pay for security, peace, and order as products of civil government are a small loss incurred to prevent a great one. Such is the only sensible and correct view of taxes. They are never anything but loss and diminution of wealth, and it is as impossible to convert them into productive forces as it would be to make destruction create, or waste save. Every tax is on the defensive, so to speak. It is necessary to justify every cent which is drawn from the community by taxes, and to show that all the capital thus consumed is necessary, under the existing order of things, to secure the protection of society, on the cheapest terms, against the forces which would disturb security, peace, and order. If the taxes were large enough, they might, as in Egypt or Turkey, almost take the place of the evils against which governments pretend to guard society. Every unnecessary cent of taxation is, therefore, a pure evil. Government in Egypt and Turkey, and in much of Asia, is not an organization to defend society against evils. It is only an organization by which some plunder all the rest, and taxes are the means by which they do it. Wherever any taxes are laid for any other purpose than to provide civil order, peace, and security, government approaches by just so much towards the Turkish pattern. Such is the case whenever protective taxes are laid.

"Taxes which ward off greater evils at the lowest practicable cost are economical. They do not lessen the average comfort of the people. Taxes which do not conform to this description do lower the average comfort of all classes of the people. The wages class has no separate interest in the matter which either can be or ought to be considered by itself. It is pure demagogism to say that it is the business of the government to make wages high. If I discuss the effect of taxes on wages, it is only by way of meeting the question in the form in which it is raised. Protective taxes do not aim to produce good government, or to accomplish any civil purpose at all. Their aim is industrial. They are planned to help some people to get a living. They interfere, on behalf of certain persons, with the conditions of production and the relations of competition. A man who engages in a protected industry has some other reliance in his business than his own capital, energy, enterprise, prudence, &c. The man who is in an unprotected industry has something more to guard against and contend with than the problems of his industry and the difficulties of the market. One of these parties has a special advantage created by law at the expense of the other party, who is therefore under a special disadvantage. These protective taxes, therefore, cannot be defended or justified under a sound view of the function and justifiability of taxation. They waste labor and capital, and keep the wealth of the country less than it might be for the labor and capital which have been expended. Let us examine in particular their effect on wages."

In these Mr. Sumner lays down several propositions which are incorrect in fact, and several which have been repudiated by Mc-Culloch, Mr. John Stuart Mill, and the other great authorities in political economy. He implies that the only permissible functions of government are the providing of security, peace, and order. This contradicts all the great economists who affirm that government has many other duties. He then draws attention to the fact that taxes which are levied in Egypt, Turkey, and Asia are squandered without giving the security, peace, and order under pretence of giving which they are collected; that they are an organization by which some plunder the rest. Then he says that wherever there are protective taxes the case is similar.

PROTECTIVE TAXES.

This was the title of an article, by Mr. Sumner, in the March number of the "Princeton Review" of 1881. As it was calculated to mislead the public, backed as it was by the weight of a great institution of learning, I replied to it in those terms of studied respect which were due to the office of teacher. In my reply I said: "A protectionist cannot even pass by the title without objection. A tax is not necessarily a burden. If the money be well and economically expended, and gives us good roads, good water-works, good police, and good government for what they ought to cost, then a tax is a great blessing and saving; but, unfortunately, the money is often expended recklessly and foolishly, and so, *through abuses*, the very name of tax becomes offensive.

The free-trader, who writes about "protective taxes," avails himself of this existing prejudice, with the effect of disgusting the reader with protection in advance of all argument in respect to it. The word *tax* also gives two false impressions: first, that all protected articles cost the consumer more than they would if not protected; and second, that when they cost more, the consumer gets no counterbalancing or greater overbalancing advantage."

The effect of the taxes which are paid for government services press with double weight when doubled, with treble weight when trebled. A duty laid on for protection has, and can have, no such effect. If thirty per cent would shut out the foreign article, all is done which can be done by the tariff. Forty or fifty or sixty per cent can do no more. I also pointed out that, even *if* our cottons, woollens, and iron cost the consumers one thousand millions, while they could be imported for seven hundred millions, still we have our cottons, woollens, and iron, and we keep seven hundred millions annually at home, which would otherwise have gone abroad, and could not have been balanced by any alternative occupation upon the land, since the land even now cannot sell to advantage all that it can produce.

Mr. Sumner, however, continues to avail himself of the catchword of "protective taxes;" and the whole of his address to the Tariff Commission assumes and presupposes that the pressure of a tariff upon the consumer is in proportion and equal to the rate of duties imposed, and that these duties inure to the benefit — in fact, go into the pockets — of the protected manufacturers who, according to him, hold a monopoly.

In pursuing this line of argument, after full notice of its inapplicability, Mr. Sumner proves one of two things. He is either ignorant of the political economy of the latter half of the nineteenth century, and incapable of comprehending the reasoning of Say, Ricardo, McCulloch, and Mr. John Stuart Mill, or else he shuts his eyes to the truth under the influence of personal or party passion. He is welcome to either horn of the dilemma. It is no satisfaction to me, or to any fair-minded American, to see him in such a position; but, on the contrary, it is a source of mortification and humiliation. To us professor connotes all

that is honorable, dignified, temperate, benignant, and wise.
When he condescends to enter the arena of politics, the passions
of the crowd stand overawed by the calm and majestic presence.
The bandying of libellous crimination and recrimination, the
unjust imputation of base motives, the giving and taking of the
lie, — all are hushed. So would Harvard's Kirkland, or Everett,
or Walker, or Sparks, or Peirce, or many others in such a position, calm and sway and elevate the people. We have come to
expect this; and the opposite action of Mr. Sumner affects us
like some horrible discord in music, or some frightful want of
harmony in colors.

In short, there are proprieties attaching to every position in
life, and we could not tolerate an actor who, in the garb of Socrates, should, upon the appearance of a fierce mastiff, descend
upon all fours and endeavor to outbark and outbite the ferocious
animal.

When a professor appears we feel that he should be able to
show propositions to be unsound, if they really be so; and when
he denounces them as " lies " we can only distrust his ability to
make good his assertions. In paragraph 7 he says : —

"Anything which lessens the number of persons competing for wages, or
which increases the amount of capital which may be divided in wages, increases wages. In a new country in which there is an immense amount of
unoccupied land, and in which the amount of capital required for tilling the
soil is small, any man who has a pair of stout hands, although he has no skill
and very little capital, may become a landowner and agriculturist. He is then
withdrawn from the wages class ; he lessens the supply of labor in the labor
market; and, as an independent producer, he contributes all the time to the
capital of the country. Every man of the unskilled labor class, therefore, has
an alternative offered to him. He is never driven by starvation into a desper-
ate competition with others in the same predicament to work for low wages.
He is on the right side of the market. Supply and demand are in his favor.
He owns a thing for which there is a high demand in the market. The comfort he could win on the land fixes a minimum below which wages cannot fall.
If they do temporarily fall below that minimum, the laborers take to the land,
as they did in the hard times a few years ago. Since the comfort obtainable
from an abundance of cheap and fertile land is high, the minimum of wages
is high. This makes the average wages of the country high. High wages,
therefore, simply mean that the soil of this continent is rich, the climate is
excellent and well varied, the rivers are large and convenient, the mountains
are full of metal and coal, the people are industrious and energetic and are

eager to accumulate, the public order is fairly secure, and the general intelligence is good. The conditions of production are, therefore, good, and we produce a great deal. We accumulate capital far more rapidly than any other people in the world."

I beg the reader to look again at this paragraph. He will see that Mr. Sumner admits that what a farmer can make from his land is equal to the minimum of wages. When skilled artisans and manufacturers from any cause fail for a length of time to obtain this *minimum*, they take to the land. He does not seem, however, to perceive what was so plain to Adam Smith, to wit, that the normal condition of agriculture, where there was plenty of land, was less profitable than the non-agricultural industries, *because* the farmer's position is more independent, and one in which the mere possession of food is certain. Those greater advantages are counterbalanced by a smaller profit, just as the high dignity of a professor causes his salary to be less than that of just the same sort of man employed as a treasurer to a mill. Adam Smith has an interesting chapter upon this point, which has been accepted by all subsequent economists, and which I recommend to Mr. Sumner's attention.

The word *minimum* presupposes and admits a normal something greater than the minimum. It concedes the point that in a community like ours the non-agricultural industries are more productive than the agricultural; that under the action and reaction of demand and supply among ourselves, the man who works at a trade or carries on a manufacture adds more to the gross annual product than the farmer does. The latter takes out the difference in feelings of independence and perfect security. But here Mr. Sumner would object that he has nothing to do with the play of industrial forces among ourselves; that he refuses to consider them; that political economy regards the whole world; that there is a country called Great Britain which will take our agricultural products and give us in exchange finished products at a much better bargain than our artisans or manufacturers can or will give. And this position he immediately demonstrates in the following manner. He picks out some article such as iron or fine woollens, and shows that at the present prices for cotton or for wheat here, and the present prices for iron and woollens there, the imported article without duty would be a good deal cheaper than the domestic product. But this argument assumes that if we had occasion to sell more largely abroad we should obtain as high a price as now, and that if we had occasion to buy more largely abroad we should buy as cheaply as now. If Mr. Sumner will propound the propositions embodying these assumptions to any merchant he will be set right, or he can be set right without going out of Yale, by turning to Mr. John Stuart Mill's chapters upon International Trade.

Our non-agricultural industries add at least three thousand millions to the value of the materials they deal with. We now find a market abroad for some seven hundred millions of raw products; but we find it with difficulty, and only when the food crops of all Europe are short.

The idea of selling three thousand millions more at any price, or one thousand millions more without a reduction of forty to fifty per cent in our prices, is an idea which no well-informed merchant and no well-informed economist would entertain for a moment.

His premises do not lead to his conclusion that "high wages simply mean that the soil of the continent is rich, the climate is excellent and varied," &c. These things do not, by his own showing, account for the high wages that exist, but only for a high minimum of wages, high as a minimum, but a good deal less than what we enjoy. His observation that "we accumulate capital far more rapidly than any other people in the world" is *prima facie* evidence that our present organization of industries, as brought about by a protective policy, is better than that of any other nation; but it is totally irrelevant with regard to an entirely different arrangement such as Mr. Sumner would prefer.

It is tedious to be obliged to refute such sophistries. Paragraph 8 says: —

"It is one of the humors of the tariff that the politician appears at this stage and says, 'Oh, no! you are quite wrong in attributing the prosperity of the country to those causes. It was I who did it, with my little taxes. The country has prospered because I taxed it vigorously. If I had not put on my taxes the country would have been ruined.' He argues that an industrious people on a fertile soil could not have got food and clothing out of it if they had not had the right taxes. A further touch of the ridiculous, however, is added by those politicians who declaim about the dignity of the American laborer. To listen to the speeches and read the editorials, one would think politicians formed a standard of comfort which they thought suitable for the American laborer, and then just passed the right laws to get it for him. It is said that *our* laborers ought not to be on the standard of comfort of European paupers. It must be, then, that the American sovereign can formulate his demands on nature. He makes up his mind what is suitable to his own majesty, and serves notice on nature to provide it. His attorney, the politician, justly indignant that nature does not respond, passes a law to secure the becoming thing for his noble client, the American laborer. In this view of the matter certain persons are 'nature's noblemen' in a sense not heretofore used. A little examination shows us, however, that we are only dealing with an old fraud under a new face. The old-fashioned nobleman drew his drafts, not on nature but on his fellow-citizens, and, as his friends were in control of the government, they got payment for him. The American sovereign can get nothing from nature which he does not earn. If the politician meddles in the matter, he can only rob one sovereign to favor another. That is all that he ever has done. That process has never made us any richer, but only poorer."

The protectionists do not argue that an industrious people on a fertile soil could not get food and *some* clothing out of it, &c. They argue that fifty millions of people, situated like those of the United States, could not have got food, and anything like their actual present quantity of clothing, and all other conveniences, had the foreign products been left free to come in.

The American sovereign, it is true, can get nothing from nature which he does not earn; but he will earn twice or three times as much under a rational distribution of industries as he can if confined to the production of raw products, for which there is no adequate foreign demand, and for which the growth of a domestic demand is prevented by the constant presence of foreign products ready to be sold for money. Mr. Sumner is in error in alleging that if the politician — say rather statesman — meddles in the matter he can only rob one sovereign to favor another. The statesman who promotes measures which bring about a suitable diversity of employments can cause, and in the United States has caused, the total annual product per head to be doubled and trebled, thereby doubling and trebling the aggregate of all wages, all profits, and all rents. He can cause and has caused a prosperity which shall endow great institutions of learning and fill them with instructors whose salaries are vastly higher than they could have been under a free-trade policy. Mr. Sumner's argument could be buried out of sight by evidence drawn from all recognized authorities, whether those on the protectionist or free-trade side of the question. But Mr. John Stuart Mill will suffice. Although breathing every day an atmosphere surcharged with free trade and consequently prejudiced in that direction, his "Political Economy" is full of passages the reasonings of which followed out to their full consequences prove all that any protectionist maintains. As to Mr. Sumner's dogma that any change wrought in society by the united action of the whole must be injurious, let the reader consult Book I. Chap. VIII. §§ 2, 3, and also Book V. Chap. XI. § 12, of Mr. John Stuart Mill's "Political Economy." Paragraph 9 says : —

"Under the conditions of the United States, a tax on immigrants would probably lower wages, not raise them. The country is underpopulated. So long as there is an immense amount of unoccupied land, the immigrants do not go to swell the wages class ; they go upon the land ; they open it up, win wealth from it, and contribute to the capital of the country. Each new-comer who is industrious counts more as a pair of new hands to produce than as another mouth to consume ; and he may well add to the average wealth per head. Taxation has not even, therefore, in this country the field which it might have in some countries, if it were used to keep competitors out of the labor market."

I agree that under the present condition of the United States a tax upon immigrants would not raise wages, but not for the reason given by Mr. Sumner. The immigrants from European countries quickly assimilate themselves to us. They distribute themselves throughout the industries, and speedily *produce and consume* as much as others. The country simply grows symmetrically like a crystal or a tree, and so it will be until in the far distant future there comes to be a scarcity of land, mines, &c., in comparison with the population. Paragraph 10 reads : —

"If a tax on laborers could not raise wages, certainly no tax on commodities can do so. Protective taxes aim to keep certain foreign commodities out of the country. An army of custom-house officers must therefore be supported, not to collect revenue, but to prevent revenue from being collected. This device is kept up in order to secure the home market to the home producer. The home producer carries on his business at a loss. He says that he would lose capital if it were not for the tariff. His industry, he says, would not exist if it were not for the tariff. It is therefore conducted at a loss all the time, only that the loss is not borne by the persons carrying on the business, but by the consumers of the goods. The protective system, therefore, involves the following expenditures : The pay of all the custom-house expenditures to keep up the system ; wages and profits to all those who are carrying on the productive industries ; the losses incurred by the protected industries. All these outgoes must be borne by the non-protected in order that there may be less goods of all kinds in the country than there might be under free trade. How then can protection increase wages, or the average amount of these goods which can be obtained by each laborer in the country ? There could not be a more flagrant error. If there is anything cheap anywhere, the protectionists spring into activity to keep the American people from getting it. If there is an abundance of food, clothing, furniture, and other supplies which is offered to the American people on easy terms, the protectionists call it an 'inundation,' and run to set a barrier against it. A few weeks ago I saw a hundred women waiting for hours on the sidewalk for the opening of a store at which some fire-damaged goods were to be sold cheap. A protectionist must hold that those women were insane, or that they were selfishly ruining the country. It is impossible to raise wages by opposing cheapness and abundance. The protective system lessens wealth ; and until somebody invents an arithmetic according to which 10 will go in 70 more times than it will in 100, it is certain that a smaller dividend will give a smaller share to each person. The protective system, therefore, lowers wages."

This whole paragraph is based, as already pointed out in my former reply to Mr. Sumner, upon the fallacy of division. Under our present industrial organization we have our own food and raw materials, and export, at present prices, say seven hundred millions of raw products. Our farmers sell these seven hundred millions abroad, and they sell twelve hundred millions at home. Mr. Sumner's microscopic vision sees only the present. He assumes that if our farmers had to sell nineteen hundred millions abroad instead of seven hundred, they would get the same price. With the seven hundred millions of raw products, we now buy abroad say three hundred and fifty millions, which we could not produce, of tropical products, and a like quantity of the finer manufactures which we cannot yet produce under existing duties. If we did not produce finished products for ourselves, we should have to buy not only what we now buy, but many times that quantity. Mr. Sumner assumes that under such circumstances the price of imports would be the same as now! Or, leaving out the reference to price, he assumes that whereas now we exchange three hundred and fifty million dollars worth of raw products for the like amount of finished commodities, we could exchange at the same advantage, if we were under the necessity of selling and buying abroad, four times as much! Neither Mr. John Stuart Mill, nor any other economist of capacity to take in the whole problem, would maintain such a proposition. Under the supposed change we not only should obtain our finished products at a much less advantageous exchange for raw products than we do now, but, over and beyond this, we should not be able to obtain more than probably a third part as many. Our total gross annual product would not be 100 to 70, as Mr. Sumner deduces, but as 70 to 100 rather; and until somebody invents an arithmetic by which 10 will go into 70 more times than into 100 it is certain that a smaller dividend under free trade will give a smaller share to each person. Free trade, therefore, would lower wages. Paragraph 11 says: —

"Let us next look at the effect of protective taxes on the alternative which is open to the American laborer to go upon the land. The protective taxes enhance the cost of all articles of clothing, furniture, crockery, utensils, tools, and machinery. They also increase the cost of fuel and transportation. They therefore reduce the amount of all the commodities mentioned which a farmer can get for a certain amount of farm products. They therefore lessen the profits of agriculture in all its forms, and lessen the attractiveness of the land. Whatever lessens the attractiveness of the land lowers the minimum gain of all manual laborers, increases the number of competitors in the labor market, and reduces the amount which the employer needs to bid in order to counteract the advantages of the land. Protective taxes, therefore, take away from the laborer the advantage which he has by nature in this country; that is to say, they take away from him part of his advantage in the labor market. Consequently they lower wages."

Underneath the whole of this paragraph lies the above fallacy, which assumes that present prices of exports could be obtained if we had need to sell four times as much, and that imports could be obtained as cheaply if we had occasion to buy four times as much. Theory, as laid down by the greatest economists, negatives this assumption, as can be seen by reference to the passages in Mr. Mill's work already indicated. Experience contradicts this, as shown by the quotation already made from Andrew Jackson. The truth is as follows: Protection prevents a vast number of people from flying to the land, and makes them consumers in-

stead of producers of raw products. It diminishes the aggregate
of the farmer's products, and increases the demand. They therefore increase the profits of agriculture in all its forms, and increase the attractiveness of the land. Whatever increases this
increases the minimum gain of all manual laborers, and increases
the number of competitors for labor, and increases the amount
which the employer needs to bid in order to counteract the
advantages of the land. Protection therefore secures to the
laborer the advantage which he has by nature in this country,
and increases it by diversifying employments. Consequently it
raises wages above what they could be under foreign competition.
At the same time it hastens the moment when increasing skill
may compensate for the higher moneyed cost of labor; for high
wages lead to greater efforts and intelligence on the part of oper-
atives, and to greater care in selecting the most skilful on the
part of employers, and to a more extensive use of the very best
machinery.

For the theory of this I appeal to Mr. Mill. For the verification
of the theory I appeal to the experience of the United States, where
the growing efficiency of labor has already in some cases overcome
the effect of its greater cost per man, as is shown by the very many
manufactured goods which we export, and by the approximation to
a similar cheapness in nearly all which are used by the great bulk
of the people. Champagne, fine broadcloth, silks, satins, gloves,
feathers, &c., the objects of ostentation and luxury, are much
dearer. Is it desirable to change our legislation in order to
cheapen these? I beg the reader to carefully compare this reply
with the paragraph to which it is an answer. Paragraphs 12
and 13 read : —

"It has been affirmed by protectionists that their system increases capital.
Two ways have been alleged in which it does this, — (1) by improving the
organization of labor, (2) by bringing capital into use which would otherwise
be idle.

"1. The people of this country are all the time exercising their utmost ingenuity to organize their industry to the highest advantage. Partly they do
this by instinct. Plenty of people never heard of the 'organization of industry,' but they are constantly arranging their business to save labor, and so
gain time and prevent waste. They are also constantly laboring intelligently
to secure a better organization of industry. But, after they have exhausted

their ingenuity, the protective system assumes that some other persons, viz. politicians and legislators, can see some better organization than the persons engaged in industry have themselves been able to devise. If one part of the American people have not invented the best organization of labor, we have no one else to call upon than some other portion of the American people, and we must appeal from the men of business to the politicians. The politicians, then, as an incident to their own occupations, rectify the errors and shortcomings of the business men. The mode they employ is taxes. It is the same old magic. But the business men have to bring intelligence to bear on the organization of labor, while the protectionist legislator never has brought any intelligence at all to bear on the problem, and he never can. Protective taxes have never been laid in view of any true knowledge of the industrial circumstances, and they never can be. A thousand commissions, sitting for ten years, and actually engaging in a real study of the industries of this country, could not win a knowledge of our industrial system ; and if they could acquire such knowledge of the industrial system as it exists on a given day, their knowledge would not be good for anything the day after, on account of the new inventions, discoveries, processes, lines of transportation, financial arrangements, and so on."

Here we have the antique doctrine that a man must know his own business better than any statesman can know it, and that the interests of the man are identical with the interests of the state. This was entirely refuted by John Rae (see pp. 1–32) some fifty years ago ; moreover, as pointed out by Mr. Mill, there are cases in which the interests of the whole nation and that of the individual coincide only when all can be made to act in a certain way.

The case of bankers is in point. Every intelligent banker sees that it is for the public interest and for his own that *all* bankers should keep a sufficient reserve ; but if some do and some do not, the reckless in fair weather take away the business of the others, and when a storm comes their failure throws a portion of the consequent loss upon those who have been prudent.

Protection is still more in point. Fifty millions of people may believe, and believe truly, that it is better for them to buy of one another, — that by such means a greater annual product can be reached, and hence a great benefit to *all* classes ; that there will be more produced, and hence more to divide. But the recipients of rents, profits, and fixed salaries see that *after they have got* their incomes, — after, in short, they have got the profit arising out of protection, — it would be an excellent thing if they could get their commodities abroad. A and B and C wish to be paid very high profits or salaries by the rest of the alphabet, but not to give any employment in return. They do not see that under such an arrangement the rest of the alphabet would be quite unable to pay their profits and salaries. If a protective law binds the whole to the profitable course, it will be followed; otherwise, not. Each will say to himself, "The action of one individual can have no appreciable effect upon fifty millions; and whether it has or not, I want my fine broadcloth to be cheap: those bloated manufacturers are robbing, cheating, swindling, pillaging me," &c.

There are cases in which the intelligence of the statesman can promote the public good in a way that is unattainable in any other manner. This is admitted by Adam Smith in passages where he is not arguing for free trade, and is distinctly laid down by Mr. Mill. The argument, then, of Mr. Sumner is too obsolete to be repeated in the year 1882. Paragraphs 14 and 15 say:—

"We have here now fifty millions of people spread over a continent with great varieties of climate and soil, and we constitute the most energetic, restless, and indefatigable nation which has ever existed. To try to plan a system of artificial relations of industry for such a nation is the most ridiculous undertaking that could be proposed. Any one who talks of reaching a permanent adjustment of the tariff to fit the needs of all interests and do injustice to none is talking the wildest nonsense. Nothing less than the impersonal forces of nature can adjust interests under such conditions, and there is only one thing which can be predicated of any steps taken by the statesman, that is, that he will make mischief. A man who is running a railroad easily sees what crude nonsense people talk about railroading when they know nothing of the business. A banker makes the same observation. So does every other man in his own line. What chance is there, then, that politicians can deal wisely with the thousands of industries and interests in this country in all their manifold and complex relations to each other? We might as well try to establish, by legislation, a system of health which would prevent the people of the United States from ever being sick any more.

"Furthermore, the politicians never try to deal with the whole combination of industrial interests. They listen only to the most clamorous. They heed only those who win influence and so secure the position of favorites. They never bring any intelligence to bear on the question. How much assistance is needed? There never is any adjustment of means to ends. No tests are ever applied; no guarantees are ever given; no subsequent reports are ever made by the recipients of favor to show results for the expenditure. Each interest comes forward and asks for favor, and gets it for no reason save because it asked for it. The petitioner thinks that about so much per cent will do, and does not himself know or ever try to calculate what will be the effect of that much protection to him when offset by all the taxes to which he must submit in behalf of others in order that the system may be completed. Mr. Peter Cooper says that the tariff ought to just about offset the difference between American and European wages. If that could be done and were done, it would just take away from the American laborer those superior advantages which made him or his ancestors come across the ocean. Now, from this tangle of absurdities and contradictions and ignorances and guesses, it is expected that guidance will come which shall lead the American producer to a better organization of industry than he could arrive at if left alone, so that greater accommodation of capital and larger wages would follow. From such causes no result, save waste and loss, can ensue with reduction of capital and lowering of wages."

According to Mr. Sumner, the politician — say rather statesman — has never brought any intelligence to bear upon the question of how to deal with the whole combination of industrial interests! Well, now, let us order out an immense pair of scales. Into one we will put Franklin, Washington, Jefferson, Madison, Monroe, Jackson, Webster, after he had studied the subject, — in short, we will put a large majority of the statesmen of the United States for a hundred years; and into the other we will put Mr. Sumner, backed by theories which all the great economists repudiate. Is it easier to believe that all these great intelligences were ignorant and corrupt, or to believe that Mr. Sumner's dialectics have led him, and tend to lead others, into fatal error? Let any one who desires the truth peruse their speeches, messages, and letters; or let him read Mr. Hamilton's report on manufactures, and compare its prophetic wisdom with Mr. Sumner's production now under review. Let him note the objects for which Hamilton recommended the protection, and then let him look at the United States and see whether those objects have or have not been attained; let him compare Massachusetts with the more fertile Canada, — Canada, too, which has been aided by our protective policy, which has prevented the foreign markets from being overwhelmed by the immense mass of our raw products which are similar to hers. Paragraphs 16 and 17 read : —

"2. It is alleged, in the second place, that protection brings capital into use which would otherwise be idle. Every one of us who has any capital is anxious to put it to productive use without delay. It is impossible, in the nature of things, to keep all capital all the time employed. Improvements (such as a better credit system) which make this more fully realizable are eagerly adopted. The argument I have quoted means that in spite of this eagerness, and in spite of the chances for employing capital on a new continent, some portion of the capital now in protected industries would not be in use if it were not for protection. Such a notion is beneath discussion.

"There is, then, no way in which protective taxes can produce capital. Every analysis shows that they waste it. Not a cent can come to A by the action of the tariff which does not come from B. The consequence of universal borrowing, or stealing, or gift-making, however, is not to increase capital but to waste it. Hence protective taxes lower wages. The laborers have been exhorted to vote for protection, lest their wages should be reduced to European rates. I have shown that the rate of wages obtained here is due to the economic forces at work in this country. There is only one thing which could reduce American wages to European standards, and that is protective taxes applied long enough and with sufficient weight."

In Mr. Sumner's article in the "Princeton Review," already alluded to, he said: "*The rest is all phrases intended to occupy attention while the thimblerig is going on.* If this is not so, let some protectionist analyze the operation of his system, and show by reference to undisputed economical principles where and how it exerts any effect upon production to increase it."

He himself threw down the glove; I picked it up, and, shutting my eyes to the imputation of dishonesty, I replied in an article which was, at all events, courteous. Mr. Sumner says that it is beneath discussion. I am content to reaffirm my arguments, and to leave it to competent judges to decide whether or not they are beneath discussion. Possibly they are not so much beneath discussion as above refutation. In the article in question, which can be found in all the great libraries of the United States in a volume entitled "Free Trade and Protection," I pointed out the precise manner in which, in a country already possessed of a great variety of industries, the floating capital, converted to a fixed form, was almost instantaneously reproduced, so that the nation became owners of the fixed capital, either merely by calling out more labor or by turning to the production of capital what otherwise would have gone into new carriages, furniture, houses of luxury, &c., and that the result came about generally by the former rather than by the latter means; the fixed capital resulting from a fuller employment

of the people, and not by a mere diversion from one work to
another.

Mr. Sumner thought he had me alone to deal with, but he
has another infinitely more formidable antagonist in Mr. John
Stuart Mill. Let any one turn to Book IV. Chap. V. of Mr.
Mill's "Political Economy." Mr. Mill had in mind, to be sure,
the effect of an abstraction of capital by government for purely
unproductive purposes; but the reader will see at once that the
argument is much stronger with regard to measures leading to
the construction of fixed capital, which would forever after be
productive of commodities. A does *not* get his capital from B,
for A can, upon the average of years, obtain only the profits
current in the community. A gets his capital out of his own
abstinence. If the manufactured article at first costs more, it
must, with increasing skill, cost less and less, and by necessity,
enforced by competition, be sold for less and less. If B, whose
wages or salary is in money, pays more, C, D, and the rest of
the alphabet, practically pay less, for they can pay with commodities they produce, and for which the new industry occasions an
additional demand and a better price. Even B is compensated,
and more than compensated, by an augmentation in his salary
or his profits, growing out of the general increased prosperity of
the country.

It is easy to call this "thimblerigging," or a "bungle of absurdities, contradictions, ignorances, or guesses;" but calling names
is not economical reasoning. If there be anything wrong in the
deductions, some one can show with precision and courtesy the
exact point in which they are wrong. It is not the protectionists
who shrink from bringing doctrines to the test of the methods
of economic reasoning laid down by the greatest recognized
authorities.

Mr. Sumner says he has shown that the rate of wages now obtained here is due solely to economic forces at work in this country. In this he is in error. He has only shown that the *minimum*
of wages cannot be less than food and such small modicum of
clothing and other conveniences as a nation producing raw products could obtain from foreign markets eternally glutted with
such products. He has not shown, nor can he (without admitting

the effects of protection) show, how the much higher existing rate
of wages has come about. The intimation that higher or long-
continued protection could reduce wages involves the economic
absurdity which supposes that, in a population of fifty millions,
under free competition, the profits upon protected industries can,
upon an average of years, be higher than upon others. Upon this
point I appeal from Mr. Sumner to Adam Smith, Ricardo, Mr.
John Stuart Mill, to the universally accepted conclusions of
economic reasoning, and to common sense. They are all upon
one side, and all against Mr. Sumner. Paragraphs 18, 19, and 20
read thus : —

" There is, however, another argument which must be considered in this connection. It is said that under free trade all our population would go into
agriculture, and that wages and all other remuneration for labor would be reduced until we should all be in poverty together. Hence the agriculturists,
and the mechanical laborers, too, are exhorted to support a wide protective
system in order to diversify industry and prevent ruinous competition.

" We have seen above that the direct cost of keeping up the protective system consists of three items : (1) payment of custom-house officers to keep
goods out ; (2) support of laborers, and profit on capital in protected industries ; (3) the losses of the protected industries. These costs must be paid to
buy off competition.

" In the first place, it can pay no one to buy off competition unless he has
a monopoly. Protected industries have done it sometimes. American farmers
share the world's market with a number of strong competitors. If they buy
off the competition of American manufacturers they must bear all the cost of
it ; and they must share the gain, if any, with all the agriculturists in the
world. That means that if they try it they will put themselves at a great
disadvantage with their own competitors in the world's market."

The expense of custom-house officers is too trivial to be considered. The support of laborers and profit on capital in protected
industries is paid out of the exchangeable value of their products :
the *losses* of the protected industries consist of the higher cost of
their products, calculated upon present prices here and abroad.
It amounts even now to very little. The gain to the nation is
the whole value of what must have been sent abroad to purchase
those products. The gain to the agriculturists is a certain home
market, already twice as great, and destined in twenty years to
be four times as great, as the market of the world affords him.
They now sell abroad say seven hundred millions, and twelve

hundred millions at home, or nineteen hundred millions. This is the market required by half the population. The whole population employed on the soil would require a market for forty-eight hundred millions. Nowhere on this planet is there a market for one half the amount; and in twenty years the case would be twice as bad. But it is not necessary to take an extreme case, although Mr. Sumner challenges it. We need only inquire into the effect of offering abroad twice as much as we do now, to be convinced that the purchasing power of raw products would be vastly less than it is now. The farmer does not lose, but gains, and gains immensely, by that better distribution of the community which the necessities of his argument compel Mr. Sumner to describe as " buying off the competition of the manufacturers." By favoring such a distribution they have not put themselves at a disadvantage, as compared with their competitors in the foreign market. On the contrary, the resulting wealth of the whole nation has overflowed upon them, and given them much more and better clothing, tools, and machines than they could possibly have obtained under a *régime* of free trade. The arrangement has helped other agricultural countries, doubtless ; but that need not distress us. It has helped ourselves vastly more. Paragraph 21 says : —

" In the second place, all the protected industries of this country are now parasites on the naturally strong industries. Agriculture now supports itself and all the rest and all their losses. Therefore, even if it were true that all the population would, under free trade, take to agriculture, it is mathematically certain that agriculture could support them all better directly than under the present arrangement."

To this I must add a sentence already quoted in paragraph 3. It is this : —

" No wonder the protectionists are enraged at the economists who are still stupidly teaching that we can produce nothing except by applying labor and capital to land."

There is nothing in this to enrage, but there is much to astonish and amuse. The doctrine is that of the Physiocrats of France, and has been supposed to have been disposed of by Adam Smith in his lectures one hundred and thirty years ago.[1] All the

---

[1] See Wealth of Nations, Book IV. Chap. IX. § 28, &c.

world thought it had been decently buried, but Mr. Sumner with sacrilegious hand has disinterred it.

Let us add a word to what Adam Smith says. As already pointed out, the United States produce annually seven thousand millions worth of finished products. Agriculture and mining furnish the raw materials, worth three thousand millions ; manufactures and the mechanical arts bring these into a shape suitable for consumption, and trade and transportation place them where they can be consumed. Each class is indispensable to the production of the vast aggregate. It is in vain to argue that the other industries could do nothing without raw materials ; for it is equally true that agriculture and mining, such as they are to-day, could not exist without the machines, the admirable tools, the clothing, the barns and stores and dwellings, and the transportation afforded by the other industries. Nor will it do to affirm that these fifty millions engaged in agriculture could procure those things cheaper and better from abroad.

No such conclusion can be arrived at either by the theoretical deductive reasoning of any recognized political economy of to-day or from the inductive reasoning of practical men. Mr. John Stuart Mill, were he alive, would feel for it as little respect as is felt by statesmen and business men. It not only is not practical wisdom or a guide to practical wisdom, but it is not political economy of any school, save one which has been forgotten for more than a hundred years.

Agriculture, then, does not support itself and all other industries, and therefore it is not mathematically certain that it would support us all better directly than under the present arrangement. It is, on the contrary, as certain as anything can be made by means of economical reasoning or by reasoning from observation, that a reversion to agriculture and trade alone would reduce by one half the amount of necessaries, conveniences, and luxuries now enjoyed by the people of the United States. Paragraphs 22–28 read : —

" The farmers would indeed gain a great deal if the protected people would keep still and not do anything, for then they would at least waste nothing. The earnings of farmers and the wages of laborers would then not be reduced so much as they are now. The protectionist theory, however, is that it increases wages to keep on an occupation which wastes capital and lessens all the time the goods within reach of the population. It is interesting to apply this theory to some other cases.

"On the protectionist theory it would be a means of raising wages to keep up a big standing army. All the soldiers would be withdrawn from competition in the labor market, and would consume while producing nothing. In time of peace they would not be destroying anything ; but in time of war they would be just like a protected industry, — they would be wasting capital all the time. In that case, then, they would raise wages all the more.

"On the protectionist theory a leisure class of idle, rich people make wages higher than they would be if the same people should go to work. By the same reasoning women who now consume without producing would lower wages if they should go to work, and while consuming, as they now do, should compete in the labor market. Indeed, this view of the matter is very often taken, and perhaps the popular view is that the rich make wages high, if they not only keep out of the labor market, but also consume luxuriously, and do not save anything.

"On the protectionist argument paupers living in an almshouse raise wages as compared with what wages would be if the same persons should no longer consume unproductively, but should come out and compete in the labor market while consuming as before. On the same argument paupers who produce something, though less than they consume, lower wages compared with what would be the case if the paupers did nothing; still more as compared with the case in which the paupers should destroy.

"On the protectionist argument, convicts in the state prison raise wages by consuming the product of taxation in idleness, and lower wages if they go to work, and, while consuming as before, produce something, because in the latter case they compete in the labor market. In fact, criminals out of state prison would satisfy the protectionist reasoning still better. They always destroy far more than they produce, and they do not compete with laborers. They would, therefore, raise wages by their operations. It would be a limitation of their beneficent action to put them in prison as consumers in idleness, still more so to set them to work at a useful industry.

"On the protectionist view of the matter the trade-unionists are right when they adopt wasteful processes, practise shiftlessness and neglect, study not to be skilful or effective, and try to make work, as they call it, believing that they thus raise wages. The protectionist and the trades-unionist both mistake toil for wages. They think that when they increase the difficulties which intervene between us men and goods they increase wages, and that to make goods abundant is to lower wages.

"On the protectionist theory those men in the riot at Pittsburgh, who exulted in the destruction of the city because they thought that it would make work, which they confused with making wages, were right from their point of view. No man wants work ; that is, toil, or irksome exertion. Least of all does the man who has no capital want toil. He supplies toil. He cannot supply and demand the same thing. He demands capital on which to live. When capital is destroyed and toil is necessary to reproduce it, the ratio in which toil must be given for capital is rendered more unfavorable to the laborer ; that is, wages fall. If they do not fall on the spot where the destruction took place they must fall elsewhere whence the capital is drawn to replace the capital destroyed. If Pittsburgh had to be rebuilt other cities could be built up just so much less. If Pittsburgh had not been burned up the capital which went to replace it would have been used to employ laborers in adding so much more to the comfort and possessions of the country. The country is poorer for all time by the capital there destroyed, with all its accumulations. Just so every year that this nation, on account of the protective system, attains to the possession of a less amount of goods than it could have obtained under freedom, the effect is the same as if we had produced a city and had seen it burn up ; and anybody who believes that the protective taxes raise wages must believe that to burn up cities raises wages. All these notions are miserable fallacies, which sin against the first elements of common sense. He who believes that the way to raise wages is to hinder people from getting at things easily and cheaply, or to refrain from the most profitable modes of obtaining goods, must believe that workmen raise wages when they stop working and go out on strikes, and lower wages when they go to work again. Trades-unionism and protectionism are falsehoods. The way of prosperity for human society is by industry, economy, thrift, skill, energy, painstaking, excellence, liberty, abundance, and not by some crafty and artificial devices to produce scarcity and bad work. The protectionist system requires a new set of proverbs which have never yet found their way into any popular philosophy, such as these : Want makes wealth ; destroy and prosper ; taxes are wages ; to have much produce little ; blessed are the bad workman and the foolish capitalist, for they shall get abundance."

I have already shown that according to the protectionist theory the whole amount which would be sent out of the country to buy the goods now made in it by protected industries, — this whole amount less the amount by which home-made goods exceed in cost the foreign, is a gain to the country, even taking prices at their present point ; for the labor now employed would, if transferred to the land, reduce the exchangeable value of the totality of raw products, — it would be a minus quantity. Protection therefore increases capital, and increases all the time the goods within reach of the population. The theory of protection, then, is absolutely the reverse of what Mr. Sumner alleges it to be, and it is a theory in perfect accord with methods of reasoning always adopted by the great economists excepting when they are arguing for a preconceived opinion. It is a theory also which is in harmony with facts. It explains the past and the present. It explains with precision and in an intelligible manner the poverty of Ireland and Portugal and Turkey and India, and why all purely or disproportionably agricultural nations and states are poor, &c. It is not necessary, then, to follow Mr. Sumner into the side issues of paragraphs 22–28. They all fail to be analogies in every point but one, and it would require many pages to examine them in detail. I will notice only one sentence. Mr. Sumner says that "the way of prosperity for human society is by industry, economy, thrift, skill, energy, painstaking, excellence, liberty, *abundance.*" But abundance in political economy is prosperity. The way of prosperity then, according to Mr. Sumner, is by prosperity. This is an identical proposition. But, abstaining from taking advantage of this, let us strike out the word *abundance.* The other means he enumerates would certainly not lead to abundance or prosperity if we insisted upon producing only or even more largely the raw products with which the world is already oversupplied, and abstained from producing the finished products we ourselves require, and which can be had in abundance only through our own labor. The new set of proverbs which Mr. Sumner offers to protection are borrowed from Bastiat's "Sophisms of Protection," a book which a great lawyer once said to me was in his opinion the most sophistical work he had ever read. The new proverbs are totally inapplicable, and protection declines to accept them.

The precise point in which Mr. Sumner's reasoning is faulty is the assumption that prices of finished products abroad would remain the same under a vastly increased demand, and that the prices of raw products abroad would remain the same under a vastly increased supply. None of the great economists would indorse such an assumption; on the contrary, the methods of reasoning adopted by them all justify the protectionist conclusions, and warrant them in affirming that the exchangeable value of the annual product of the United States is vastly increased by protection. But we have the authority of Adam Smith and Say and Mr. Mill for the conclusion that the exchangeable value of the annual product is precisely equivalent to the totality of the individual incomes. Protection then raises all incomes, and wages among the others. There does not appear to be a particle of doubt that, according to the accepted economical reasoning, we ought in the United States to have high wages in consequence of protection; and experience shows that we have high wages which bring to us annually three fourths of a million of people from almost every country of the earth. Paragraph 29 runs : —

" Let us now look at the other dogma : High wages make protective taxes necessary. It is the very opposite of the truth. If wages are high, that is the reason why no protective taxes are needed, even if they might be in some other case. In Germany the protectionists generally allege that lower wages in Germany than in England are a proof that Germany is industrially inferior, and needs protection against England. The protectionist argument never flags on account of any little variation in the facts."

This argument is, I believe, borrowed from Mr. David A. Wells, and is thus answered by a free-trade writer, Professor Cairnes : " Mr. Wells shows that labor in England, though much higher than in most European countries, and in particular than in Russia, is still so much more efficient here than there, that the high English rates are practically cheaper for the English capitalist than the lower continental rates for the capitalist of the Continent. What is the bearing of this upon the American demand for protection against England? Will Mr. Wells maintain that, as the efficiency of English labor is to that of Russia, so is the efficiency of American labor to that of English? If not, how does his objection to the protectionist criterion of costs, founded upon the different degrees of industrial efficiency, affect the argument?"

In short, Mr. Wells's argument was this: If in the case of England a high rate of wages is the result of greater skill or other greater advantages in the iron and textile industries, then a still higher rate of wages in America is a proof of still greater skill or other advantages in the iron and textile industries, or generally in the conversion of raw into finished products! It is this absurdity which his words suggest and insinuate, although when confronted with it he would say, "Oh, no! I only mean that if high wages are paid it must be because the products of the country find a market at home and abroad which makes it possible to pay such wages. If the liberal wages now paid in the United States to the iron and the textile industries could not be paid under free trade, this only proves that those industries are carried on at a loss, which loss must fall upon the unprotected industries." The answer to this is, that the industries in question produce about seven hundred and fifty millions, or one tenth of the annual product, and so support directly and indirectly one tenth part of the population. Were it not for these industries our production of raw materials must be increased by one tenth, that is to say, by an amount equal at present prices to three hundred millions, and the demand for iron and textiles in the outer world would be increased by seven hundred and fifty millions. There would be, then, an advance in finished products and a sharp decline in raw products, and the exchangeable value of what we had to offer would be diminished enormously. Agriculture not only would not gain, but it would lose immensely. Paragraph 30 reads : —

"In the arguments under this head of the subject, it is constantly assumed that wages are the controlling condition in production, or that there is some direct connection between the wages paid and the value of the product or the profits of the capitalist employer. These assumptions are false. Suppose that an individual comes forward and claims that he cannot compete because he pays higher wages than a foreign producer. When has any examination ever been made to find out whether such person has an adequate capital, or has a competent knowledge of the business, or diligently attends to his business, or has located his establishment wisely, or has organized his business economically, or has bought his raw material judiciously, or has kept up with improvements in machinery, or has not speculated with his product unsuccessfully, or has not violated some one of the other conditions of success ? The wages paid are but one, and often one of the least important conditions of production. If it is alleged, as it constantly is in this controversy, in a sweeping way, that American industries need protection because American wages are higher than foreign wages, it is a case of joining a very wide inference to very inadequate premises. What are the comparative conditions of industry in America and elsewhere as regards convenience and cost of raw materials, quality and cost of machinery, rent of land used, character of the climate as affecting the requirements of various industries, national character as respects industry, diligence, sobriety, intelligence, &c., of laborers, distance from the market or convenience and cost of transportation, convenience and cost of natural agents (coal or water), taxes and tax system, the security afforded by the excellence or otherwise of the government, &c. ? Surely it is plain that these things are the conditions of production ; and the comparative money rates of wages, taken apart from the purchasing power of money, or the efficiency of labor, to say nothing of all the other conditions enumerated, are by no means a criterion for a decision whether an industry can be carried on successfully or not. The lists of comparative wages which have been made, and which are relied upon by protectionists, and are often accepted by free-traders as pertinent to the issue, and perhaps as decisive of it, have no value at all for the purpose. The employer alleges that he can make no profits because he pays high wages. He assumes, apparently, that wages and profits displace each other.. It is ,certain that they do nothing of the kind. There is no ascertainable relation between wages and profits. Wages are paid out of the capital during the period of production. The employer tries to keep wages down, just as he tries to keep down cost and waste of raw material or wear of machinery, because he wants to economize on his outlay. He, of course, tries to minimize every outlay, because that is the road to success in the competition of the market, and to maximum profits. The price of his product, when he gets it done, will be determined by supply and demand on the market. He must replace his capital, and then he will find out what profit he has. No law whatever can be established between this profit and the wages which were paid to the men while they were making the article. Profits and wages may both be high or both low at the same time, or one may be high and the other low. The fact is, that instead of one being displaced by the other, they most always go together, both high or both low at the same time."

In this paragraph Mr. Sumner succeeds very well in confusing the reader by enumerating a great many other things which affect the cost of commodities, perplexing the subject by using the very reverse of the method employed, when we seriously desire to ascertain the plus or minus effect of a certain cause.

The true method is to isolate the cause, and see how it must act when taken alone, or with other things equal. Well, then, a commodity being produced is offered in the market and sold at a certain price. From this price F, the foreigner, has to deduct the cost of materials and x wages, and what remains is profit. From this price A, the American, has to deduct the cost of materials and say x plus y for wages. The additional y incapacitates A from contending with F. Higher wages, then, are indisputably a reason for protection, especially when we recollect that they enter into the cost of forming fixed capital and into the cost of repairing fixed capital, as well as into the sums paid directly for the work performed in shaping the commodities. It is of course necessary to success "that a man should have adequate capital, a competent knowledge of his business, must diligently attend to his business, must organize his business judiciously, must have kept up with improvements in machinery, have abstained from speculating with his product unsuccessfully, and have not violated some one of the other conditions of success;" in short, he must be well enough to get out of bed and sane enough to keep out of the lunatic hospital. But all these things are as necessary to F as to A. They have nothing to do with the question of the effect of a higher price of labor, into the discussion of which they are brought.

If Mr. Sumner means that we cannot contend with England in manufactures because we do not attend to our business, it may be noted that we are the same race of men as beat the pauper farm-laborers of Europe in their own market. It is fair to suppose that we should use as much diligence in the one occupation as the other. If he says no, because protection makes the protected manufacturer careless, the answer again is that all, or very nearly all, protected articles are very much cheaper, upon an average of years, than the foreign article with duty added; and in not a few the domestic article is cheaper than the foreign article without any duty. If the duty made the protected industries thriftless, in spite of internal competition, we should have prices remaining continually only very slightly below the point at which they can be imported and pay duty. If, on the contrary, he means that we are more careful, more skilful, or rapidly becoming more skilful, than the foreigner; that our general high rate of wages causes a careful selection of the most skilful, and great attention to have the best machinery, &c.; and that this being so, we ought to be able to manufacture as cheaply as the foreigner in spite of the difference of wages, — the answer is, that the fact of prices being already much less than the foreign commodity with duty added, is sufficient proof that the duty is not preventing our *advance* in the desired direction; that we have already reached the goal in common cottons, locomotives, agricultural machinery, tools, &c., and nearly reached the goal in such woollens as are used by the great mass of the people. The duty troubles nobody much except the users of the finer cottons and woollens and other luxuries. The men who get their one, two, or three dollars a day feel the tariff only through its beneficent effects upon their wages; it is the men who get their ten and twenty and thirty dollars a day who are very erroneously thinking themselves oppressed. If they really were oppressed, it might be reason even for class legislation; but they and their families would spend just as much in ostentation were there no custom-house in the country. Paragraph 31 says: —

" It is much more to the point to notice that profits are higher in this country than in Europe. We ought not to take too low views of human nature; but when an employer pretends to bull wages, we shall not believe him without examination. When we notice that profits are high in this country, we can understand the applicants for tariff favors, without assuming any disinterestedness. No capitalist will go into a business which gives less profit than some other which is open to him. The American producer does not want to put up with the rates of profit which his European competitor is satisfied with. He wants the rate which he could get if he went into one of the industries which are favored by nature in this country. Instead of going where he could get it on a natural basis, he wants the law to tax his fellow-citizens to give it to him. The talk about wages is all for effect. It is only so much smoke and noise imported into the contest to obscure the issue. It has had no little effect, because no one has taken the trouble to expose it in detail. The competitor whom we fear most is England, in which country wages are higher than anywhere else in Europe. How does England pay high wages and beat all the others, if high wages are the controlling consideration? And if she pays higher wages than the continental countries and beats them all, because other considerations come in, why may we not pay higher wages than she and beat her, at least in our home market, because other considerations come in? The nearest approach to pauper laborers in Europe are agricultural laborers. Our farmers send their products, raised by men remunerated at American rates, and pay transportation, and beat the pauper laborers in their own home market. How can this be done if the criterion of possible competition is the comparative rate of wages?"

Mr. Sumner here intimates that the manufacturer who tells the workingman that the tariff sustains and tends to increase wages is deluding the latter with a statement he does not believe, because his own interest is to have wages low. Yes; but it is also his own interest to sustain a policy which makes his industry possible in spite of the high wages. But the manufacturers are not the only men whom Mr. Sumner accuses of dishonesty in this matter. The highest statesmen of the land he believes to be simply telling lies when they speak in the manner he disapproves. He cannot believe that there are any men who, looking forward to the time when population must begin to press upon subsistence, feel it to be of the greatest possible importance that high wages should continue from now till then, and that the change should find a people so long used to good living as to refuse to descend into beggary. I am sorry he thinks such sentiments to be hypocrisy. He differs from Mr. Mill in this as much as he does in political economy.

Mr. Sumner asks, If England can pay higher wages than the Continent and beat the Continent, why cannot we pay higher wages than England and beat England ? Answer : Because England's superiority in skill more than counterbalances the lower wages of the Continent, while we have not a similar superiority over her. He also asks how our farmers compete with European, if the criterion of possible competition is the comparative rate of wages. The answer is, that nobody ever said that wages were the criterion, but only one of the elements. The English farmer has to pay three times as much in rent as the American farmer pays for wages, and he has to use vastly more labor per acre, and he has to use fertilizers. When manufactures and the mechanical arts have a similar advantage, they certainly will need no protection. Paragraph 32 reads : —

"If it is said that we cannot compete, what is meant ? These phrases are allowed to pass without due examination. I cannot compete with my inferiors or with my superiors. I cannot compete with an Irish laborer at digging a ditch, and I could not compete with the late Mr. Scott in running a railroad. Could any taxes enable me to run a railroad as Mr. Scott did, and to earn such remuneration as he earned ? Certainly not. No taxes can possibly enable a man to compete with a superior. Could any taxes enable me to compete with an Irish laborer at digging a ditch ? Indeed they could. They might interfere between me and the laborer, and prevent me from getting his services, and I might be forced to dig my own ditch, turning away from other and better paid occupations to give my time to an inferior occupation. That would impoverish me. Such is the only way in which protective taxes can make competition possible. They drive us down to compete with those who are far worse off than we instead of allowing us the full use of our natural advantages."

If the condition of things were such that, without a protective law, so many persons would crowd into professorships as to depress the *exchangeable* value of their services below those of ditch-diggers, then a law which should cause some of those would-be professors to dig ditches would increase the annual product, and raise the rate of wages. Paragraph 33 says : —

"If we have high wages, then they are a proof of industrial superiority. They prove that there are some lines of industry open to us, as a nation, in which great returns for both labor and capital may be obtained. To argue from high wages that we need protection is like arguing that a man needs charity because he is rich, or needs help because he is strong."

If we have high wages, they are a proof that we have a wisely distributed variety of industries ; that we have not, by overdoing the production of raw products, thrown away our natural advantages, so as to go half clad in the midst of fertile fields. To argue from high wages that we do not need protection is like arguing that a man's methods of business must have been bad because he has become rich, or that the organization of a victorious army had been pernicious, and that greater success would have come if each man had waged the war by himself. Paragraph 34 says : —

"A true analysis of the facts therefore shows us that protective taxes lower wages, and that high wages are not a reason why protective taxes are necessary. We get the remuneration of labor by using our natural advantages. The remuneration of labor is high because the advantages are great. It will be highest if the laborer is let alone to use the advantages without any restraint or interference. If we get a high remuneration by the use of our advantages, our strength in competition will come from the very advantages of nature which gave the high rewards of industry. Thus every aspect of the matter is consistent and straightforward, clear and natural. The more we study the case in all its aspects, the more thoroughly is the free-trade solution of it confirmed ; for, instead of entangling ourselves in ridiculous absurdities, we find that all the relations are simple and consistent."

He who studies Hamilton's report upon manufactures will see that he expected general prosperity — that is, high wages — to flow from protection, and why he expected it. He who studies the United States to-day will see that the event has justified his theory, and he will see that his theory accords with the wisest thought of the great writers upon political economy. We get a great remuneration to our labor by using and not throwing away our natural advantages. The remuneration of labor is high because we do not press those advantages beyond the ability of the world to absorb their products. We should entirely throw away those advantages if the laborers, instead of acting in concert for the greatest good of all, had each acted independently. If we get a high remuneration under protection, that is evidence that protection was needed, and will be needed until we gain a skill so much greater than others as to overbalance the greater cost per man of our labor.

Thus every aspect of the matter is consistent, straightforward, clear, and natural. We are not, like the free-traders, confounded by the presence of prosperity in the United States in spite of and in contradiction of all our theories, nor by the presence of the direst poverty in Ireland, Portugal, Turkey, and India. Paragraph 35 reads : —

"The application of these ideas to the matter in hand is simple and direct. I have spoken wholly as a political economist whose business it is to study theoretical questions. If it is proper to do anything about wages, the right thing to do is to abolish all protective taxes, and that will let them rise where they ought to be."

The author of this review of Professor Sumner's paper has written wholly as a political economist whose business it has been for many years to study theoretical questions. It is of the utmost consequence to sustain wages, and this will be done by continuing the protective policy. Otherwise the growth of our non-agricultural industries will be checked, and the country will become disproportionately addicted to farming, with a constant diminution of the profits of that occupation and of wages and profits in all occupations.

We have now finished Mr. Sumner's paper. He had afterwards a long conversation with the Commissioners, in which he repeated that protection lowered wages, declared that New England would have been greatly richer had there never been any tariff, and that the South was about to greatly harm herself by introducing manufactures; and he scoffed at the theory of Franklin, Adam Smith, and Mr. Mill which teaches the great advantages of frequent industrial centres to the farming population. This he dismissed by calling it the famous Truck Farm argument. It is not necessary to go through those conversations, as they evolved no new point, and as the positions above referred to are not warranted by any reasoning in accordance with the political economy of the latter half of the nineteenth century as set forth by Mr. Mill and by many authors on the protectionist side.   I believe there is not a particle of doubt that protection sustains and gradually raises wages; that New England and the whole country is greatly richer by reason of it; that the South is doing very wisely in introducing manufactures; and that the "Truck Farm argument" is sufficiently justified by the authorities I have named, by all sound economic reasoning, and by common sense.

"PROGRESS AND POVERTY."

I.

In "Progress and Poverty" Mr. Henry George has given to the world a brilliant work, admirably written, full of eloquence, radiant with the noble aspiration of diminishing human suffering, and absolutely devoid of that too common cowardice which stops at each sentence to consider whether the words about to be written will be in harmony with opinions avowed upon the other side of the Atlantic.

But the ability and earnestness of the author and the tremendous importance of his subject make it all the more necessary to examine with care every doubtful premise and every questionable deduction, and to collect what evidence we can as to the exactness or carelessness of his methods of reasoning. Of these we have some specimens in an article published by Mr. George in the *Popular Science Monthly* for March, 1880, entitled "The Study of Political Economy." In this he says : —

"The effect of a tariff is to increase the cost of bringing goods from abroad. Now if this benefits a country, then all difficulties, dangers, and impediments which increase the cost of bringing goods from abroad are likewise beneficial. If this theory be correct, then the city which is the hardest to get at has the most advantageous situation ; pirates and shipwrecks contribute to national prosperity by raising the price of freight and insurance ; and improvements in navigation, in railroads and steamships, are injurious. Manifestly, this is absurd."

It is certainly absurd, but the absurdity must be looked for in Mr. George's reasoning. The true statement should be this: *One* of the effects of a tariff is to increase the cost of bringing *certain kinds* of goods from abroad. Nevertheless a tariff is said to be beneficial.   If so, then everything which increases the cost of bringing from abroad not only those certain goods, but all goods, must likewise be beneficial.   The obstacles he mentions not only raise the price of a particular kind or kinds of goods, but of all goods, and that of passage also, and they diminish the value of all exports.   The railroad and the steamship facilitate every sort of exchange, but this does not prove that every sort of exchange is beneficial.   Rum, opium, small-pox, and leprosy do not become desirable because distributed by rail and steamer ! A tariff does not stop all exchanges, but only some.   That would be a droll syllogism which ran : " If to stop some exchanges be beneficial, then to stop all exchanges would be beneficial." Mr. George continues thus : —

"And then I looked farther.   The speaker had dwelt on the folly of a great country like the United States exporting raw material and importing manufactured goods which might as well be made at home, and I asked myself, What is the motive which causes a people to export raw materials and import manufactured goods ?   I found that it could be attributed to nothing else than the fact that they could in this way get the goods cheaper, — that is, with less labor.   I looked to transactions between individuals for parallels to this trade between nations, and found them in plenty : the farmer selling his wheat and buying flour ; the grazier sending his wool to a market and bringing back cloth and blankets ; the tanner buying back leather in shoes, instead of making them himself.   I saw, when I came to analyze them, that these exchanges between nations were precisely the same thing as exchanges between individuals ; that they were in fact nothing but exchanges between individuals of different nations ; that they were all prompted by the desire and led to the result of getting the greatest return for the least expenditure of labor ; that the social condition in which such exchanges did not take place was the naked barbarism of the Terra del Fuegians ; that just in proportion to the division of labor and the increase of trade were the increase of wealth and the progress of civilization.   And so, following up, turning, analyzing, and testing all the protectionist arguments, I came to conclusions which I have ever since retained."

The reader who is familiar with the Free-Trade and Protectionist controversy will need no one to point out the weakness of the above paragraph.

To get goods cheaper is not the equivalent of getting them for less labor.

To get the greatest return for the least expenditure of a small portion of its labor is not the proper aim of a nation, but to get the greatest Gross Annual Product obtainable by the whole of its available labor. This is a very different matter.

That exchanges and division of employments find place in all but savage societies, does not prove that there must be division of employments between nations. It is not necessary that England should make up all our raw materials while we confine ourselves to agricultural pursuits. We are numerous enough to derive from the division of employments every possible advantage among ourselves. No man can be certain that the increase of wealth and the progress of civilization are "just in proportion" to the division of labor and the increase of trade, because these two last are not the only nor even the chief elements in civilization; but even if they were, we are not promoting the division of labor nor the increase of trade in the *United States* by confining ourselves to raising raw material.

THE OBJECT OF INTERNATIONAL TRADE.

The object *aimed* at in trading with a foreign nation is to get what is wanted cheaper in the sense of for less labor, certainly; but this object is attained only when the reciprocal desires balance. When they do not balance, the party whose needs are the greatest in amount must give up more and more of any advantages arising from the exchange, and may have to give up the whole, — yes, and a good deal more than the whole; for if he does not possess the skill and the fixed capital he cannot begin to manufacture (which is his only defence) until the other party has extorted from him twenty or thirty or more per cent over the rate at which he might manufacture for himself if he had the skill and fixed capital. And this is not the worst: B needs more of A's goods than A will take of his. He must pay in treasure while this lasts. He may produce, if you please, a hundred millions of treasure a year; but if he pay out two hundred, he will soon find the basis of his machinery of exchange gone, only to be recovered after years of loss and misery, and

he will find that he must go *without* a large part of what he
might have enjoyed through his own industry. He can permanently obtain from abroad only so many goods as will pay for
that quantity of his commodities which is needed in the outer
world at the lowest price at which he can afford them. These
are the conditions which the *World* offers to fifty millions of
people, soon to be a hundred millions. If it were bargaining with
five millions of people it might have to offer better terms. This
is not merely protectionist doctrine, but is a necessary deduction
from the propositions regarding international trade laid down by
Mr. John Stuart Mill. But Mr. George reasons as if the matter
of proportional demands or requirements had no place in political
economy.

The reader may at first think that all this has nothing to do
with " Progress and Poverty ; " but it has much to do with Mr.
George's habits of thought, and these have shaped his book. If
we find him making about free-trade deductions which involve
a syllogism with four terms, — or a universal conclusion drawn
from a particular premise, or the like, — we shall be prepared
and on the watch for similar inaccuracies in the book we are
about to examine ; and before going to the main subject it
is well to quote from page 270 of " Progress and Poverty "
the following : —

"To these must be added, in the United States, the robbery involved in the protective tariff, which for every twenty-five cents it
puts in the treasury takes a dollar and it may be four or five out of
the pocket of the consumer."

Now the duties collected have some years been over two hundred millions ; there must then, according to Mr. George, have
been at least eight hundred millions, and perhaps four thousand
millions, taken by the tariff from the pockets of the consumers.
These Munchausen figures would have set any honest man like
Mr. George upon a re-examination of the statements which the
allies of the Cobden Clubs have the audacity to repeat year after
year in the face of repeated refutations ; but he did not stop to
see where his allegations would carry him, — and this is a lamen-
table fact, as it throws his evident uprightness and earnestness

into the scales which are heavily weighted with falsehood and frivolity. The fact is noted in no hostile spirit. The internal evidence which "Progress and Poverty" contains of the pure, single-hearted, and noble motives of its author are overwhelming; and his object, "the alleviation of human misery," is one with which every true man must sympathize; but the higher the object the more important it becomes not to fall into error as to the cause of the evil or as to the remedies which may be advantageously applied to it.

THE AMERICAN PROBLEM.

Mr. George describes eloquently this century's increase in wealth-producing power, and thinks that if a Franklin or a Priestley had seen it in a vision he would have expected the very poorest to be lifted above the possibility of want, — he would have expected to see

"Youth no longer stunted and starved; age no longer harried by avarice; the child at play with the tiger; the man with the muck-rake drinking in the glory of the stars! Foul things fled; fierce things tamed; discord turned to harmony! For how could there be greed when all had enough? How could the vice, the crime, the ignorance, the brutality, that spring from poverty and the fear of poverty, exist when poverty had vanished? Who should crouch where all were freemen; who oppress where all were peers?"

But Franklin and Priestley were far from rhapsodists; they were cool and wary thinkers and observers. They saw about them much vice, crime, ignorance, and brutality that were the cause of poverty, instead of being caused by poverty, as Mr. George assumes. They saw much poverty which need not then exist, had the sufferers been as free from vice, crime, ignorance, and brutality as they might have been under the then conditions of society; they saw, indeed, much vice, crime, ignorance, and brutality which even then had not the apology of poverty: moreover, they would have foreseen a vast increase in cities, where temptations are more numerous and restraints less powerful; where there is much wealth to be preyed upon, and comparatively great opportunity of escaping detection; where Charity rushes about eager to relieve the deserving, and often carelessly giving to the undeserving the funds which should have been better bestowed; where men may live for months or years without knowing who lives in the next house; where there are a thousandfold more opportunities for self-indulgence than in the village in which every one knows every one, and each man and woman is a wholesome restraint upon the rest. Franklin and Priestley, then, would hardly have expected as much as our author believes they would have expected: possibly they would not have expected even as much as has been accomplished. If they could have foreseen the condition of society to-day, and compared it, class for class, with what existed in their times, they probably would have gone down to their graves with bright hopes of the future. They would have seen great cities become as healthy as the village was in their days, and they would have seen a great and a general advance in the real wages of all classes of those who are able and willing to work. The change in this respect is most striking, and is within the scope of the personal observation of all who can look back thirty or forty years with a clear and distinct memory. To such no statistical proof is needed; but such proof is at hand, for we have careful estimates of the gross annual product of the United States each ten years, and by these we find that there was earned enough to give each individual $61 in 1840, $69 in 1850, $83 in 1860, at least $110 in 1870, and at least $140 in 1880. Let us add 15 per cent to 1840 on account of possibly shorter enumerations then than now. Still we have only $70 in 1840 against $140 now. But for 1880 we have not only estimates of the gross annual product: we have also those of the total value of the nation's accumulations, and made by the same hand (Mulhall). These make the property of the United States to have been forty thousand millions; and this valuation was made at a time when Government could borrow at 4 per cent, and when few investments could be made to safely yield 5 per cent, and when farmers in the far west could borrow at 6 per cent. If, then, we take into consideration the fact that much property in real estate gave no return, but was merely held for a market, it will be seen that to assume the whole forty thousand millions of property to have paid its owners 6 per cent will be to err so much on the side of too high a rate as to cover any possible error which may have crept in from undervaluation of the property at forty thousand millions. But 6 per cent upon forty thousand millions gives twenty-four hundred millions (out of the seven thousand millions of gross annual product) as the amount going in the first place to rent and profit.

But what becomes of rent and profit? On the average of years the annual product is used up, leaving at the end of each year the same percentage of stocks of commodities. Rent and profit are completely passed over to the renderers of services which do and services which do not issue in commodities. They are totally spent either for services, or for commodities, or for property which is expected to bring in an income, and which is formed by labor. Nearly all of the seven thousand millions gets into the hands of those who render services, of those who produce commodities, and of those who form those instruments of production and of convenience which are expected to yield a power of appropriating a portion of the enhanced annual products of future years. The recipients of rent and of profits enjoy the comfort, the consideration, and the luxury which the services of a large mass of the population can afford, and in return they pass over to this portion of the population nearly the whole of their share of the gross annual product. They retain nothing to the exclusion of the rest of the community except the raw materials which enter 'into the commodities they and their immediate families consume. Even the gross total of their receipts is regulated by demand and supply, and can only be a *portion* of that which the community derive from the use of the capital (the fixed and floating instruments of production and instruments of convenience) which has been formed out of their savings. Without the aid of these instruments even Mr. George (see p. 72) concedes that the total annual product could be only a small fraction of what it is now; in other words, that it is of supreme importance that these instruments should be kept in repair, and that new ones should be formed to meet the demand of the rapidly increasing population. They are kept in repair by those who live within their incomes. New ones are formed by those who save.

Without the instruments of production now in use Mr. George declares that the product could not be a tithe, or a tenth part, of what it is now; that is, the capital produces nine tenths, and, if our calculations be correct, the whole people get two thirds of this advantage, and the owners of the capital get one third; but this one third they spend in such a shape as to cause the existence of various classes who are not employed in producing necessaries, and whose demand for necessaries enables those who do produce them to procure by exchange a vast amount of conveniences and luxuries, and to be thus stimulated to make the earth yield a greater amount of necessaries.

PROPERTY AS AN INCENTIVE TO PRODUCTION.

Out of the institution of property, then, has grown both the present great productive power and also the distribution of the population into various grades of wealth, each of which stimulates the next poorer to strive to better its condition; and this beneficent effect should be seen most fully in the United States, where the almost universal sentiment of the people demands the equal or nearly equal division of properties among the children at the death of the possessor. Enormous estates are said to have destroyed Italy and the provinces of the Roman Empire; but it does not follow that there should be no estates and no landlords, and it is to be feared that Mr. George is giving fatal advice to the already sufficiently miserable Irish. Native landlords living on their estates and using Irish products would speedily change the whole aspect of that island. The abolition of landlords will indefinitely postpone her resurrection.

For the purposes of this discussion an improved farm is as much an instrument of production as a power-loom, and so is a store in Broadway. The position of this last may be such that the land, apart from the building, possesses great exchangeable value; but the totality of such ground rents form but a small part of the value of the annual product, — nine tenths of which product Mr. George calculates to be due to the efficiency lent to labor by capital. Such ground rents are what Mr. Wm. Lucas Sargant calls *ascending* rents. They spring from the *improvement* of the productive forces of the community, and in this are

totally unlike the *descending* rents, which may come into existence where population presses upon the means of subsistence.
The former are the accompaniment of national growth and prosperity; the latter are an indication of national decay.

Out of the twenty-four hundred millions which is assumed
as having, in 1880, gone in the first place to rent and profits,
probably one half went for services not issuing in commodities,
— such as those of actors, artists, barbers, clergymen, clerks,
copyists, hotel-keepers, dentists, designers, draughtsmen, domestic servants, civil engineers, gardeners, government officials (in
taxes), hostlers, intelligence-office keepers, journalists, laundresses,
librarians, lawyers, managers, musicians, nurses, physicians, professors, restaurant-keepers, teachers, surgeons, and so on.

The other half must have gone to the butchers, bakers, con-
fectioners, carriage-makers, furniture-makers, blacksmiths, carpenters, tailors, etc., etc., who furnished commodities; and a little
reflection will show that less than half of the value of these
would upon the average consist of raw materials. We have then,
at most, only six hundred millions consumed by the owners of
property to the exclusion of the rest of the community; six hundred out of seven thousand, which last is, according to Mr. George,
ten times more than could be produced without capital. This
includes the cases of all recipients of profits and of all recipients
of rent, and the latter includes the rent of improvements as well
as ground rent. The reader will then see that ground rent, from
the abolition of which Mr. George expects the return of the golden
age, is altogether too minute to produce any perceptible harm;
while the commission of so stupendous a breach of public faith
would be likely to lessen the general confidence in the stability
of individual fortunes, and in this way to diminish the effective
desire for accumulation which lies at the very foundation of
national prosperity.

WAGES INCREASE WITH PRODUCTION.

We appear, then, to have arrived at the conclusion that more
than nine tenths of the gross annual product goes directly or indirectly to those who labor with the hands or with the head;
and this is so near the whole, that, for purposes of comparison,

we may say that the great wage fund of the entire community is the gross annual product, or, at all events, that in comparing different periods the wages fund is in proportion to the annual products. Now the most we could make out for 1840 was an average of $70 per head for the whole population; the least which seems probable for 1880 is $140 per head. Gold may have depreciated since 1840, but not enough to account for a quarter part of this difference; and we are forced to the conclusion that real wages must have risen immensely; and this is what the personal observation of each individual and what statistics in detail bear witness to. The question then —

"Why, in spite of increase in productive power, do wages tend to a minimum which will give but a bare living?" which Mr. George propounds as "the riddle which the Sphinx of Fate puts to our civilization, and which not to answer is to be destroyed,"— this question appears to have no existence out of his imagination. Wages, fees, salaries, emoluments of every kind, have risen every ten years. They were higher in 1850 than in 1840, again higher in 1860, and very much higher in 1880. At each period there was more to divide, and every portion of the community obtained a larger dividend, — every portion, that is, in which no exceptional or temporary causes overcame the general swing of financial events.

The problem, then, for the solution of which Mr. George wrote his eloquent book seems not to exist. It appears that wages do *not* tend to a minimum, but that, on the contrary, they are constantly and steadily increasing if we examine them at considerable intervals and under similar circumstances: it would appear that "where population is the densest, wealth greatest, and the machinery of production and exchange most highly developed," we do *not* "find the deepest poverty, the sharpest struggle for existence, and the most enforced idleness." His proposition is universal, and is demolished the moment we compare Ireland with England, or Portugal with France, or the farmer of fifty years ago with the farmer now, or the domestic servant and 'longshoreman of those days with the same classes to-day.

II.

BUT although it appears quite certain that all classes who are able and willing to work have shared in the great increase of opulence which has during the last century resulted from the greater security of property and the introduction of machinery and the division of employments, still it is equally certain that the progress has not been continuous. It has been in waves. Each wave has run higher than the last ; but, during the reflux, there has been distress enough to wring the heart of any one who observed it at its focus in the poorer quarters of a great city. It is in vain to answer that this is a trivial matter compared to the famines and consequent pestilences that used to attend short crops, and that still attend them in nations which modern trade prevents from attaining a diversity of occupations. It is in vain to point to Ireland and Orissa and Behar and the Punjab with their many millions of victims ; for, although we have passed from the scene of such horrors, the evil which remains is great enough to demand that we use every effort to discover and remove its causes.

THE REAL PROBLEM

would seem to be to ascertain why, during the advance of modern society from one plane of opulence to another, there should occur periods of depression in which a considerable portion of the population suffers want of employment and all consequent evils for periods of several consecutive years.

At the bottom of the whole trouble lie the imperfect information and consequent imperfect judgment of individuals.

A market, which has been for some time closed, is opened. A manufacturing and commercial nation hastens to send goods

to it. They pay a profit. Then all prudence is cast to the winds;
immense supplies are poured upon the market and forced upon it
by long credits and all the devices of trade. The thing is overdone. The comparatively agricultural nation has taken vastly
more than it can pay for in goods. It has to pay in treasure,
and this sort of trade at last comes to an end; but not until the
buying nation has suffered a disarrangement of its machinery of
exchange which keeps it in a state of paralysis for years.

We suffered this after the war of the Revolution and after the
war of 1812–15.

But there is another field in which the inaccurate judgment
of men would bring about excitement and subsequent depression,
even if there were no such thing as trade.

The efficiency of modern labor springs, in a great measure,
from the aid given by fixed and floating capital; and the disposition to save — or to form capital — is stimulated by the
manifold instruments of convenience and luxury which increasing opulence bestows.

AMERICAN CAPITAL AND POPULATION.

But, in a country like the United States, the desire to save finds
wide scope. The population, and its effective demand for capital,
increase at the rate of three per cent annually. If, then, we take
the value of all capital and of all improvements on land to have
been $30,000,000,000 in 1880, the average demand for new capi-
tal and improvements would be to the amount of $900,000,000;
that is, commodities would every year be exchanged, not for other
commodities, but for labor employed in forming new property,
to this enormous extent.

At the commencement of a period of excitement more than
this would be invested, and with profit; then more, while the
prudent shook their heads. But perhaps, nevertheless, a profit
would ensue; and so on until the formation of instruments of
production and convenience is carried beyond the point where
society can and will pay for their use enough to satisfy the desire
for profit current in the community. Up to this point there has
been a greater and greater demand for commodities, and consequently for labor to form commodities. Now, suddenly, the

movement to form more improved farms, more mills, forges, machinery, etc., is diminished, and the labor which was forming them is set adrift and is unable to consume as largely as before; and so less commodities are required, and less labor to form commodities. Here we have a glut, a panic, and a period of depression.

Rent has had nothing to do with the movement except as one of the closing effects. As the keener-sighted see that too much fixed capital is being formed, they may rush upon real estate as a means of securing some income; and this speculation may run very wild, because when A buys B's real estate his doing so does not diminish a particle the aggregate of funds seeking investment. He simply transfers them to B. But such a speculation is an effect, not a cause, of the movement which is about to culminate in a collapse. This would come to pass just the same if real estate were never either bought or sold.

THE MOTIVE OF GEORGE'S BOOK.

A collapse of this kind, aggravated by over-importations and by a simultaneous contraction of the currency, occurred in 1873, and continued in greater or less intensity until 1879; and it was during these years that Mr. George saw the misery which caused him to write his eloquent book. Unhappily, he seems to have entirely missed the nature and causes of the disease, and to have equally erred in the remedy he prescribed.

During this period of depression he saw "gaunt Famine side by side with the gilded palace," etc.; but the construction of the gilded palace in no way hastened or contributed to the collapse. *On the contrary*, it tended to postpone and moderate the collapse; and the construction of a thousand such at the proper moment, accompanied by similar expenditure in other directions, might have totally averted the miseries, losses, and wreck which filled the period from 1873 to 1879. They could not have been averted nor have been postponed for a moment by the confiscation of landed property or any other property.

Let us pass now to what Mr. George has to say about capital.

Mr. George is particularly unfortunate in his use of the *reductio ad absurdum*.

In examining his free-trade notions we have seen him brush aside the opinions of Washington, Franklin, Hamilton, Jefferson, Jackson — in short, of the majority of the statesmen and people of the United States — by a few phrases which to him appeared to be a *reductio ad absurdum*, but which a brief examination showed to be only a false syllogism. In writing of "Capital" he dismisses all previous political economists, both free-trade and protectionist, in a similar manner. He finds their propositions absurd — in holding labor to be supported by capital — "because they involve the idea that labor cannot be exerted until the products of labor are saved, — thus putting the product before the producer," and this he repeats several times in different words. Let us put this into a syllogism.

The producer of capital cannot be dependent for support upon the subsequent product.

Labor is the producer of capital, therefore labor cannot be dependent for support upon capital; but labor in the minor premise is undistributed, while in the conclusion it is distributed. It is a false syllogism.

The labor which precedes and produces certain capital is not the labor which is supported by that same capital, but quite another labor. There is nothing absurd in supposing that the crops raised by certain labor in 1882 may support and be absolutely necessary to the support of that other labor which raises the crops of 1883. The confusion of thought lies with Mr. George, and not with those whom he criticises.

Through many pages upon "Capital" he labors to show that "wages are not drawn from capital at all, but come *directly* from the produce of the labor for which they are paid." But the real wages of the laborers are the food, raiment, shelter, etc., for which they spend their wages. These are produced *before* they are used. They are advanced by the capitalist, who is reimbursed only when the articles or the property formed by labor are finished and put upon the market and sold.

That industry cannot exceed the amount which previously existing means can support, is plain enough ; but in point of fact there always exists in an industrial society sufficient commodities to carry the community to the next harvest and *somewhat beyond*.

Industry, then, is not limited by capital, but both it and capital are limited by the *field of employment*.

Underneath this, and limiting it, lie the desires for the gratification of which the community, as a whole, will work and save. If it desire only bananas and bamboo huts, or mere necessaries, it will remain without progress and without wealth. If it desire the manifold conveniences, luxuries, and amusements now enjoyed in the United States, it will continually work towards the attainment of them as increasing skill, dexterity, judgment, and capital bring nature more and more under dominion. But at no point of time, between the two conditions, has it been true that there existed an unlimited demand for any one or for all the commodities known to the community. At any given moment the demand is limited to such quantity of commodities as can be obtained by a given amount of effort; and it is still further limited by the desire to provide for the future, — the desire to save.

Without this desire there can be none of that progress which grows from the greater efficiency given to labor by fixed and floating capital; that is, by those instruments of production and of convenience which, according to Mr. George himself, enable the community to produce a product ten times greater than it could unaided. But, at any moment, capital is of limited efficiency, and demand and supply will award it only a portion of that which it adds to the annual product. With a given population and a given efficiency of capital the latter cannot be increased indefinitely. Beyond a certain point a larger amount must either rest unemployed, or divide with that before existing the same portion of the annual product, — thus diminishing the profits of the whole. There is, then, in every industrial community, at each point in its development, a limit to the field of employment, even if it be in possession of immense undeveloped resources. The English economists generally (and Mr. George follows their lead) suppose that there is only one limit; namely, that which is found in a scarcity of land, mines, etc. Whether this limit has ever been reached in any existing industrial community seems doubtful; that it has not been reached in the United States seems quite beyond doubt.

It is idle, then, to attribute the fluctuations in amount of employment to a deficiency of land brought about by speculation.

The normal limit to the field of employment is *passed* when the desire to save forms capital faster than the population and its effective demand increases. The excess of employment in this direction causes an excess of production of commodities, and a farther excess in the employment of what is called productive labor.

During the corresponding depression employment shrinks beneath its normal limit, and continues less than the average until the population has gained upon capital or has changed its habits of expenditure. Unemployed capital and labor, during a period of depression, are constantly looking for new commodities and new services with which to tempt the savers (great and small) to increase their expenditure; the savers, meanwhile, vie with each other for the possession of any property which yields a sure income; and those in whom the desire to save is least are crowded out and give up trying to accumulate, — until at last it begins to be apparent that more fixed capital is needed. Then commences another expansion, to be followed, after a longer or shorter period, by another collapse.

The violence of these fluctuations will doubtless diminish in proportion as the community obtains correct views of the relative *magnitude* of the industrial forces, — of the amounts of fixed and floating capital, — the average quantity of unemployed capital in the shape of unsold stocks of commodities and of materials awaiting conversion into commodities, etc.; and, meanwhile, some considerable mitigation might be afforded if, *during times of excitement*, the general and State and city and village governments abstained, as far as possible, from expenditures for improvements, and reserved their means for times of depression.

To lay all taxes upon real estate would give governments enormous revenues during periods of excitement, when to use them would be prejudicial, and leave it without a large portion of its necessary revenue during periods of depression, when expenditures would be beneficial. How much could be collected from taxes upon land during periods when land is so depressed that mortgaged property sold under foreclosure fails generally to pay its debts?

CONFUSIONS OF THOUGHT.

In his chapter on "Capital" Mr. George accuses all past economists of confusion of thought; but his own errors in this respect seem to outweigh those of all other writers put together.

He thinks it foolish to suppose that the capital produced in 1882 should support the labor of 1883, but finds nothing unreasonable in saying that the man who is at work upon an unfinished steamship "virtually produces the things in which he expends his wages."

But the things for which he expends his wages were created *before* he did his work, created by the previous joint efforts of antecedent labor and capital. They belonged to capital, which had furnished the instruments of production and advanced the wages and kept the instruments of production in repair. If what remained was more than the profit usual in the community, it would indicate that population had outgrown capital, — that more capital was needed. To construct this capital more labor would be called for, and wages would rise.

That is, labor (of all kinds) and capital and rent divide between them the total gross product. When this increases, wages and profits and rents increase. When this diminishes they all must submit to a diminution. The proportions of the gross product which go to one or the other are determined by demand and supply. If capital be relatively scarce, capital takes a larger percentage; if relatively abundant, it takes a smaller percentage. And so with respect to different classes of the community. If any be in excess, it receives a smaller share of the annual product; otherwise, a larger.

With the increase of the annual product, growing out of more efficient labor and more efficient capital, the totality of wages must necessarily advance. If it advance less in any particular class it can only be because that class is relatively in excess. The amount per head which goes *directly* to labor of every sort in 1882 is more than the *whole* product of 1840, and the amount that goes directly and *indirectly* to labor of every sort in 1882 is double that which went to labor of every sort in 1840.

Mr. George argues rightly that, at any particular moment, industry is not limited by capital, for there are always surplus stocks ready to support more labor, and likely to be speedily made good by quickened production; but, indirectly, and in the long run, industry is very much affected by the increasing efficiency of capital, for on this depends the magnitude of the total annual product, and on this the rewards of industry. To secure this, together with a greater diversity and division of employments, and to secure to our own labor as large a proportion of the best possible field of employment — that, namely, which is found in satisfying by our own efforts as many of our desires as possible, — was the avowed object of the

PROTECTIVE POLICY

as set forth by Alexander Hamilton; and under this policy, when thoroughly carried out, we have attained that high rate of wages which attracts two thirds of a million of men annually to our shores, and which gives us warrant to hope that, before population can press upon the means of subsistence in these United States, our people will have become accustomed to so high a scale of living as to ensure the exercise of that prudence which will become necessary in the altered conditions of the nation.

Mr. George can see nothing in the policy but a foolish effort to make certain classes rich!

Few things, however, are so settled in political economy as that "no industry can for any length of time obtain a higher rate of profit than that which is common in the community." If it could, it would be doubly desirable to have those industries which might be turned into monopolies within reach, and not upon the other side of the Atlantic! Let it be ascertained that a monopoly exists among us, — likely to be permanent, not likely to be speedily destroyed by internal competition, — and the remedy would be the easiest conceivable. A reduction of the duty would put the would-be monopolists upon their good behavior. But if, upon a false or mistaken cry of monopoly, we destroy some of our own industries, and transfer the scene of monopoly to foreign shores, we shall be thenceforth without remedy.

The outcry of monopoly as to industries easily inaugurated by moderate amounts of capital is generally passed over as the product of insincerity; but Mr. George is above suspicion in this respect. He writes what he believes.

We come now to what he has to say about the Malthusian Doctrine.

III.

Mr. George quotes as follows from Mr. John Stuart Mill: —

"A greater number of people cannot, in any given state of civilization, be collectively as well provided for as a smaller. The niggardliness of nature, not the injustice of society, is the cause of the penalty attached to over-population. An unjust distribution of wealth does not aggravate the evil, but, at most, causes it to be somewhat earlier felt. It is in vain to say that all mouths which the increase of mankind call into existence bring with them hands. The new mouths require as much food as the old ones, and the hands do not produce as much. If all instruments of production were held in joint property by the whole people, and the produce divided with perfect equality among them, *and if in a society thus constituted industry was as energetic and the produce as ample as at the present time*, there would be enough to make all the existing population extremely comfortable; but when that population had doubled itself, as with existing habits of the people it undoubtedly would in little more than twenty years, what would then be their condition? Unless the arts of production were in the same time improved in an almost unexampled degree, the inferior soils which must be resorted to, and the more laborious and scantily remunerative cultivation which must be employed on the superior soils to procure food for so much larger a population, would, by an insuperable necessity, render every individual in the community poorer than before. If the population continued to increase at the same rate, a time would soon arrive when no one would have more than mere necessaries, and soon after a time when no one would have a sufficiency of those, and the further increase of the population would be arrested by death."

To this Mr. George replies: —

"All this I deny. I assert that the very reverse of these propositions is true. I assert that in any given state of civilization a greater number of people can collectively be better provided for than a smaller. I assert that the injustice of society, not the niggardliness of nature, is the cause of the want and misery which the current theory attributes to over-population. I assert that the new mouths which an increasing population call into existence require no more food than the old ones, while the hands they bring with them can, in the natural order of things, produce more. I assert that, other things being equal, the greater the population the greater the comfort which an equitable distribution of wealth would give to each individual. I assert that, in a state of equality, the natural increase of population would constantly tend to make each individual richer instead of poorer.

"I thus distinctly join issue and submit the question to the test of facts."

Now, let us look at his facts. They are these : That, in our times, communities have increased faster in wealth than in population; that it is in the densest populations we find "costly buildings, fine furniture, luxurious equipages, statues, pictures, pleasure-gardens, and yachts, men of income and of elegant leisure, thieves, policemen, menial servants, lawyers, men of letters, and the like; and that capital overflows for remunerative investment from these densely populated to sparsely populated regions." These things, he says, "conclusively show that *wealth* is the greatest where population is densest; that the production of wealth to a given amount of labor increases as population increases."

But these things do not prove the contradictory of Mr. Mill's propositions. Mr. Mill would not deny that, in countries so greatly underpeopled (having regard to the existing skill and knowledge of mankind and the available land) as were our colonies when, as Adam Smith relates, a widow with half a dozen children was looked upon as an heiress, — he would not deny that in such cases a mere increase of population would bring increase of wealth. Mr. Mill was speaking of communities in which to support a widow who had six children would be a good deal more difficult than to support a widow without any; and, with respect to such, he says that a great increase of population would bring great misery, unless, *at the same time*, the arts of production were

improved in an almost unprecedented degree.   This, Mr. George
thinks, he disproves by adducing the experience of the last forty
years, in which the arts of production *have* been improved in an
almost unprecedented degree.

Wealth has increased in consequence of these improvements,
— not in consequence of the greater population.   The greater
wealth and the greater population are joint effects; or rather the
improvements brought greater wealth, and this brought greater
density of population.   This answers his point as to the general
advance in wealth and population in our times.   With respect
to the comparison he draws between countries now underpeopled, — those in which that density of population which can be
maintained to the best advantage with the skill and the productive instruments known in our time has not been reached, —
it is quite true that greater wealth would ensue from greater
population up to a certain not very well defined point.   More
capital can be used to advantage as population increases; the
steamship and the railroad become paying instruments where before they could not be used, and capital speedily appears, either
from home savings or from other communities, when the conditions exist for its safe and paying investment.   And with the
application of more capital comes the possibility of satisfying new
desires, — the desires for " costly buildings, fine furniture, luxurious equipages, statues, pictures, pleasure-gardens, yachts, elegant
leisure, protection by means of police, menial servants, instruction
in the law, in religion, in literature, and the like on the part of
the rich, and for better food, better clothing, better houses, better
schooling, and more amusements on the part of the rest of the
community."

It is the existence of those desires and the possibility of gratifying them that leads to the accumulation of those instruments
of production of which Mr. George himself says: —

" If the farmer must use the spade because he has not capital enough
for a plough, the sickle instead of the reaping-machine, the flail instead
of the thresher ; if the machinist must rely upon the chisel for cutting
iron, the weaver on the hand-loom, and so on, — the productiveness of
industry cannot be a tithe of what it is when aided by capital in the
shape of the best tools now in use."

Well, then, these instruments of production, which do nine tenths of the work, can be brought into existence and kept in repair only by abstinence. Somebody must save what he otherwise would have squandered in present enjoyment. Instead of orgies with boon companions he prefers to improve his farm, to buy better tools, to build a mill, etc. The instruments of production into which he transforms his savings are part of those which increase tenfold the gross products to be divided. He is clearly entitled to some portion of the increase his savings have effected: what that portion shall be will be decided by perfectly impartial umpires, — demand and supply. If of any one kind of the instruments of production there are less than the community can use to advantage, the rent for their use will be high, the profits to be derived from constructing more will be great, and many will be constructed; until at last there will come into existence as many as will command such annual rent or equivalent profit as will satisfy the existing effective desire for accumulation. If he cannot get income enough from his instruments of production to make it worth while to save in this shape, he will form instead instruments of convenience: he will improve his dwelling-house or build a new one; or, abandoning saving, he will use better food, better clothing, go oftener to the shows or the play; and if he be rich, he will call together a number of carpenters, masons, and other artificers, and build him a "gilded palace." In building this he will pass over to the artificers a portion of the annual product which came to him as rent for his part of the community's property, and the artificers will eat it and drink it, and put it into clothing, or obtain some amusement with it, or put a portion in the bank. Every particle of the value of the gilded palace and its luxurious furniture will, when it is finished, have passed into the hands of labor, and the greater part of it will have been consumed by those who were able and willing to work. Thereafter the gilded palace will stand as a striking witness to the fact that in some previous year or years there were funds which could be devoted to unproductive purposes. The totality of such costly edifices, yachts, etc., which existed in San Francisco in 1879 were the accumulations since 1849. They struck the eye and excited the

imagination, and they led Mr. George to very erroneous conclusions.

Mr. George says : —

"There is no necessity for abstract reasoning. The question is one
of simple fact. Does the relative power of producing wealth decrease
with the increase of population ?"

But he wishes to establish the universal fact that the production of wealth increases faster than population. This he endeavors to prove by inferences from other facts, — that is, by
abstract reasoning. He could not do it in any other way, except
by appealing to statistical facts, and is therefore not to blame
for the method. What he appears to err in is the way in which
he applied his method. He looks at a very sparsely peopled
community, and sees that in it a canoe is a more suitable instrument than a steamer, a common road than a railroad ; that, in
short, there is a limit to the application of modern devices in
that community. With a greater population, more capital could
be applied ; and, to a certain point, with increase in the annual
product as compared with the population. Where he errs is
in concluding that what is true to a certain point is true indefinitely. He is so sure of this that he instances California. He
says : "In 1849, $16 a day were only ordinary wages. Now,
men are glad to work a week for that sum, and money is loaned
by the year for what would not have hardly been deemed extor-
tionate by the month." But, strange as it may seem, Mr. George
does not think that wages are lower because labor yields less
wealth. He says : —

"On the contrary ! Instead of the wealth-producing power of labor
being less in California in 1879 than in 1849, I am convinced that it
is greater ; and it seems to me that no one who considers how enormously during these years the efficiency of labor in California has been
increased by roads, wharves, flumes, railroads, steamboats, telegraphs,
and machinery of all kinds, — by a closer connection with the rest of
the world, and by the numberless economies resulting from a larger
population,— can doubt that the return which labor receives from nature
in California is on the whole much greater now than it was in the days
of unexhausted placers and virgin soil ; the increase in the power of

the human factor having more than compensated for the decline in the power of the natural factor. That this conclusion is the correct one is proved by many facts that show that the consumption of wealth is now much greater, as compared with the number of the laborers, than it was then. Instead of a population composed almost exclusively of men in the prime of life, a large proportion of women and children are now supported, and other non-producers have increased in a much greater ratio than the population ; luxury has grown far more than wages have fallen ; where the best houses were cloth and paper shanties are now mansions whose magnificence rivals European palaces ; there are liveried carriages on the streets of San Francisco, and pleasure yachts on her bay ; the class who can live sumptuously on their incomes has steadily grown ; there are rich men beside whom the richest of the earlier years would seem little more than paupers, — in short, there are on every hand the most striking and conclusive evidences that the production and consumption of wealth have increased with even greater rapidity than the increase of population, and that if any class obtains less it is solely because of the greater inequality of the distribution."

This quotation is an example of the eloquence with which Mr. George states his conclusions, and of the unwariness with which he adopts them and considers them proved.   .

Wages had fallen to one sixth, and the interest upon capital to nearly a twelfth ; yet he thought the annual product must certainly be greater per man than it was in 1849 ! One would think he would have asked, If this be so, what becomes of it ? Rent, profits, and wages must take the whole ; and rent and profit again spend nearly the whole of their shares upon wages. How, then, could it be that wages had fallen to one sixth part of what they were ? Having come to this question, it must have occurred to him to look into the census of 1870 and see what *were* the earnings of labor and capital, — that is, the gross product out of which the share of rent must come. Looking into this, he would have found that the value of all farm products, including betterments and additions, was $50,000,000, and that the number of hands employed was forty-eight thousand, giving $1,040 a year to each ; or, dividing by three hundred days, $3.50 a day. Turning now to mining, he would have found the gross product $8,300,000, and the hands employed seventy-six hundred, giving to each $1,090 a year, or $3.60 a day. Turning again to manufactures, he would have found the gross product $68,000,000, the materials being $27,000,000, leaving $31,000,000 as the value added to materials by forty-nine thousand persons; giving $633, or $2.11 a day.

The agricultural and mining gross products included of course more rent, and the manufacturing less rent; but they all three contained funds which went to non-productive labor, — that is, to the seventy-six thousand persons who were engaged in professional and personal services. The thirty-three thousand persons engaged in trade and transportation could hardly have much increased the average. We will call their earnings $4 a day, or $1,200 a year, for each person, or $39,000,000 altogether.

We have, then,

48,000 persons engaged in agriculture and producing	$50,000,000
7,600 in mining, producing	8,300,000
49,000 in manufacturing	31,000,000
33,000 in trade and transportation	39,000,000
76,000 in professional and personal services	
213,600	$128,300,000

We have, then, $128,300,000 to be divided among two hundred and thirteen thousand six hundred persons, or just about $600, or $2 a day against $16 a day, earned by each man in 1849.

Nobody supposes that the census enumerations are absolutely exact, but on the other hand nobody believes that they err by fifty per cent; and it will be seen then how wild, beyond belief, were the conclusions which Mr. George considered *proved* by his method of reasoning.

He believed that labor, assisted by capital, was earning in California over $16 a day; and his book would tend to make the laborer feel himself wronged if he did not receive that amount. But all that labor and capital together earned was about $2.11 a day, as shown by the statistics of manufactures; and out of this and the shares of rent in agriculture and mining, the persons engaged in professional and personal services had to be supported.

With the total annual product, such as it was, the laborers could not possibly have had more than they obtained; and it is a pity they and their innumerable well-wishers in other classes should have been disquieted by Mr. George's generous and eloquent but exceedingly inaccurate reasoning.

Analyzing Massachusetts in the same way as California, we find : —

Engaged in agriculture	73,000	with products worth		$32,000,000
Engaged in manufactures	279,000	" " "	$554,000,000	
		Deduct materials	334,000,000	220,000,000
Engaged in mechanical and mining occupations	14,000	Supposing these to earn as much as those engaged in manufac-		
Engaged in trade and transporta- tion	83,000	turing		76,000,000
				$328,000,000
Engaged in professional and personal services	131,000			

580,000 persons, among whom $328,000,000 being divided gives $566 a year, or $1.89 a day.

But the estimates in Massachusetts were in currency, which was at 15 per cent discount, so that the daily earnings in that State come down to $1.61 against $2 in California. With all her machinery, and all the economies resulting from a denser population, Massachusetts in 1870 could not divide among her workers as much as thinly settled California.

And here we come to a distinction as to the wealth of States, which seems nowhere present to the mind of Mr. George.

A State may possess a vast accumulation of public and private edifices, and a vast aggregate of tools, machinery, mills, etc. These strike the eye and impress the imagination forcibly. The beholder infers at once that he is in an enormously rich community, and his next inference is that in such a community the wages of labor ought to be very high. It seems as if where there was so much visible wealth every one ought to have a great abundance. But the value of these visible portions of wealth has already been consumed once. At the time of their construction, nearly every cent of their cost passed directly or indirectly into the hands of some kind of laborer. They have been eaten up once; they cannot be eaten up again. All that they can hereafter be made to contribute is that which their assistance adds to the annual product. This is every year divided between rent, labor, and capital, in such portions as demand and supply determine; but the part which goes to rent and capital nearly all, as we have already seen, goes (through the hands of the landlords and capitalists) to labor.

What, then, can be annually divided among the members of a community is the annual product of commodities; and that nation is the wealthiest which can give to each of its members the largest amount of the "necessaries, conveniences, and luxuries of life." This dividend bears no necessary proportion to the visible accumulated property, which is the result of the savings of many years, and which may have much, or may have very little, influence upon the annual product.

The repeated references of Mr. George to the magnitude of these accumulations, as showing what ought to be, or could possibly be, the annual reward of labor, — these are at the bottom of much that is misleading in his book.

Mr. John Stuart Mill, as every one knows, was a person of the highest integrity, a great logician, as much interested in the future fate of the poorer classes as any man who has lived in our times. His positions, as quoted in the beginning of this chapter, seem not to have been shaken by Mr. George in the slightest degree.

We have now gone through the first two books of "Progress and Poverty," and have found what appear to be good reasons for dissenting from every one of his distinctive doctrines.

It appears that wages do *not* tend to decrease as wealth (in the sense of the gross annual product as compared with population) increases, but that, on the contrary, wages increase *pari passu* with wealth. It appears that although productive labor, when employed, adds generally, by the assistance of capital, a value which is greater than its wages, still this value is not available until the product is finished and put upon the market and sold, so as to give a general purchasing power. It seems, therefore, that wages are certainly advanced by capital, without which the greater portion of the work of industrial communities could not be carried on. It appears that under favorable circumstances population *does* increase as rapidly as Malthus and Mr. Mill declared; and although, with increasing skill and capital to the very extraordinary extent that has been seen in our days, the annual product in the United States has increased much more rapidly, and so led to an equal advance in wages, still it is by no means certain that improvements can continue indefinitely at the same rate.

We see that the same causes have not produced an equal advance in wealth and wages in older communities, and we see that in California there has been a very marked decline. It seems probable, then, that in the course of another century, or half a century, population with us will press upon the means of subsistence. It is the hope of protectionists that the high scale of living which has been established in the meanwhile will prevent the descent of any large class of the people to transatlantic poverty. Mr. George sneers at protection as being contrived and intended to favor monopolies; but this is as untrue, as offensive, and as unjust as it would be to stigmatize him as a selfish communist and demagogue, whose only aim was notoriety. This is not true; neither is that.

IV.

How to deal with the remaining chapters.of "Progress and Poverty" without wearying the reader is "the riddle which the Sphinx of Fate puts" to the reviewer, and which not to answer is — not to be read! The fallacies are so numerous that to reply to each in full would be to exceed reasonable limits. All that can be done is to take the principal ones *seriatim*, and get rid of each as speedily as possible.

He says that one thousand men working together will do much more than one thousand times the work of one man.

This is true when they have unlimited subject-matter to work upon. Double the population of the United States, and all might be better off. Would they be better off if multiplied by a thousand? Up to a certain point the mutual helpfulness of men outweighs the relative but not absolute scarcity of materials, such as land, mines, etc.; but only up to a certain point. He makes the old error of arguing "*a dicto secundum quid ad dictum simpliciter.*" This is all that there is in his argument, that the joint product of labor and capital continually increases faster than population increases, and that *therefore* the laborer must be robbed if in a densely peopled country he earns less than the wages usual where lands, mines, forests, etc., are more abundant.

He repeats that capital does not employ labor, but that labor employs capital, and adduces in proof the fact that capital was originally formed by labor; but when the first capital was being formed few could exist upon a given space, and society bore no analogy to present communities in which, according to his own dictum, nine tenths of the product is due to the assistance of capital.

RENT AND CAPITAL.

He asserts that "rent is the price of monopoly, arising from the reduction to individual ownership of natural elements which human exertion can neither produce nor increase." But human agency has already vastly increased their capacity and can increase it still farther; ten acres with sufficient capital will yield as much as fifty without. Rent, then, is kept in check by capital. Moreover, he would have us believe that rent has actually swallowed up much that belonged to labor in the United States, and that to this cause we must trace the panic of 1873. Now, with respect to Economic Ground Rent, there seems reason to doubt whether it has begun to exist in the United States, as far as the great mass of farms and plantations are concerned; there seems, indeed, reason to believe that the farms do not yield a full interest upon the mere improvements existing upon them. The formation of this particular kind of instruments of production has been over-stimulated by our homestead laws, and by the action of that very common desire of men to acquire an absolute right to a portion of land and to be each his own master, with a certainty, as nearly complete as possible, of never being in want of food and seldom in want of a moderate amount of conveniences and luxuries.

The competition of seven millions of individual farmers ought surely to be a sufficient guarantee against monopoly; they will not even obtain a fair return for the labor they have spent in improvements, until increasing population and the action of the protective system build up a sufficient market for their products. Free trade, by forcing them to offer a greatly increased quantity of raw products to the outer world, would infallibly, under existing conditions, reduce very much the exchangeable value of their produce, and impoverish them for several generations.

It appears evident, then, that the panic of 1873 could not have been brought about by a scarcity of raw products. Many millions of farmers — each with more land than he habitually used, each eager to raise more when prices warranted — were a sufficient guarantee against any such catastrophe.

But it may be said, " There are the rents of houses and stores in the cities; these become exorbitant and make the production of something or other too expensive, and so something or other is not made, and hence we have a diminution in the aggregate demand."

But this idea is contradicted by the facts, well known to practical men, that during a period of excitement real estate is one of the last things to rise, and that when a period of depression comes it is one of the last to fall. The facts are empirical, and so may be questioned until we discover a reason for them. This is not far to seek. People do not enlarge their quarters until they have experienced high wages and high profits for some time, — until, in fact, they have got used to them, and have come to consider them as practically permanent. The individual takes a larger house or more rooms because he feels he can afford it, and he takes more space for the accommodation of his business because he feels that an increasing business demands more, and that, after paying more rent, he will have a larger sum left at the end of the year. High rents in the cities appear to be a *consequence* of the fuller occupation of the population; and even if, towards the end of a period of excitement, they become so high as to materially affect the profits and consequent expenditure of a portion of the dealers, they can only transfer to the owners of houses and lands the very same sums that are taken from the dealers, and the recipients must in their turn either spend them or save them; and in saving they spend only upon different people. It is only when it begins to be seen that saving has been overdone, — that more instruments of production and convenience cannot be formed with a chance of their yielding the rate of profit usual in the community, — it is only then that the industrial movement begins to decrease. Then laborers are thrown out of employment, and with this comes a diminished demand for commodities and a necessity for dismissing still more laborers, and so on in a widening circle.

RENT NOT RESPONSIBLE FOR PANICS AND POVERTY.

In a country depending largely upon the export of manufactured goods, like Great Britain, a panic may be brought

about by a failure of the crops of some of her principal purchasers, and a consequent inability to buy ; but this does not
arise from extravagant rents in either country.

Again, in a country which exports largely of raw products, a
period of depression might be brought about by large crops and
low prices in some other part of the world; but here again rent
has nothing to do with the matter.

Mr. George appears, then, to have failed in his attempt to fix
upon rent the responsibility for panics. That rent is not the
cause of general poverty in the United States is apparent enough
from the fact that if from the Gross Annual Product of 1880
per head we subtract the whole of rent and the whole of profits,
there remains much more than the whole product per head
of 1840. That is, labor alone in 1880 took more than labor,
rent, and profits together took in 1840. And besides this, rent
and profits again spent three quarters or more of their share
upon labor.

His algebraical formula, then, Produce = Rent + Wages + Interest, therefore Produce — Rent = Wages + Interest, proves
nothing. We should rather say, Produce = Rent + Wages + Interest; therefore Produce — (Wages and Interest) = Rent. As
long as men and capital, taking the whole country together, are
scarcer than land, they must be paid first, and rent must take
what they leave. When, in the far future, men and capital are
the more plenty, and land the less, then, and then only, will his
interpretation of the formula be true. But when, if ever, we
approach such a point, it is fair to expect that a population
long accustomed to conveniences and luxuries will exercise sufficient self-restraint to prevent the loss of them.

There are two cases in which the rent of land, and the rent of
capital also, become oppressive and the source of poverty. One
is when the owners are absentees. This case Mr. George recognizes. The other is when the owners, instead of buying their
conveniences and luxuries of their fellow-citizens, buy them
abroad. This case Mr. George entirely ignores. But this is
semi-absenteeism. If, for instance, rent and profits together
receive in the United States twenty-four hundred millions out
of seven thousand millions annual product, in consideration of

the use by the rest of the community of their land and capital, and if they proceed immediately to redistribute three fourths or more of the twenty-four hundred millions to other classes of the community, we speedily come to have vast masses of men who are engaged in producing conveniences and luxuries and services, and who bring conveniences and luxuries to the doors of those who produce necessaries.

' But if the owners of land and of capital were allowed to send their twenty-four hundred millions abroad after *cheap* conveniences and luxuries, the inevitable effect would be to break down the foreign market for our raw products, to make what we did buy exceedingly dear instead of cheap, and, in the end, to limit us to a small portion of what we now have by our own direct industry. A vastly diminished gross annual product would ensue, and rents, profits, and wages all suffering together, an impoverished people would no longer be able to support the stately universities that are now in league with the Cobden Club to destroy our industries.

It is not charged that the colleges are doing this intentionally; but their good intentions cannot alter the result.

Mr. George draws a picture of the growth of a village into a city, and tells us what "some hard-headed man of business, who has no theories, but knows how to make money," would say *if* he were assured that the village would in ten years become a city. He would say, "Go and buy lands and you will be rich." But if some one thinking, not knowing, that the village would become a great city, should ask the advice of the same hard-headed business man, he would reply, —

"Speculation in land is an exceedingly unsatisfactory business in the aggregate. If your village become a great city in ten years, and if your land happen to be in the right path of it, you may become rich without any exertion on your part; but where one man judges correctly, fifty judge wrong, and find at the end of twenty or thirty years their piece of land worth very much less than what the first price of it would have grown to if placed at interest. Land speculation is a great lottery, and has an inordinate number of blanks. When a man or a family draws a prize, all the world knows of it. When he draws a blank, he keeps it to himself."

Mr. George says :—

"In the city where I write is a man — but the type of men every-where to be found — who used to boil his own beans and fry his own bacon, but who, now that he has got rich, maintains a town house that takes up a whole block and would answer for a first-class hotel, two or three country houses with extensive grounds, a large stud of racers, a breeding farm, private track, etc., etc. It certainly takes at least a thousand times, it may be several thousand times, as much land to maintain this man now as it did when he was poor."

But the question is not how much land he keeps vacant. That can be of no consequence in a State which has but two or three persons to the square mile. What we have occasion to know is what portion of his income he can or does keep the rest of the community out of. His houses and the improvements of his pleasure-grounds have been paid for years ago to labor. They do not form any portion of his annual expenditure. His stud of racers is the only great expense which does not almost entirely go to labor at once; and much of this does. So does the greater part of the additional expenditure for more delicate food. The longer you look at it the more improbable does it appear that he does or can keep the rest of the community out of a tenth part of his income, even counting in all that he pays for foreign com-modities.

But more important than all this is the bad logic of calling this man "a type of men found everywhere."

How many out of the seven millions of land-owners and as many more capitalists in the United States keep studs of horses? What has such a man as this or a hundred such to do with the general sweep of the nation's life?

FREE TRADE NOT THE CAUSE OF PROSPERITY.

Mr. George says that "free trade has enormously increased the wealth of Great Britain!"

Other events, more especially the discovery of Californian and Australian gold, occurred about the time she entered upon the career of free trade, and those events have caused a general ad-vance in wealth among industrial nations; but as protectionist

France and the United States have advanced much more rapidly
than Great Britain, it is not easy to see what free trade has
had to do with it.   It is the policy of England to exaggerate her
prosperity, and to impute it all to free trade.   But if it were
even so, the outside barbarians would inquire what free trade
had done for India, Japan, Turkey, Ireland, etc.   *If* it has benefited Great Britain, if it has not even made the advance of her
prosperity less than it would otherwise have been, the other
parties to the exchanges made by her show no signs of having
shared in the profits.

LABOR PROFITS BY IMPROVEMENTS.

At page 225 Mr. George gives what he considers a demonstration that any and all improvements enure to the advantage
of rent, and in no way benefit the laborer.

He supposes that population remains the same, but that improvements in production take place so as to

"reduce by one tenth the expenditure of labor and capital necessary to produce the same amount of wealth.   Now either one tenth of
the labor and capital may be freed, and production remain the same as
before ; or the same amount of labor and capital may be employed,
and production be correspondingly increased.   But the industrial organization, as in all civilized countries, is such that labor and capital,
and especially labor, must press for employment on any terms.   The
industrial organization is such that the mere laborers are not in a position to demand their fair share in the new adjustment, and that any
reduction in the application of labor to production will, at first at
least, take the form, not of giving each laborer the same amount of
produce for less work, but of throwing some of the laborers out of
work and giving them none of the produce.   Now, owing to the increased efficiency of labor secured by the new improvements, as great
a return can be secured at the point of natural productiveness represented by eighteen as before at twenty.   Thus the unsatisfied desire
for wealth, the competition of labor and capital for employment, would
insure the extension of the margin of production, we will say to eighteen, and thus rent would be increased by the difference between eighteen and twenty, while wages and interest in quantity would be no
more than before, and in proportion to the whole produce would be

less. There would be a greater production of wealth, but the land-owners would get the whole benefit (subject to temporary deductions, which will be hereafter stated)."

Possibly this might happen in a country where, as in Ireland, landlords were in the habit of sending abroad for their conveniences and luxuries and exporting raw products to pay for them; but in a country like the United States, where the whole population is accustomed to many conveniences and luxuries, produced for the most part by our own labor and capital, the result would be very different. The moment any additional labor was applied to the land there would be an over-supply of raw products; and the exchangeable value of these, as compared with highly finished commodities composed largely of labor and capital, and as compared also with services, would decline. There would be an increased demand for services not issuing in commodities, and an increased demand for conveniences and luxuries on the part of the whole community. Labor and capital would be turned to the production of these, and the end of it all would be a community consuming the same abundance of necessaries as before, and a much greater abundance of conveniences and luxuries.

If, before the change, rent and profits took one third of the product and again distributed three quarters of that third to labor for services and for commodities, then rent and profits would not be likely to retain any greater share of the increased product after the change, for the demand of rent and profits for raw materials was already satisfied before.

It would seem then that, so far from the whole increase going to rent, eleven twelfths of it would go to labor, and part of the other twelfth would go to capital, and a part of the remainder would be rent of improvements and not at all ground rent. By labor is here meant every kind and description of labor, both that with the head and that with the hands. The annual product pays them all, and those get the largest share who are the least numerous as compared with the demand for their work.

Wherever, then, the productive efficiency of th population becomes greater per head it would seem that w s must increase, whether the greater efficiency spring from augmented skill, or more abundant capital, or from the mutual helpfulness and greater economies which attend a greater density of population. If these advantages continued to increase indefinitely, as Mr. George imagines, then wages would increase indefinitely but, unfortunately, greater numbers upon a given space and with given skill and capital come at last to press upon the means of subsistence; and then, however disagreeable it may be to face the fact, the only recourse by which the population can avoid increasing poverty is to avoid increase in numbers.

All the eloquence in the world, all the passionate declarations that such an opinion impeaches the goodness of God, etc., will not change the disagreeable fact. It is just as well to admit it and act accordingly; and this is exactly what every working-man does who considers before he marries whether he can or cannot support a family and bring up his children so that they will be good and useful and happy members of society.

Mr. George in effect tells this good citizen to make no such calculations; that, in all cases, there comes with each additional pair of hands a more than equal means of production: but Mr. George's conclusions, though inspired by a very good heart, are arrived at by a very bad logic, and he gives fatal advice, which can only impoverish and destroy those whom he desires to lift up and enrich. *Up to a certain point* each additional pair of hands increases the average production; *beyond a certain point* it is diminished. No one who dispassionately reflects upon this matter for an hour can be in any doubt with regard to it.

The next and last chapter will be devoted to what Mr. George has to say about the wickedness and impolicy of individual property in land, etc.

V.

WE now come to Mr. George's views as to justice. He says : —

"If we are all here by the equal permission of the Creator, we are all here with an equal title to the enjoyment of his bounty, — with an equal right to the use of all that nature so impartially offers."

Afterwards he says : —

"Though the sovereign people of the State of New York consent to the landed possessions of the Astors, the puniest infant that comes wailing into the world, in the squalidest room of the most miserable tenement-house, becomes at that moment seized of an equal right with the millionnaires. And it is robbed if the right is denied."

Many intelligent readers, who are not afflicted with a little knowledge of formal logic, but who retain, unimpaired, their natural common-sense, will see at a glance that the above passages contain a vast amount of rhetoric. It is *assumed* that the value of land of these United States is the product of nature ; but nearly the whole of it is the product of capital slowly acquired by self-denial. Mr. George himself estimates that of the present annual product nine tenths are due to the efficiency which capital lends to labor. Take away then the capital, — take away the farm improvements, the tools, the mills, the machinery, the forges, the houses, etc., and it would seem that a very large portion of the population must perish. They do not perish, because those who have gone before have labored and saved. But for this antecedent labor and thrift no piece of ground would command any rent. The whole value then would seem to belong of right to those who are here.

6

We welcome annually to our shores, it is true, nearly a million of persons, — from every nation that will assimilate with us and adopt our habits, — feeling that there is still room enough for many more.   But what would the people of the United States think if each of these immigrants, not satisfied with an equal chance to share in our opportunities to labor to advantage, should, upon landing, claim for every man, woman, and child a *pro rata* right to the land of the country ?

The contrast which Mr. George avails himself of, between the puny infant and a wealthy millionnaire, is rhetorical in the highest degree.   It appeals at once to our natural and laudable compassion for the poor, and to our natural but not laudable envy of the rich.   To pillage the latter and pass the plunder over to the former, gratifies at once two strong passions.   But how if, in thus gratifying our blind inclinations, we should miss our aim, and prevent that development of society to which alone the puny infant can look for a chance of unfolding its faculties and rising in the world ?   How if, in robbing the rich, we rob a thousand times as many deserving persons who cannot afford to be robbed ?

RENT NOT MONOPOLY.

Let us look at some illustrations which, if a little rhetorical in the opposite direction, are still many times nearer the true statement than is that of Mr. George.

Here is a brave-hearted woman, sixty years old, left destitute, with three children, long years ago.   With thrift, intelligence, and self-denial, she faced the world.   She saved, after many years, a few thousand dollars.   She bought a house in a city, paying half the cost, and being able, upon its security, to raise the other half upon mortgage.   She has denied herself fine clothing, amusements, — every kind of unthrift.   She has brought up her children to be good members of society.   She has barely enough to support her without charity until she passes away.   Mr. George proposes to take her all in the name of justice.

Again : There was, forty years ago, a young man, son of a New England farmer, who had many children.   The young man loved a young woman, and she loved him, — loved him enough to face every hardship, if it were with him.   They two went into the wilderness, knowing that a life of privation was before them, but knowing that in course of time the country would become settled, and that their farm would in the meanwhile be their bank, in which many years of labor might, under the laws of their country, be safely deposited. They looked forward to an independent old age, and something with which to give their children a start in life. Even now, in their declining years, their farm has no rent which can be distinguished from the rent for improvements. Then, says Mr. George, let the rent of all be taken. And this in the name of justice!

To the mind of Mr. George, rent is monopoly. He imagines one man owning all the land, and infers that under such circumstances the whole population would be his slaves. But what light does such an imagining throw upon the case of the United States, where there are certainly many millions of land-owners? The land-owners of the country cannot possibly combine to make food scarce, nor can the land-owners of the city combine to make commodities dear. There are plenty of other sites for cities, and there are plenty of competing cities already. The rents which are paid are paid simply because the sites are worth more than is paid for them. They would not be any lower if they were paid to the government instead of to individuals; and if city governments are the sinks of corruption Mr. George believes them to be, the transfer of the funds into their hands would not seem to be in the interest of civilization. It would be infinitely better to leave them in the hands of the present owners, to be by them distributed — as they must be — for services and for commodities, and for the formation of new capital, by which the annual product may be still further augmented.

Mr. George instances several cases in which land-owners in Great Britain have manifestly abused their power and pushed the rights of property beyond their just limits. Such instances are proper for legal restraint. It is not necessary to confiscate all property in land in order to prevent some abuses. To turn Mr. George's favorite illustration upon him: it is not necessary to burn down your house because there is a pig in it. The pig can be driven out.

RENTS IN A GROWING COUNTRY.

Our author appears to have knowledge of only one kind of rent — that of Ricardo — which arises from a pressure of population upon subsistence forcing inferior lands to be taken into cultivation, and is thus an evidence of diminishing comfort. But there does not seem to be any rent of this description in the United States. The rent of farming lands generally is as yet the rent of improvements, and the rent in cities and the vicinity of cities is spontaneous ascending rent arising out of an improvement, not out of a diminution, of the productiveness of labor. Capitalists set themselves down beside one another and carry on certain industries at so great an advantage that more capital can be applied to the adjacent farms, and their product be greatly increased. The distant farms produce just as much as before. As the city grows, rents in some portions increase; and some capitalists, enticed by this chance, build stores and houses rather than engage in manufacturing. For the opportunity to do this they are willing to pay high prices for land, and the capital they would otherwise employ themselves is employed by others, from whom they buy land.

Some persons or families who have made fortunate or sagacious investments of this sort have benefited largely; they have drawn the prizes in the Land Lottery. But others, many others, draw blanks. I have in mind not a few. One where $50,000 were loaned upon property, the property foreclosed, and, after twenty years, sold for one third of the sum advanced, not a cent of interest having been ever received. Another, a case of property held twenty years and not yet salable at first cost, having never yielded any income, and being taxed all the time at its full value. These cases were in a city. The city in the latter case grew the wrong way! That it is best for society that property in land should be under individual management is so manifest that even Mr. George admits it; but he proposes to take the income of it for the State, because every infant born in the world has an equal right to his individual proportion of the planet!

To the writer the proposal appears to be unwise, useless, unjust, and wicked. That abuses of the rights of property ought to be restrained, and that a limit might be, and perhaps ought to be, fixed to the quantity of land that any one man or family may engross, may be admitted; but the suggestion that society may repudiate its own titles, without compensation, under the subterfuge that the present generation cannot be bound by the past, is one which so evidently upright a person as our author could never have made if he had not been carried out of himself by the imagination that he had discovered the source of all social evil.

Would that he had! With fifty years of moderate economy we could buy back our concessions, and, thereafter, there would be no more poverty or wickedness upon earth! But, alas! his supposed cause (the rise of real estate before a panic) is not a cause, but a concurrent effect of quite another cause.

THE LAWS OF WAGES.

But if our examination of "Progress and Poverty" shows that we must abandon the belief in the discovery by our author of a panacea for all social evils, it shows, on the other hand, that we may dismiss his fears of wages tending to a minimum, and of rent devouring the whole annual product.

So long as this annual product increases, wages also must increase; and there appears to be no reason to apprehend that they will not increase for a long period unless the people, misled by fallacious advice, should abandon the protective policy and permit the recipients of rent and of profits, and the non-productive classes, who are supported out of rent and profits, to send abroad for the greater part of their commodities. So long as the men who get their ten or twenty or thirty or more dollars a day from fees, salaries, or profits, are content to buy their commodities from the men who get their dollar and a half, or two dollars, or three dollars a day, so long (until, at all events, population presses on the means of subsistence) will the annual product, and the consequent remuneration to every kind of labor, continue to augment. The progress will not be continuous, but in waves; and during the retrocessions there will be severe distress among all classes who have not laid by something for the "rainy day."

How these periods of depression may be shortened and made less frequent is worthy of the profound study of the intelligent and philanthropic; and, meanwhile, it is some consolation to see clearly that such periods are by no means mere aggravations of a general course of economic deterioration, as Mr. George supposes, but that they are, on the contrary, only temporary pauses in a general course of economic improvement.

And now, having performed the disagreeable task of picking flaws in "Progress and Poverty," let us gratefully admit, once more, that it is a brilliant book, glowing with a noble philanthropy, courage, and self-devotion. All that we have read in fable, or history, or the records of science, is brought again to mind in admirable sentences, and there is much of most interesting and suggestive thought and speculation. If political economy could all be strained out, there would remain a volume which every critic would applaud, and which the general reader would turn to again and again as a source of improvement and pleasure. As it is, the book is well suited to fascinate and mislead the inexperienced, the impatient, the many who judge by the heart rather than by the head, and all those who, in seeking an imaginary right, are willing to commit a certain and irretrievable wrong.

University Press: John Wilson & Son, Cambridge.

www.ingramcontent.com/pod-product-compliance
Lightning Source LLC
Chambersburg PA
CBHW030315270326
41926CB00010B/1374